Skyline 4

Teacher's Guide

Carol Lethaby

MACMILLAN

Macmillan Education
Between Towns Road, Oxford OX4 3PP
A division of Macmillan Publishers Limited
Companies and representatives throughout the world

ISBN 0 333 92755 9

First published 2002
Original design by Caroline Johnston
Editorial, design and picture research by
Lodestone Publishing Limited (design: Mind's Eye Design)
Illustrated by Kathy Baxendale, Fred Van Deelen, Celia Hart,
Sue Potter, Andy Warrington, Geoff Waterhouse
Cover photo by Stone

Adapted extract from Amazon.Com Book Review 'The Mozart Effect'
from www.arkanar.minsk.by/medinice/118/Mozart_Effect.htm,
reprinted by permission of the publisher; Adapted extract from 'One
Thousaaaaahhhhh… Shit' by David Banks, from Parachuting with
Barry from www.pyteeoh.demon.uk/extreme/parachut.htm reprinted
by permission of the author; Adapted extract from 'Barbie's Girl Power'
by Jessica Callan from The Electronic Telegraph 28.01.99, copyright ©
Telegraph Group Limited 1999, reprinted by permission of the
publishers; California Dreamin' words and music by John Phillips and
Michelle Phillips © 1965 Wingate Music Corporation, USA.
Universal/MCA Music Limited, 77 Fulham Palace Road, London, W6,
reprinted by permission of Music Sales Ltd. All Rights Reserved.
International Copyright Secured; Give Me a Little More Time words
and music by Gabrielle, Andy Dean, Benjamin Wolff & Ben Barson,
© 1995 EMI Music Publishing Ltd/Polygram Music Publishing Ltd &
Perfect Songs Ltd, London, WC2H 0QY & Universal Music Limited,
77 Fulham Palace Road, London, W6, reprinted by permission of
EMI Music Publishing Ltd, IMP Ltd and Music Sales Ltd. All Rights
Reserved. International Copyright Secured; I Will Always Love You
words and music by Dolly Parton © 1973 Velvet Apple Music,
reprinted by permission of Carlin Music Corp, London, NW1 8BD.
All Rights Reserved; Ironic words by Alanis Morissette music by Alanis
Morissette & Glen Ballard © 1995 Music Corporation of America
Incorporated, Vanhurst Place, MCA Music Publishing & Aerostation
Corporation, USA. Universal/MCA Music Ltd, 77 Fulham Palace Road,
London W6, reprinted by permission of Music Sales Ltd. All Rights
Reserved. International Copyright Secured; Oops I Did it Again words
and music by Max Martin and Rami © 2000 Zomba Music Publishers
Ltd, reprinted by permission of the publisher; Tears in Heaven words
and music by Eric Clapton & Will Jennings © 1992 & 1995 E.C. Music
Limited, London, NW1 and Blue Sky Rider Songs, reprinted by
permission of Music Sales Limited and Hal Leonard Corporation. All
Rights Reserved. International Copyright Secured; The Logical Song
Hodgson/Davies © 1979, reprinted by permission of Universal Music
Publishing Ltd; Walking in Memphis words and music by Marc Cohn ©
1991 Museum Steps Music and W B Music Corp, USA Warner/
Chappell Music Ltd, London W6 8BS, reprinted by permission of IMP
Ltd. All rights reserved.

The author and publishers would like to thank the following for
permission to reproduce their photographs; AKG pp42(t), 44(br),
66A(Lessing), 66E(Binder); AP pp19(E), 19(F)(Maakjterrill), 46, 52,
66C(Djansezian), 86(r), 90(t), 109(Yu); John Birdsall p10A; Bridgeman
Art Library p43(l)(© ADAGP, Paris and DACS, London 2002), 43(r)(©
Succession H, Matisse/DACS 2002); Bubbles p68(Woodcock); Corbis
pp42(b), 72D(Thompson), 86(c)(Bettman), 87, 88(Rowell), 90(b); Eye
Ubiquitous pp10E(Skjold), 19(C)(Grau), 32(C)(Fairclough),
34(Hawkins), 72C(Wilson), 98A(Skjold); Genesis/NASA p116; James
Davis Worldwide pp32(B), 125, 111(G,H); Kobal pp19(D)(20th
Century Fox/Paramount), 51(Rank), 104(b)(MGM/United Artists),
105(MGM/United Artists), 118(B); Mary Evans Picture Library p44(bl);
Moviestore p104(t)(MGM/United Artists); PA Photos pp18(tl),
19(A)(EPA), 61(l)(EPA), 61(r)(Melville), 66D(Abaca), 106(l), 107(r);
Popperfoto pp54(Reuters/Behrakis), 63(Reuters/Braley), 86(l),
118(A); Powerstock/Zefa pp9, 10B, 14(tl), 19(B), 32(C),
37(Enticknap), 38, 55, 80(tr), 81(l,r), 84, 96(tr), 98B, 111(B,C,D,E);
Redferns p66B(Hutson), 114(Hutson), 118(C)(Michael Ochs Archive);
Rex Features pp48(Weus), 66F(Adebari), 79(Sipa), 121(Meddle);
Stock Directory (TCL) p80(b)(Mo); Sylvia Cordaïy pp96(tl)(Whiting),
111(A); Telegraph Colour Library pp7(Krasowitz), 10C(Fruchet),
10D(Gelot), 14(tr)(Traza), 44(t)(Adams), 66(l)(Hippisley),
69(Childs), 70(r)(Tilley), 72A(Scott), 106/7(Simpson),
111(F)(Croucher); Tografox pp6(A,B), 70(l), 96(br), 100(Williams);
Travel Ink pp18(tr)(Enoch), 72B(Badkin); John Walmesley p80(tl),
98(C,D).

Commissioned photographs by Robert Battersby pp6(C), 62,
64, 78, 96(bl); Nick Webster p60.

Printed in China

2006 2005 2004 2003 2002
10 9 8 7 6 5 4 3 2 1

Contents

Introduction

Welcome to **Skyline**, a stimulating program for adult learners of English. **Skyline**'s extensive range of materials offers a fresh, easy-to-use approach to learning and teaching English.

The following Frequently Asked Questions are designed to serve as an easily accessible introduction to the course.

What do we know about how people learn a language?

Nobody knows exactly how languages are learned. However, researchers, methodologists, teachers and successful learners all generally agree that the following conditions are virtually indispensable.

- Motivation: learners need reasons for learning the language and a sense of success.
- Learners' differences: learners will approach what they learn and how they learn in different ways.
- Communicative input: learners need abundant exposure to comprehensible and interesting language.
- Focus on the language itself: learners need to notice and understand the meanings, forms and uses of the language.
- Use: learners need opportunities to produce the language as well as understand it, and above all to use the language for genuine communication.
- Trial and error: all learners have to risk making errors (and do make them!) as they progress in their command of the language.
- Feedback: learners need information about their performance so they can correct themselves and see their progress.

How does *Skyline* create opportunities for this to happen?

We've developed the *Triple A* approach to learning English. We think this is an easy and memorable way of describing the important characteristics of an approach that reflects what we now know about language learning. The three As are: *Access, Analysis* and *Activation*.

- **Access to language** – learners are exposed to language in clear, interesting contexts which are relevant to their broad interests and needs.
- **Analysis of language** – learners are encouraged to look in detail at the meanings, forms and use of language taken from context.
- **Activation of language** – learners are continuously given opportunities to use language and skills through a wide variety of motivating task and text types.

How does the *Triple A* approach work in practice?

The *Triple A* approach is closely linked to the structure of the Students' books, but learners are encouraged to access, analyze and activate their English throughout the book. The approach is linked to the structure of each unit as follows.

Access: In lesson 1 of each 4-lesson unit of **Skyline**, learners listen and read about interesting and relevant topics in English they can understand. They respond to this input through motivating tasks using the English they already know, as well as meeting new language items in appropriate contexts.

Analysis: In lessons 2 and 3 of each unit of **Skyline**, learners are helped to notice and understand the meanings, forms and uses of new language items taken from context and practice them. This practice provides opportunities for the teacher, and the learners themselves, to monitor their learning of the new language items. Along with this focus on new language, learners continue to develop their English in varied skills activities.

Activation: In lesson 4 of each unit of **Skyline**, learners use their growing repertoire of English in activities related to their real needs and interests outside the classroom – study, professional and personal. This lesson, the *Language for Life*, includes a motivating variety of authentic text types and realistic tasks and activities. It provides opportunities for the teacher to monitor learners' 'real English' – the English they would use to communicate outside the classroom – and then plan appropriate remedial work.

What is *Skyline's* approach to accessing language?

Learners are exposed to language through a variety of reading and listening texts. However, exposure in itself is not enough. It is important that this input is comprehensible, so in **Skyline** learners are led to meaning through a wide variety of task types, for example matching pictures to a reading or a listening. On one level they are accessing language, and on another level they are developing their ability to cope with reading and listening. This second element of skills development is also key to **Skyline**'s approach.

What is *Skyline's* approach to analyzing language?

Skyline approaches the planned teaching of individual language items in two ways.

- Inductively: learners look at a contextualised language item, complete awareness-raising tasks, and come to conclusions. They then try to apply these in practice.
- Deductively: the teacher presents a pattern, rule or definition and the learners try to apply them in practice.

We give inductive teaching-learning priority for three reasons. Research and experience show that people tend to remember what they discover for themselves better than what is explained to them. Most adult learners of English have had the basic grammar of English presented to them deductively before and a new approach is likely to be more interesting and effective. Learners become more independent, developing a variety of strategies to analyze language for themselves; this is essential for continuing progress in language learning outside the class. However, a deductive approach can still be appropriate at times, depending on the difficulty of the language item and the type of learners. It is simply better to reserve it for when it is really needed rather than always requiring the learners to pay attention to a teacher presentation.

What is *Skyline's* approach to activating language?

A lot of communicative language teaching still puts the programmed presentation and controlled practice of individual language items firmly at its center. Such accuracy based work is important and **Skyline** has a clear linear language syllabus at its core. But learners also need to develop a feeling of English as a working communication system which can be used for the learners' own real purposes. They need to experiment with language in a number of different ways and in a number of different situations. The wide variety of activities in **Skyline** demand learners' engagement in purposeful, communicative tasks with clear outcomes. This is key in developing their fluency.

This fluency applies to the four language skills. In the real world no single skill is used in isolation and throughout **Skyline** the four skills are integrated. Skills integration and development are central features of the course. The goal is to enable learners to become more proficient in the four skills so that they can communicate with other speakers of English – native and non-native.

How does *Skyline* involve learners in their own learning process?

Skyline encourages learners to be involved by:

- providing topics and situations which are interesting and relevant to learners
- asking them to bring their own experiences, knowledge and opinions into the classroom
- having them work out meanings and find answers for themselves wherever possible
- encouraging learners to analyze how they learn and what they learn
- pushing them to stretch their English through a variety of task and text types
- helping them relate what they do inside the classroom to their lives outside the classroom
- encouraging them to work outside the classroom.

How can *Skyline* help learners improve their English outside class?

- Music is of interest to most people, so learners should be encouraged to listen to songs in English. This will provide further opportunities for learners to activate language they have learned. This is why **Skyline** has six classic pop songs at the end of each Student's book.
- Apart from language summaries and practice exercises, the **Skyline** Workbooks provide further skills development work, particularly in reading.
- The Internet provides an inexhaustible source of information in English. **Skyline**'s own website (http://www.skyline-english.com) suggests projects for learners to undertake using the Internet.
- All these activities help point learners towards a real world of English outside the classroom. It is helpful to encourage learners to pursue this further, by means of movies, TV, magazines, newspapers and songs. In fact, whatever interests each learner individually will be of most use in supporting their acquisition of English.

Contents

unctions	Vocabulary	Pronunciation
Making polite requests for information Talking about causes and effects / situations and decisions Reporting other people's ideas	● Compound and paired words ● Expressions related to the home ● Adjectives to describe character	● Rhythm
Talking about processes / past events Defining what / who you're talking about	● Words / expressions related to jobs ● Financial	● Word stress
Confirming / questioning information	● Appliances / technology ● Environment ● Cars	● Contrastive stress ● Intonation – question tags
Talking about setting up / carrying out projects Talking about habits and states in the past	● Multi-word verbs ● Describing interiors	● Intonation – questions
Talking about background facts / past circumstances Talking about previous events	● Crime ● Law	● Past tense forms
Reporting what people have said, opinions they have given Debating points	● Nouns as adjectives ● Reporting verbs ● Expressions for discussions	● Word stress

Contents

Songsheets

Irregular verbs
Pronunciation chart

unctions	Vocabulary	Pronunciation
Describing people / places / things / events	● Clothing ● Shopping items ● Music / instruments	● Linking
Talking about obligation and necessity Indicating time	● Weddings and graduations ● Inviting	● Intonation – showing interest
Talking about past conditions / cause and effect Expressing regret	● Gender ● Practical / ethical issues ● Discussion	● Sentence stress – conditionals
Speculating about past events / actions	● Experiential ● Historical	● Weak forms – modals
Talking about future events	● People: from cradle to grave ● Linking words	● Linking
Getting ideas across clearly Analyzing / discussing language	● Language of prediction ● Computer words and expressions	● Intonation and emotion

Unit 1 Relationships and communication

1 Parents and children

1 Speaking and listening

a What do you think is happening in each photograph below?

b Listen to three pieces of conversation. Match each with the appropriate photograph.

1 ....   2 ....   3 ....

c In groups, discuss the following question.

What topics do parents talk about with their 15–16 year-old children?

2 Listening and speaking

a Listen to Claudia, 15, and her mother talking. Check (✔) the topics you hear.

money ◯	time on the phone ◯	messy bedroom ◯
school grades ◯	watching TV ◯	getting home late ◯
taking care of pets ◯	volume of stereo ◯	homework ◯

b Try to complete the following four house rules for Claudia. Listen to the conversation again and check.

1 No .... if the volume is too high.

2 No allowance money if she doesn't ....

3 No TV before she ....

4 No phone calls longer than ....

Relationships and communication

Helping the learner: using previous knowledge and experiences

Activate what students already know before you focus on something new.
• Activating students' previous knowledge of grammar and vocabulary helps them when reviewing and practicing new language.
• Using pre-reading and pre-listening activities activates students' background knowledge of a topic and builds confidence.

Further reading:
Gower, R., Phillips, D., Walters, S., (1995) *Teaching Practice Handbook*, Macmillan Heinemann ELT, Ch.2

Lesson 1   Parents and children

Aims: To develop students' speaking, listening, reading and writing skills.
To review past tenses and the present perfect.

1   Speaking and listening

Aim: To introduce the topic of parents and children.

a • Have students work in pairs and guess what is happening in each photograph.

b • Now have students listen to the conversations on the tape, and match them to the appropriate photograph. Check the answers.

Answers   1 C   2 A   3 B

Tapescript

1 *Mom:* Look at the state of your room! You're supposed to keep it neat.
Teenager: All right. I'll clean it, OK?

2 *Mom:* Can you see the dog?
Child: This one.
Mom: Yes. He lives with two little cats. See?
Child: Here. Meow.

3 *Child:* And the capital of France is ...
Dad: Yes?
Child: Uh ... Rome?
Dad: Come on!

Child: Uh ... Paris?
Dad: Right. Paris, France. Rome ...?
Child: Italy.
Dad: Right!

c • Put students in groups and ask them to discuss the question.
• Get feedback and write the answers on the board.

2   Listening and speaking

Aim: To practice listening for the main idea and specific information.

a • Tell students they are going to listen to a teenage girl and her mother talking.
• Compare the topics with the list you wrote on the board from exercise 1c.
• Play the tape and have students listen and check the topics discussed.

Answers   money, time on the phone, watching TV, volume of stereo, messy bedroom, homework

b • Have students try to complete the four house rules.
• Play the tape again and have students listen to the conversation to check their answers.

Answers   1 music   2 keep her room neat   3 has finished her homework   4 15 minutes

Tapescript

Mom: Claudia! Claudia! Claudia! Low music or no music! You know the rules.
Claudia: Yes, Mom. I've turned it down. Sorry.
Mom: Oh! Look at the state of your room! You know you're supposed to keep it neat. You won't get any allowance money if you don't. Your dad says ...

Claudia: I was cleaning my room when you called me.
Mom: Sure, sure ...
Claudia: I was! Really!
Mom: All right. Have you done your homework?
Claudia: Uh ... I've almost finished it.
Mom: But you have to finish your homework before you watch TV. You know that. Why's the TV on?

Claudia: Uh ... don't know. It was on when I came in. Perhaps Mickey ...
Claudia: Hello. Oh, hi, Erica!
Mom: And don't spend hours on the phone. Fifteen minutes maximum, remember.
Claudia: What? Susan went out with Jimmy? No ...
Mom: Fifteen minutes – starting now!
Claudia: Sure, Mom. Erica, tell me more!

3 Grammar builder: review of past tenses and present perfect

Aim: To review the use of past tenses and present perfect.

Helping the learner   Activate what students know, by eliciting the names of the past and present perfect tenses; write them on the board. Elicit examples of the tenses before students do the exercises.

a   • Put students in pairs.
    • Have them look at sentences 1–3, and match them with sentences a–c.
    • Check the answers and discuss.

Answers   1 c (past progressive - interrupted action)   2 a (present perfect - completed actions in the past with results in the present)   3 b (past simple - completed past action in finished time)

b   • Now ask students to complete the text in exercise 3b with the appropriate forms of the verbs in parentheses.
    • Get them to check their answers in pairs or groups.

Teaching tip   Encourage students to discuss why they chose the different tenses.

    • Check the answers.

Answers   1 has attended   2 was (past simple – completed past action in finished time)   3 has visited (present perfect for general experience)   4 improved (past simple – specific time in the past)   5 was staying (past progressive – background action)   6 has read (present perfect – action started in the past which continues up to the present)

4 Pronunciation: rhythm

Aim: To practice identifying stressed syllables.

a   • Tell students they are going to listen to sentences from exercise 2 and focus on the rhythm.
    • Play the tape and get students to listen to the example.
    • Ask them to listen to the other sentences and to underline the stressed syllables.
    • Check the answers.

Answers / Tapescript   1   I've **turned** it **down**.
2   **Look** at the **state** of your **room**!
3   I was **clean**ing my **room** when you **called** me.
4   Have you **done** your **home**work?
5   **Su**san went **out** with **Jim**my?

b   • Students now practice saying the sentences with the same rhythm.
    • Ask some students to say the sentences for the whole class.

    • **Optional step:** Ask students to make up their own sentences using past tenses and present perfect and then get them to underline the stressed syllables.

5 Speaking, reading and writing

Aims: To practice talking and reading about effective parenting.
       To practice writing a short account.

a   • Tell students they are going to talk about being a good parent.
    • Put students in groups.
    • Have them make a list of ways of being a good parent.
    • Get feedback and write students' ideas on the board.

b   • Tell students to read the excerpt and see how many things they included in their list in exercise a.
    • Elicit other examples of being a good parent from the excerpt.
    • Ask students if they agree with these examples. Encourage them to discuss.

c   • Ask students to write a short account of something that happened between them and their parents.
    • Put students in pairs and get them to exchange accounts and discuss what they have written.

3 Grammar builder: review of past tenses and present perfect

a **Look at sentences 1–3. Match them to sentences a–c.**

1 I was cleaning my room.   a) Look how clean it is. I've done it three times this week.

2 I've cleaned my room.   b) Well … uh … last week.

3 I cleaned my room.   c) You called me, so I stopped.

b **Complete the following text with appropriate forms of the verbs in parentheses.**

Claudia (1) ……………………… (*attend*) her present school for three years. Last year she (2) ……………………… (*be*) first in her class in French. She (3) ……………………… (*visit*) the French-speaking part of Canada three times. Her French (4) ……………………… (*improve*) a lot while she (5) ……………………… (*stay*) there with a family last summer. She (6) ……………………… (*read*) several books in French since then too.

4 Pronunciation: rhythm

a **Listen to these sentences from the conversation between Claudia and her mother, and notice the rhythm. Underline the stressed syllables, as in sentence 1.**

1 I've turned it down.   4 Have you done your homework?

2 Look at the state of your room!   5 Susan went out with Jimmy?

3 I was cleaning my room when you called me.

b **Practice saying the sentences with the same rhythm.**

5 Speaking, reading and writing

a **In groups, make a list of ways to be a good, effective parent.**

Talk to your children about things that interest them.

Be consistent.

b **Read this extract from a pamphlet about ways to be an effective parent. How many of these ideas did you include in your list in exercise a?**

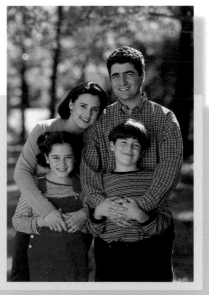

3 **Set rules and be consistent**
Discipline is necessary in every family. It can help children to behave acceptably and learn self-control. House rules might include no rudeness, no hitting and no TV until homework is done. Always follow through with consequences when rules are broken.

4 **Make time for your children**
There are fewer opportunities today for parents to be with their children. Do your best to be available when your children, including older teens, want to talk or participate in family activities. Attend concerts, sports events, etc. with your teens – if they like you to!

5 **Make communication a priority**
Children want and deserve explanations of their parents' decisions and behavior. If you don't take time to explain, they will not appreciate your values and motives. Discuss problems with older children openly and find solutions together. When children participate in decisions they are much more likely to carry them out.

c **Write a short account of something that happened between you and your parents, or one of your parents, when you were in your teens. Exchange your compositions in pairs and discuss them.**

2 In the workplace

1 Speaking and reading

a In pairs or groups, discuss these questions.

1 What do you consider the main advantages of e-mail?

2 Do you think there are any disadvantages?

b Now read the article on the right and compare your ideas with it.

c Read the text again and list the positive and negative aspects of e-mail.

Positive	Negative

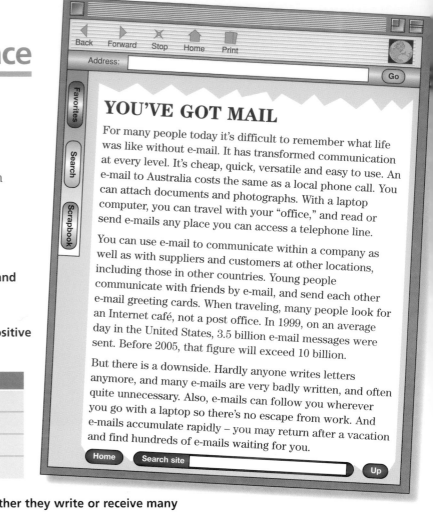

YOU'VE GOT MAIL

For many people today it's difficult to remember what life was like without e-mail. It has transformed communication at every level. It's cheap, quick, versatile and easy to use. An e-mail to Australia costs the same as a local phone call. You can attach documents and photographs. With a laptop computer, you can travel with your "office," and read or send e-mails any place you can access a telephone line.

You can use e-mail to communicate within a company as well as with suppliers and customers at other locations, including those in other countries. Young people communicate with friends by e-mail, and send each other e-mail greeting cards. When traveling, many people look for an Internet café, not a post office. In 1999, on an average day in the United States, 3.5 billion e-mail messages were sent. Before 2005, that figure will exceed 10 billion.

But there is a downside. Hardly anyone writes letters anymore, and many e-mails are very badly written, and often quite unnecessary. Also, e-mails can follow you wherever you go with a laptop so there's no escape from work. And e-mails accumulate rapidly – you may return after a vacation and find hundreds of e-mails waiting for you.

d Ask four or five other people whether they write or receive many of the following.

- personal letters
- business letters
- personal e-mails
- business e-mails

In groups, compare the results of your informal survey.

2 Word builder: compound and paired words

Form as many compounds / pairs as you can with one word from box A and another from box B.

bedroom

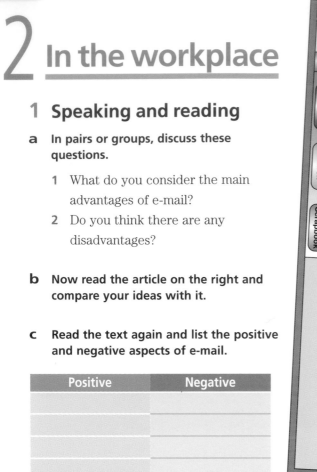

A

bed	down	greeting
home	house	Internet
laptop	telephone	post
school	self	work

B

room	café	call	cards
control	computer	
grades	line	office
place	side	work

> **Learning tip**
>
> The compounding of nouns (e.g. *bedroom* and *bus station*, **not** *room for sleep* or *station of buses*) is typical of the English language. A major aspect of successful language learning is noticing such typical patterns. Can you think of some more examples that are different in English and your language – or very similar?

Lesson 2 In the workplace

Aims: To develop students' knowledge about communication in the workplace.
To practice compound and paired words.
To review and practice polite requests.

1 Speaking and reading

Aim: To practice speaking and reading about the topic of e-mail.

a • Ask the students if they use e-mail and why they use it.
   • Put students in pairs or groups and get them to discuss the questions.
   • Ask for feedback, writing the main advantages and disadvantages of e-mail on the board.

b • Now have students read the article and compare their ideas from exercise a.

c • Have students read the text again and list the positive and negative aspects of e-mail in their notebooks.
   • Check the answers.

Answers Positive: cheap, quick, versatile, easy to use; you can attach documents and photographs; you can travel with your work as you can access e-mail anywhere there is a phone; you can use e-mail with work colleagues and with people outside a company; young people can communicate with their friends.
Negative: hardly anyone writes letters anymore; e-mails are badly written; a lot of e-mails are unnecessary; you can't escape from work; e-mails accumulate rapidly.

d • Tell students they are going to conduct an informal survey.
   • Have them move around the classroom asking each other about the different types of letter / e-mail. Ask them to tally the number of students who receive each type.
   • Put students in groups.
   • Tell them to compare the results of their survey.
   • Get feedback from the groups.

2 Word builder: compound and paired words

Aim: To practice compound and paired words.

Helping the learner Start from what the students already know. Elicit some examples of compound and paired words and write them on the board.

• Put students in pairs.
• Have them come up with as many different words as they can from boxes A and B.

Teaching tip You could do this as a competition. Encourage students to use dictionaries to see if they have formed real compounds.

• Get feedback and write the answers on the board.

Answers bedroom, downgrades, downside, greeting cards, home computer, home office, homework, house call, housework, Internet café, laptop computer, postcards, post office, school computer, school grades, school office, school work, self control, telephone call, work computer, workplace.

Language help Some of the words are "fixed" compounds, e.g. *homework*, and others can be "created" to fit a particular context, e.g. *I sometimes use my **work computer** at home.*

• Focus attention on the Learning tip, and elicit some more examples of compounds and paired words.
• **Optional step:** Have students write sentences to show the meaning of some of the words.

3 Listening

Aim: To practice listening for the main idea and for specific information.

a • Have students look at the photograph to establish where the conversation is taking place.
  • Play the tape and get students to listen and say what the different parts of the conversation are about.

Answers	Part 1 checking a report Part 2 John's new e-mail address
	Part 3 Monica's birthday party

b • Have students read the questions.
  • Play the tape again and tell them to listen for the information to answer the questions.
  • Discuss the answers.

Answers	1 Barbara 2 today 3 jbw@skyline.com 4 her birthday party 5 Barbara

Tapescript

Part 1
Barbara: Would you mind checking this report for me, Peter?
Peter: Sure, Barbara. I'll look at it right now.
Barbara: Thanks a lot. Do you know if John West wants it today?
Peter: This report? Uh, yes, I think he does.
Barbara: Right. I'll e-mail it to him.

Part 2
Barbara: Oh, uh … can you tell me what John's new e-mail address is?
Peter: Just a minute. Here it is. It's jbw@skyline.com.
Barbara: jbw@skyline.com. It's a nuisance when people change their address.
Peter: Yeah.

Part 3
Peter: Are you going to Monica's tonight?
Barbara: Her birthday party? Yes, I think so.
Peter: Do you know where she lives?
Barbara: Sure. Getting there is a bit complicated. We can go to the party together if you like.
Peter: Ah, that would be great.

4 Grammar builder: review of polite requests for information

Aim: To review the use and grammar of polite requests.

a • Write questions 1–3 on the board.
  • Elicit the part of each question that makes it more polite: *Do you know …? Can you tell me …?*

b • Now focus attention on the word order. Elicit how it is different from word order in direct questions – it does not invert or use an auxiliary.

Teaching tip	You may want to write the corresponding direct questions to show the contrast:
	Does John West want it today? What's John's new e-mail address? Where does she live?

c • Have students change the direct questions 1–5 to indirect polite questions. Remind them to use the different opening phrases from exercise 4a.
  • Ask them to compare with a partner.
  • Check the answers.

Answers	1 Do you know / Can you tell me where the cafeteria is?
	2 Do you know / Can you tell me if / whether it's open now?
	3 Do you know / Can you tell me what time they close?
	4 Do you know / Can you tell me if / whether you can open a charge account?
	5 Do you know / Can you tell me how much lunch costs?

5 Speaking

Aim: To practice using polite questions in a role play.

a • Check students understand the situation for the role play and that they need to ask polite questions.
  • Put them in pairs and have them practice the questions listed.

b • Have students change roles and ask more questions.
  • Elicit some examples from the class.

Preparation:
Tell students to bring photographs of their friends for the next lesson, especially any friends from elementary school.

3 Listening

a Listen to the conversation between two people in an office. What are the topics of each part?

Part 1: ....

Part 2: ....

Part 3: ....

b Read questions 1–5, below. Listen to the conversation again, and answer the questions.

1 Who has written a report for John West?

2 When does John want it?

3 What is John's new e-mail address?

4 What is happening at Monica's house tonight?

5 Who knows how to get to her house, Barbara or Peter?

4 Grammar builder: review of polite requests for information

a In the listening text, John and Barbara are fairly polite to each other. Look at the following requests for information. What part of each request makes it polite?

1 Do you know if John West wants it today?

2 Can you tell me what John's new e-mail address is?

3 Do you know where she lives?

b What do you notice about the word order of these questions?

c Change these direct requests into more polite ones.

1 Where's the cafeteria? ....

2 Is it open now? ....

3 What time do they close? ....

4 Can you open a charge account? ....

5 How much does lunch cost? ....

5 Speaking

a Imagine you are teachers or administrative staff here where you study English. Work in pairs. Student A knows the place well; student B is new and asks student A polite questions about things like these.

• Office / reception opening / closing times, and class starting / finishing times.

• Classes on Saturday morning / afternoon / etc.

• The Director / Administrator / Coordinator / etc.

• Library / self-access center / restaurant / etc.

B: *Can you tell me where the Director's office is?*

Do you know if there's a supermarket near here?

b Now change roles and ask some more questions.

3 Between friends

1 Speaking and listening

a What is the most important quality in a friend? In pairs, put the qualities below in order of importance.

fun, good company ◯   honest ◯   intelligent and talented ◯   loyal ◯
patient and understanding ◯   reliable ◯   same interests ◯   same values ◯

b Describe the people in the photographs below. Then listen to five people talking about their friends. Match each speaker to a photograph.

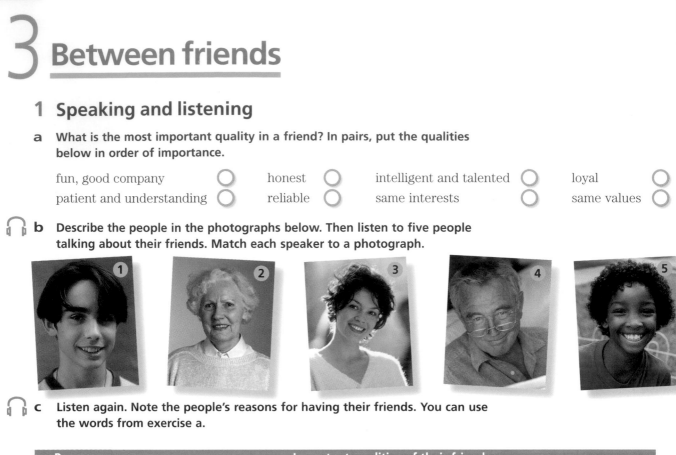

c Listen again. Note the people's reasons for having their friends. You can use the words from exercise a.

Person	Important qualities of their friends
1	
2	
3	
4	
5	

2 Reading and speaking

a Read and answer the following quiz. Then calculate your score, and read the interpretation of it.

ARE YOU A GOOD FRIEND?

1 If there were a great program on TV, and a close friend phoned sounding anxious to talk, would you:

a) make an excuse (e.g. that you were taking a shower), and say you would call back later?

b) forget the program and let your friend talk?

c) try to persuade your friend to come and watch the program?

2 Is the longest you have ever kept a close friend:

a) less than 1 year?

b) between 1 and 5 years?

c) more than 5 years?

3 If you were President, would you:

a) continue to see your present friends frequently?

Lesson 3 Between friends

Aims: To develop students' speaking, listening and reading skills.
To practice zero, first and second conditionals.

1 Speaking and listening

Aim: To introduce the vocabulary and topic of friendship.

Helping the learner Ask students if they have a good friend and what they like about him / her. This will activate vocabulary and help students approach the listening task with confidence.

a • Put students in pairs.
• Check comprehension of the qualities listed that friends might have.
• Tell students to put the qualities in order of importance for them (1 = the most important).

Optional activity Pyramid discussion

After the pairs of students have ranked the qualities, join them to form groups and ask them to decide on an order for their group.

Repeat this procedure by joining the groups until there is a whole class discussion and the students decide on a rank order for the class.

b • Have students look at the photographs. Elicit some language to describe the people, focusing on age and characteristics, e.g. *I think he's about fifteen. He looks friendly.*
• Play the tape and ask students to match each speaker to a photograph.
• Check the answers.

Teaching tip Don't forget to ask students how they knew the answers.

Answers 1 photograph 4   2 photograph 3   3 photograph 1   4 photograph 5   5 photograph 2

c • Play the tape again and have students write down the reasons the speakers give for having their friends.
• Check the answers.

Answers 1 same interests and values   2 patient and understanding, reliable   3 fun, good company, same interests   4 fun, intelligent and talented   5 loyal, affectionate, reliable

Tapescript

1 *Man:* One of my best friends is Paul. We went to school together and we've known each other for more than 40 years now. We have a lot in common. Basically we share the same interests and values.

2 *Young woman:* Sue is a really good friend of mine. She's married, with a young child like me, and she's someone I can talk to about anything. She's patient, understanding and reliable. I try to be the same for her.

3 *Boy:* Andrew and Tony are my real buddies. When I go out with them, I always have fun. They're great company ... and we all like the same things – music, sports ... and girls!

4 *Girl:* My best friend is Sophie. She's 10 like me. She makes me laugh a lot. But she's also really good at school, and she helps me a lot. She plays the piano really well too. I ... I really admire her, you know.

5 *Elderly woman:* Well, to be honest my best friend is Bernard, my dog. He's loyal and affectionate, always pleased to see me. If I'm down, he cheers me up. He's totally reliable. How many humans could you say that about?

2 Reading and speaking

Aims: To practice reading for specific information.
To practice speaking on the topic of friendship.

a • Have students look at the quiz. Elicit where the quiz is from – a magazine.
• Have them answer the quiz and check their scores.
• Have them read the relevant interpretation.

b • Put students in pairs or groups.
 • Tell them to compare and discuss the results of the quiz.
 • Ask for feedback from the class.

3 Grammar builder: zero, first, and second conditionals

Aim: To practice zero, first and second conditionals.

a • Have students look at sentences 1–3, or write them on the board. Elicit the names of the different conditionals.
 • Tell students to match the sentence with one of the meanings a–c.
 • Let them compare answers in pairs.
 • Check the answers.

Answers	1 c (zero conditional) 2 a (first conditional) 3 b (second conditional)

 • Check the grammar of zero, first and second conditionals by eliciting the tenses used in the *if* part of the sentence, and in the result clause.

Teaching tip	You might want to translate or ask students to translate the meaning of the conditionals into their native language.

b • Have students complete the sentences, using the appropriate forms of the verbs in parentheses.
 • Let them check their answers in pairs.
 • Check the answers with the class.

Answers	1 talks 2 has 3 is 4 will have 5 moved 6 would keep (first conditional – *moves, will keep* – is also possible here, depending on how likely the condition, Anne's moving, is.)

4 Speaking

Aim: To practice speaking on the topic of friends.

 • Put students in groups.

Teaching tip	Remind students to show the photographs of their friends that they brought to the lesson.

 • Tell students to talk about a friend from elementary school and their current relationship with that person. Have students refer to their photographs if relevant.
 • Ask for feedback, seeing how many students still have contact with these childhood friends.

b) forget your present friends completely in order to concentrate on your duties?

c) see your present friends one or two times a year, and send them Christmas cards?

4 When a close friend has trusted you with a personal secret, have you:

a) always kept the secret and never told anyone?

b) occasionally told the secret to another friend?

c) often told most of your other friends?

5 If you have a serious disagreement with a close friend, do you usually:

a) insist until the friend agrees with you or the friendship breaks down?

b) soon agree with your friend, or change the subject rather than let the problem grow?

c) drop the subject temporarily and try to understand your friend's point of view?

Scoring

1 a=5 b=15 c=10   2 a=5 b=10 c=15   3 a=15 b=5 c=10   4 a=15 b=10 c=5   5 a=5 b=10 c=15

Interpretation:

55–75 points – You consider friendship very important, and are good at making and keeping friends. You try hard to improve the relationships you have.

40–50 points – You consider friendship important, and are fairly good at making and keeping friends. However, you are not always as careful as you could be about maintaining good relations with friends.

25–35 points – You are probably a bit of a loner, and don't depend much on friends. However, if you do want friends, it is not difficult. If you are more sociable and help other people when you can, you will soon have friends.

b In pairs or groups, discuss your results in the quiz. Do they correspond to the facts? For example, are you a loner according to the quiz, but in fact you have many friends?

3 Grammar builder: zero, first and second conditionals

a In pairs, read sentences 1–3 below, and match them to sentences a–c.

1 If I have a disagreement with a friend, I change the subject.
2 You will make new friends if you join a sports club.
3 If I were President, I would not drop my present friends.

a) What you predict will happen as a result of a certain action.
b) What you would probably do in a hypothetical situation.
c) What you usually do in a specific situation.

b Complete the sentences with appropriate forms of the verbs in parentheses.

- Anne always (1) .... (*talk*) with her best friend if she (2) .... (*have*) a problem.
- If she (3) .... (*be*) free tomorrow, she (4) .... (*have*) lunch with some friends.
- If she (5) .... (*move*) to another part of the world, Anne (6) .... (*keep*) in contact with her friends.

4 Speaking

In groups, tell one another about your best friends in elementary school. What relationship do you have with them now?

LANGUAGE for life:

foreign *connections*

1 Are you real users of English yet?

2 Go on – try it!

Find out about your classmates, and let them find out about you! Conduct a survey using the form below. Put a check (✔) in the appropriate box for each person that answers YES or NO (there is no need for anyone's name).

Use of English outside of class	Yes	No
Uses English outside of class at least once every week.*		
Has had a conversation in English with a foreigner** in the last six months.		
Listens to English language songs almost every day.		
Has written or received a letter or e-mail in English in the last six months.		

*Homework and study excluded – must be real communicative use of English

**English teachers excluded

Compare your results in groups, and discuss your findings.

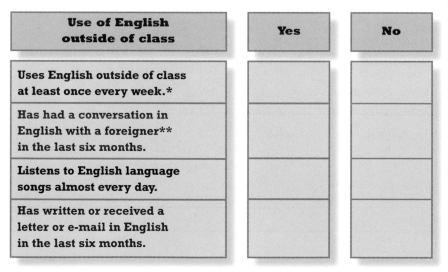

- *How many of the people you surveyed answered YES in each category – none, a few, many, most, everyone?*
  How many answered NO in each category?
- *Are there any interesting cases in the class, or in this group – for example, someone with a foreign boy / girlfriend?*
- *How could you get more practice using English outside of class?*

At some point, students of English have to become users of English if they're really going to learn the language. For some people there's no choice and no problem – from early on they have to use the language regularly for study or work. But others don't, and they need to look for or create opportunities to use English outside of class. This is essential for progress beyond elementary level. If you are an intermediate level student of English who doesn't use English outside of class, it's time to change. It's time to become a real user!

One thing you can easily do is to read and listen to English. Anyone can find English language newspapers, magazines and even books to read, or music and videos to listen to and watch. As you practice your English, you can pursue your interests, and get a better idea of how foreigners view the world. You may disagree with some of those views, but it's better to know what others are up to in this global world!

Lesson 4 Language for life: foreign connections

Note to the teacher

The fourth lesson in each unit is called *Language for life*. This is a new feature which focuses on the use of English in the real world. In order to make the material feel more authentic, it has been styled differently from Lessons 1–3. It has a magazine look, although the instructions to students are in the same style as the main text. Each section within the lesson is clearly numbered, so that the staging is easy to follow and you can use the same teaching approach as with the rest of the material. The teacher's notes for these lessons remain in the same style as the rest of the Teacher's Guide.

Aim: To encourage students to think about using English outside the classroom.

1 Are you real users of English yet?

Aim: To focus students on how much they use English, and to encourage them to explore (new) opportunities to increase their use of it.

- Tell students they are going to carry out a survey on using English outside the classroom.
- Check comprehension of the statements in the survey form.

Teaching tip Check students can form questions from the statements correctly before they conduct the survey.

- Have students move around and ask classmates the questions on the form.
- Put students in groups, and have them compare their results from the survey.
- Ask for feedback from the groups.

2 Go on – try it

Aim: To practice reading for specific information.

- Tell students to look at the cartoon. Elicit what is happening and how it is relevant to using a language outside the classroom.
- Have students read the text, and underline any specific suggestions for progressing beyond elementary level and using English outside the classroom.

Answers Read and listen to English: English language newspapers, magazines, books, music and videos.
Join Internet chat room.
Pen-pal relationship.
Speak to English-speaking foreigners who visit your city.

3 Do you agree?

Aim: To raise students' awareness of how to make progress in English.

- Put students in groups.
- Have them discuss the questions about the text they read in exercise 2.
- Ask for feedback, listing suggestions for making progress and using English outside the classroom on the board.
- Add your own suggestions to the list if appropriate.

4 Action?

Aim: To plan ways to practice English outside the classroom.

- Ask students to write down at least one way they can use English outside the classroom in the following week.
- Put students in pairs.
- Have them compare their ideas.

Teaching tip Remind students to talk about how successful their plan was and compare experiences with their classmates, during the week.

5 Breaking the ice

Aim: To think about strategies to start conversations.

Helping the learner Ask students for any ways they know to start a conversation with a stranger. Write them on the board. This gives an opportunity for students to talk about what they already know, and motivates them to learn something new.

- Have students listen to the tape for exercise 5, and note what they hear.
- Check the answers.

Answers
1 Do you speak English?
2 This is really nice, isn't it?
3 You're not from here, are you?
4 Would you like another drink?
5 Have you looked around the city yet?

Tapescript

1 *Man:* Uh ... Do you speak English?
Man: Sure. I am from France. Almost everyone ...

2 *Woman:* This is really nice, isn't it?
Man: Oh, yes – the garden, the weather ...

3 *Woman:* You're not from here, are you?
Man: No, but I've lived here for ...

4 *Man:* Would you like another drink? I see your glass is empty.
Man: Oh, thanks. Yes, white ...

5 *Man:* Have you looked around the city yet?
Woman: No, no ... Have you?

- Ask students to write down a new identity and to include their new name, age, nationality and profession.
- Have them move around the class having conversations with classmates, using their new identity.

The real problem is being able to interact with other people in English. But there are ways. Through Internet chat rooms you can now have "conversations" with people all over the world. There are still ways to establish traditional pen-pal relationships if you're a traditionalist. And in most places you can find at least a few foreigners who speak English (remember, it's not only Anglo-Saxons who speak English). If you really want to, you can use English.

③
Do you agree?

Discuss the text above in groups. Do you agree about how to progress beyond elementary level? What specific ideas are suggested in the text? What opportunities are there in your city or town to use English outside of class? Where can you:

- *get reading and listening materials?*
- *use e-mail or access chat rooms if you don't have a computer?*
- *meet foreigners?*

④
Action?

Why not plan to use English outside of class next week, and then compare your experiences?

⑤
Breaking the ice

It's not always easy to start a conversation with a stranger, foreign or not.

🎧 Listen to how some people do it, and note what they say.

1 ....
2 ....
3 ....
4 ....
5 ....

Why not practice opening – and continuing – conversations? If you all pretend to be interesting foreigners, it could be fun. (Of course, we're not suggesting that you're not interesting as yourself!)

Unit 2 Work and money

1 Working to live, or living to work?

1 Reading and speaking

a Read the two opinions below. Who works to live, and who lives to work?

"Work shouldn't dominate your life. Other interests and the time you spend with your family and friends are more important. My job's OK, but I'm not in any danger of becoming a workaholic."

"Work is central to life. If I didn't have a worthwhile and satisfying job, I'd be very depressed. In my experience, most people who aren't happy in their work aren't happy in life."

b Discuss these questions in pairs or groups.

1 Do you agree more with the woman or the man? Why?
2 How would you define the word *workaholic*?
3 Do you know any workaholics? Yourself, perhaps?

2 Listening and speaking

a Listen to Lisa and Jim talking about their jobs. What does each of them do?

b Look at the table. Listen to Lisa and Jim again. Complete the table putting plus (+) for each positive aspect of their jobs and minus (–) for each negative aspect.

	Lisa	Jim
1 salary	–	+
2 benefits (medical insurance, pension plan, etc.)		
3 nature of work		
4 working hours		
5 vacations		
6 training and development programs		
7 promotion opportunities		

c In groups, discuss the aspects of a job that are important to you. Look at the points in the table above, and suggest others, e.g. convenient location (near where you live), pleasant colleagues.

Unit 2 Work and money

Helping the learner: vocabulary building

When students are learning new vocabulary, it's a good idea to encourage them to build up a set of related words, rather than try to learn words in isolation. Encourage students to keep a vocabulary notebook and to group words according to topic. Making associations to form sub-groups helps students to record and memorize vocabulary efficiently.

Further reading:
Scrivener, J., (1998) *Learning Teaching*, Macmillan Heinemann ELT, Ch. 7

Lesson 1 Working to live, or living to work?

> **Aims:** To practice the four skills on the topic of work.
> To build up vocabulary associated with work and jobs.

1 Reading and speaking

Aim: To introduce the topic of workaholics.

a • Ask some students what they do for a living and how many hours they work.
  • Get students to read the two texts and decide who *works to live* and who *lives to work*.
  • Check the answer and ask students how they knew.

Answer the woman seems to *live to work* while the man seems to *work to live.*

b • Put students in pairs or groups and have them discuss questions 1–3.
  • Ask for feedback from the class.

2 Listening and speaking

Aim: To practice listening for the main idea and specific information.

a • Explain to students that they are going to hear the two people talking about their jobs.
  • Focus attention on the photographs, and ask students to guess what each person does.
  • Play the tape and have them note down each person's job.

Answers The woman is a junior medical research assistant, and the man is an accountant and administrator.

b • Check comprehension of the items in the table.
  • Play the tape again and have students complete the table with the positive and negative aspects of each person's job.

Answers	1	2	3	4	5	6	7
Lisa	–	+	+	–	–	+	+
Jim	+	–	–	+	+	+	–

c • Put students in groups and have them discuss the important aspects of a job, using the points in the table and adding their own examples.
  • Get feedback and write students' examples on the board.

Tapescript

Woman: I'm a medical research assistant in a college laboratory. I'm a junior assistant so unfortunately I'm not well-paid. The benefits are good, though, especially medical insurance. But it's the work that really matters to me, you know. It's very challenging and rewarding. I love it! Some people might complain and find it tiring – you know, the hours are long and vacations short – but I don't mind. I enjoy every moment of it. But there are good development opportunities too –lots of courses – and promotion opportunities. I won't be a junior research assistant for long!

Man: Well, I'm an accountant and administrator in a big plastics company. I suppose the best thing about the job is the salary - well above the pay in other companies. But the benefits aren't so good, unfortunately. The work is usually boring routine stuff, but it can get demanding and stressful at times. The hours are good, with Saturdays free, and there are generous, flexible vacations. All that is great for a family man like me. There are training programs too, but not many opportunities for promotion in my area.

3 Word builder: vocabulary for talking about jobs

Aim: To practice vocabulary associated with jobs and professions.

Helping the learner	In this exercise, students learn words that are related in meaning, but which are different parts of speech. The table format helps students record their answers in a clear and accessible way. Encourage students to use a table format when recording other vocabulary in lexical sets, e.g. Sports – Person, Verb, Place: *basketball player, play basketball, court*.
Teaching tip	Have students read the Language assistant box in exercise 3a, and elicit more examples of nouns used as adjectives, e.g. *history department, math course*. Focus attention on the Learning tip, before starting the exercise and elicit other information included in a dictionary, e.g. *pronunciation, irregular forms, collocations* and *phrases*.

a • Have students complete the table, using a dictionary when necessary.
 • Have them check in pairs.
 • Check the answers with the class.

Answers 1 accountant 2 administrative / administration 3 architecture 4 chemist
5 dental / dentistry 6 medicine 7 lawyer 8 management 9 scientist
10 science

b • Have students look at the words listed, and classify them as positive, negative, or either, when referring to a job. Have them use a dictionary when necessary.
 • Have them check in pairs. Then check the answers with the class.

Answers positive: flexible, satisfying, rewarding, varied, interesting, well-paid
negative: boring, frustrating, stressful, tiring
positive / negative: challenging, demanding

 • Encourage students to discuss in what situations the words could be positive or negative.

4 Pronunciation: word stress

Aim: To practice identifying and producing stressed syllables in words.

a • Write the words on the board.
 • Play the tape and have students underline the stressed syllables.
 • Check the answers and underline the stressed syllables on the board.

Answers / Tapescript science, scientist, scientific **arch**itecture, **arch**itect, archi**tec**tural

b • Ask students to say the words listed, and underline the stressed syllables.
 • Let them check in pairs. Then play the tape for students to check their answers.

Answers pho**tog**raphy, pho**tog**rapher, photo**graph**ic psy**chol**ogy, psy**chol**ogist, psycho**log**ical
management, **man**ager, mana**ger**ial **chem**istry, **chem**ist, **chem**ical

5 Speaking

Aim: To consolidate vocabulary associated with jobs.

 • Ask students to talk about their jobs and what they like and dislike about them compared to other people's jobs.
 • Get feedback, finding the most interesting / most challenging job, etc.

Writing

Aim: To practice writing a short job description.

a • Tell students to write a paragraph about a particular job without mentioning the name of the profession.
b • Have students read out their paragraphs and the rest of the class guess what the job is.

Preparation:
Ask students to find out information about a famous institutional building in their city or country. They need to find out when it was built, how long it took, what it was used for, etc.

3 Word builder: vocabulary for talking about jobs

a Complete this table of occupational vocabulary. Use a dictionary if you wish. Check in pairs.

Occupation "I'm a / an ..."	Activity "I work in ..."	Adjective "I'm in the ... department."
1	accounts	accounting
administrator	administration	2 ....
architect	3	architectural
4	chemistry	chemical
dentist	dentistry	5 ....
doctor	6	medical
7	law	legal
manager	8	managerial
9	science	10 ....

b Classify the following adjectives that can be used to describe jobs as normally positive (+), normally negative (–), or could be either (±). Check in pairs, using a dictionary when necessary.

boring 〇	challenging 〇	demanding 〇
flexible 〇	frustrating 〇	interesting 〇
satisfying 〇	stressful 〇	tiring 〇
rewarding 〇	varied 〇	well-paid 〇

4 Pronunciation: word stress

a Listen to the following sets of words and underline the stressed syllables.

science scientist scientific   architecture architect architectural

b Now say the following words and underline the stressed syllables. Then listen and check.

photography	psychology	management	chemistry
photographer	psychologist	manager	chemist
photographic	psychological	managerial	chemical

5 Speaking

In pairs or groups, compare your own jobs and the jobs of people you know. You may need vocabulary from the Word builder.

6 Writing

a Write a paragraph about a job (e.g. administration), but DO NOT name the job.

In this job you have to ...   You also ...   It can be very ...   The salary is usually ...

b Read your paragraph aloud to the class, and see if they can guess the job.

2 Winning and losing money

1 Word builder: financial vocabulary

a Match words 1–8 with a definition a–h.

1 gamble		**a)**	money, usually calculated in percentages, earned by an investment
2 capital		**b)**	money earned by a business or investment, after deducting expenses
3 earn		**c)**	to make money from a competition or gambling
4 profit		**d)**	to risk money in a lottery or game, or to take risks in business, etc.
5 interest		**e)**	money lost in a business project or investment
6 invest		**f)**	to make money from work or investments
7 loss		**g)**	money you have that you can put into a business project or investment
8 win		**h)**	to put money into a bank or company to earn interest

b Complete the sentences using the appropriate form of a word from the list above.

1 Enormous numbers of people .... every week in national lotteries, and a very small number .... a fortune.

2 The safest way to .... money is through a bank savings or deposit account, but the .... rates are usually low.

3 The basic idea of business is to invest .... and make a good ....

4 There is always an element of risk in business: instead of .... money, you may take a ...., and even go bankrupt.

2 Speaking and listening

a Look at the pictures. In pairs, discuss these questions.

1 What do the pictures represent?

2 Do you ever gamble in one of these ways, or in another way?

b Listen to a radio interview about gambling in Britain. Which of the three types of gambling in the pictures is the interview about?

c Answer the following questions. Listen to the interview again and check your answers. Compare your revised answers with other students.

1 What do ordinary people who win a fortune often do?

2 Why?

3 What is the most sensible thing to do?

Lesson 2 Winning and losing money

Aims:	To practice vocabulary associated with finance.
	To develop students' speaking and listening skills on the topic of gambling.
	To practice passive constructions.

1 Word builder: financial vocabulary

Aim: To introduce vocabulary associated with finances.

a • Ask students to match the words 1–8 with the definitions a–h.

Answers	1 d 2 g 3 f 4 b 5 a 6 h 7 e 8 c

b • Now have students complete sentences 1–4 with an appropriate word from exercise 1a.

Teaching tip Have students look at the words around each blank space carefully, and decide if they need a noun or a verb, and what form of the verb they need.

• Check the answers.

Answers	1 gamble, win 2 invest, interest 3 capital, profit 4 earning, loss

Helping the learner Give students the opportunity to expand the lexical set of finance by getting them to brainstorm associated vocabulary in groups. Elicit examples and then build up a word map on the board showing how the word groups fit together.

2 Speaking and listening

Aims:	To discuss the topic of gambling.
	To practice listening for the main idea and specific information.

a • Have students look at the pictures.
• Put the students in pairs.
• Tell them to discuss the questions.
• Ask for answers and feedback from the pairs.

Answers	a playing the lottery b card games c betting

• Elicit other examples of gambling from the class.

b • Tell students they are going to listen to an interview about one of the types of gambling shown in the pictures in exercise 2a.
• Play the tape and ask students to identify which type of gambling is being talked about.
• Check the answer.

Answer	playing the lottery

c • Have students answer the questions.
• Play the tape again and allow them to revise their answers.
• Put students in groups to compare their answers.
• Check the answers with the class. (The tapescript is on the next page.)

Answers	1 They often spend the money very quickly.
	2 They aren't used to having a lot of money, so they buy what they have always wanted.
	3 Invest the money and get an accountant.

Tapescript

Interviewer: Twice a week, on Wednesdays and Saturdays, millions of people in Britain listen to the lottery results and check their tickets. Sometimes, millions of pounds are won by one person. I have with me Dr. Paul Medley, a finance specialist and author of the book *Winning and Losing Fortunes.* Paul, tell us about your research.

Dr. Medley: Well, it concentrated on ordinary people who win and then lose fortunes on the lottery. Often, the fortune that was won, was lost again in a year or two.

Interviewer: Why?

Dr. Medley: The main reason is that many winners make no investment plans. They just spend and spend. If the winnings are properly invested before the winners spend much, the capital can earn enough interest for them to live on splendidly for life.

Interviewer: Why don't winners invest?

Dr. Medley: They've probably never had capital to invest before, and their first reaction on winning a large sum of money is to buy all the things they've dreamed of – a splendid house, expensive cars, jewelry ...

Interviewer: I imagine a million pounds or more can be spent very quickly like that.

Dr. Medley: Yes, sometimes in a few months. And most winners give up their jobs, which means they have lots of time on their hands, and they spend that time ...

Interviewer: ... spending money.

Dr. Medley: Exactly.

Interviewer: So what's your advice to lucky winners?

Dr. Medley: Well, the money should be invested as soon as possible. But the very first thing is to get yourself a good accountant.

d • Put students in groups.
  • Have them discuss the questions.
  • Get feedback from the groups.

3 Grammar builder: review of passive constructions

Aim: To review the structure of passive sentences.

a • Get students to look at the sentences and underline the passive structures.
  • Check the answers.

Answers 1 are won   2 was lost   3 can be spent   4 should be invested

b • Put students in pairs.
  • Have them discuss the question.
  • Ask for feedback comparing English with the students' native language.
  • Focus attention on the Language assistant box, and check students understand why the passive is used.

c • Have students complete the paragraph, using passive forms of the verbs in parentheses.
  • Check the answers.

Answers 1 was built   2 was designed   3 was used   4 be completed   5 be inaugurated
6 is recorded / has been recorded

4 Speaking, writing and reading

Aim: To practice using passive constructions.

a • Put students in groups.
  • Have them discuss what they know about an institution in their city or country.

Teaching tip Encourage students to use the information they found as preparation for this lesson.

b • Now have students write a brief history of the institution, using the model in exercise 3c to help them.
  • Join two groups together.
  • Have students exchange their histories and read what the other group has written.
  • Ask some groups to read out their versions.

d In groups, discuss these questions.

1 Do you know any people who have won a lot of money and then lost it again?

2 Have you ever won a large sum of money or a valuable prize?

3 Grammar builder: review of passive constructions

a Look at the following sentences, and underline the verb constructions as in the example.

1 Sometimes, millions of dollars <u>are won</u> by one person.

2 The fortune was lost again in a year or two.

3 A million dollars can be spent very quickly.

4 The money should be invested.

b In pairs, discuss this question.

Are there passive constructions like these in your language?

c Complete the paragraph below using the verbs in parentheses.

The Old Mill (1) .... (*build*) in 1895 by Caleb Fuller. The building (2) .... (*design*) as a textile factory, but later it (3) .... (*use*) as a hospital, a prison, and then a shopping mall. The Town Council is currently remodeling it for its new function, the Old Mill Museum and Cultural Center. The work should (4) .... (*complete*) within four months, and the Center will (5) .... (*inaugurate*) by the Mayor on September 23. The varied history of the Old Mill (6) .... (*record*) in a recently published book by Selma Brett-Howard, *If Buildings Could Speak.*

Language assistant

The passive is used to focus attention on the person or thing affected by an action, rather than on the doer of the action. Often, the doer is not known: *A Picasso painting **was stolen** last night.*

4 Speaking, writing and reading

a In groups, select an institution in your city or country (a bank, a manufacturing company, a college, etc.), and discuss what you know about its history from the time it was founded.

b Write a brief history of the institution. Look at the example in exercise 3c. Exchange your history with another group, and read their version.

3 Entrepreneurs

1 Speaking and reading

a In pairs, discuss the photographs, and the possible connections between them. What do you think is special about The Body Shop products?

b Read the article quickly, and see if your ideas about The Body Shop products were right.

c Read the text again and complete the information in the fact box.

NICE PEOPLE DO WIN

Anita Roddick, who founded The Body Shop, is one of the most successful entrepreneurs in the world. But she thinks that businesses should operate humanely and deal only in products which are environmentally friendly. There appear to be millions of women and men that agree with her.

In the many countries she visited as a young traveler, Anita Roddick noticed the natural substances the local women use to care for their skin and hair. She realized there was no need for the synthetic ingredients, cruel animal testing, and wasteful packaging that are used in the modern cosmetics industry.

The Body Shop, which produces and sells only natural skin and hair care products, first opened in England in 1976. There are now 1,500 stores in 47 countries. It has grown into a $1 billion business with 86 million customers. It was one of the first cosmetics companies that made products for men. Anita Roddick is a real businesswoman, but one who cares about the environment and social justice. She has shown that profit and ethics are not necessarily in conflict. She is an example other entrepreneurs should follow.

The Body Shop

Founded in (1) .... in (2) ....

Now a business worth (3) ...., with (4) .... stores in

(5) .... countries and (6) .... customers.

GUIDING PRINCIPLES
- All products are made from (7) .... ingredients.
- No products are tested on (8) ....
- No wasteful (9) ....

Lesson 3 Entrepreneurs

> **Aims:**   To practice reading and speaking on the topic of entrepreneurs.
> To review the grammar and use of relative clauses.

1 Speaking and reading

Aims: To introduce the topic of entrepreneurs.
To practice reading for specific information.

a • Ask students if they have heard of The Body Shop. Elicit what they already know about it and its products.
• Put students in pairs.
• Have them discuss the photographs.
• Ask for feedback on what connects the photographs.
• Write students' ideas on the board.

b • Tell students to read the article *Nice People Do Win*, quickly, and check if their ideas were correct.
• Write the main ideas that are mentioned in the article on the board.

Answers   Environmentally friendly products are popular. Profit and ethics can coexist.

c • Have students read the article again, and complete the information in the box under the article.

Answers   1 England   2 1976   3 $1 billion   4 1,500   5 47   6 86 million   7 natural
8 animals   9 packaging

2 Grammar builder: review of relative clauses

Aim: To review and practice relative clauses.

a • Write the sentences from exercise 2a on the board.
  • Have students identify the relative clauses.
  • Focus attention on the same sentences in the Student's Book and on the underlined sections.
  • Put students in pairs and ask them to try to work out the rules by matching half-sentences 1–4 with half-sentences a–d.
  • Check the answers, highlighting the rules by referring to the sentences.

Answers	1 d 2 a 3 c 4 b

b • Keep students in the same pairs and have them rewrite the pairs of sentences as single sentences, using relative clauses.
  • Have students compare answers with another pair.
  • Check the answers with the class.

Teaching tip Have students tell you what rule they applied to join each pair of sentences.

Answers	
	1 Anita Roddick is a businesswoman who has made a fortune.
	2 The Body Shop is a $1 billion company that Anita Roddick founded.
	3 The Body Shop sells skin and hair care products that / which have entirely natural ingredients.
	4 Anita Roddick has a philosophy millions of women and men share.
	5 Entrepreneurs are dynamic people who establish new, often innovative, businesses.
	6 In Europe there are many historic cities which / that American tourists often visit.

3 Speaking

Aim: To practice using relative clauses.

a • Put students in groups.
  • Have them discuss the people and things in the pictures, and say what they know about them.
  • Ask for feedback from the groups.

Answers	The pictures show Bill Gates (founder of Microsoft and one of the richest men in the world), an Apple computer, a McDonald's sign, a picture from the movie *Titanic*, starring Kate Winslett and Leonardo di Caprio, Colonel Sanders (symbol of the Kentucky Fried Chicken fast food chain), Steven Spielberg (director of such movies as *Raiders of the Lost Ark, ET, Schindler's List, The Color Purple*).

b • Elicit the kinds of people and events that students like or hate, using relative clauses, as shown in exercise 3b, and write them on the board.
  • Get students to discuss how they feel about them.

Helping the learner This is a good opportunity to build up vocabulary for describing people's characteristics, and also to review some of the qualities from Unit 1, Lesson 3. Elicit examples and write them on the board. Encourage students to form relevant word groups, e.g. Positive characteristics: *generous, good fun, reliable*, etc. Negative characteristics: *mean, boring, dishonest*.

2 **Grammar builder:** review of relative clauses

a In pairs, look at the sentences below, especially the underlined sections. Then match 1–4 with a–d.

The Body Shop deals only in <u>products</u> <u>which</u> are environmentally friendly.

Anita Roddick is a <u>businesswoman</u> <u>who</u> cares about the environment and social justice.

There are millions of <u>women and men</u> <u>that</u> agree with Anita Roddick.

The Body Shop was <u>one of the first cosmetics companies</u> <u>that</u> made products for men.

The Body Shop employs <u>the natural substances</u> <u>the local women</u> use.

Anita Roddick is <u>an example</u> <u>other entrepreneurs</u> should follow.

1	"Which" is used	**a)**	after nouns referring to people
2	"Who" is used	**b)**	when another noun is the subject of the following verb
3	"That" is used	**c)**	after nouns referring to either people or things
4	"Which / who / that" can be omitted	**d)**	after nouns referring to things

b In pairs, write the following pairs of sentences as single sentences, with relative clauses. When possible, omit *which / who / that*. Compare your sentences with other students.

1 Anita Roddick is a businesswoman. She has made a fortune.
2 The Body Shop is a $1 billion company. Anita Roddick founded it.
3 The Body Shop sells skin and hair care products. They have entirely natural ingredients.
4 Anita Roddick has a philosophy. Millions of women and men share it.
5 Entrepreneurs are dynamic people. They establish new businesses, often innovative ones.
6 In Europe there are many historic cities. American tourists often visit them.

3 **Speaking**

a In groups, discuss what you know about the people and things in the pictures below.

b Now discuss the kind of people and events that you really like or hate.

Student 1	*I hate weddings that ...*	*The reason is that ...*	*How do you feel about weddings?*
Student 2	*I love people who ...*	*I suppose that's because ...*	*What about you?*
Student 3	*I love parties which ...*	*I always ...*	*What kind of parties do you like?*

LANGUAGE for life:
armchair *shopping*

1 Home delivery

You're at home, feeling tired but hungry. There's nothing to eat in the kitchen. It's dark and raining outside. You can:

1 go to bed hungry.
2 go out to the nearest restaurant.
3 call for a pizza.

What would you usually do? Have you been in that situation? If so, what did you do?

Compare your answers in groups. Then discuss these questions.

- *Is there anyone in the group who regularly orders food by phone?*
- *Where from?*
- *Why?*
- *Is there anyone who never orders food by phone?*
- *Why not?*

2 Magic plastic

Telephone ordering of food for home delivery is just one kind of armchair shopping. People usually pay cash for their pizza. But most other armchair shopping is paid for by check or, most often, credit card. Do you know the history of the credit card? No? **Well, guess what's happening in the scene shown below. Have you ever been in a similar situation?**

Now listen to a radio talk, and decide which part of the talk the picture is illustrating. Then listen again and note the following information.

1 Year when Frank McNamara decided to start Diners Club credit cards: ....

2 Number of cards issued by McNamara in the first year: ....

3 Number of restaurants that accepted that first Diners Club card: ....

4 Bank that issued the first widely used credit card: ....

5 Year that card was introduced: ....

6 Present name of that card: ....

7 Name another credit card that was introduced in 1958: ....

8 Number of credit card holders in the United States: ....

Lesson 4 Language for life: armchair shopping

> **Aim:** To raise awareness of the use of English for buying things by mail, by phone or on the Internet.

1 Home delivery

Aim: To introduce the topic of ordering food by phone.

- Put students in groups.
- Have them discuss options 1–3 and the questions in the box.
- Get feedback, finding out how students feel about ordering food by phone.

2 Magic plastic

Aims: To discuss the topic of credit cards.
To practice listening for specific information.

- Ask students what you need to buy something over the phone or on the Internet; elicit *credit card*.
- Have students read the introductory paragraph in exercise 2.
- Ask students to guess what's happening in the scene that is drawn, and ask if they have been in a similar situation.
- Play the tape for students to decide which part of the talk the picture is illustrating.
- Check the answer with the class.

Answer Frank McNamara was in a restaurant and did not have enough money to pay the bill.

- Play the tape again and get students to note the information necessary to complete questions 1–8.
- Have students compare their answers in pairs.
- Check the answers with the class.

Answers 1 1950 2 200 3 27 4 Bank of America 5 1958 6 Visa 7 American Express 8 140 million

Tapescript

Judy: Now it's time for Jack Paltrow and the "Did-You-Know" segment. Jack.

Jack: Thanks, Judy. Credit cards are an essential part of life today, aren't they? But they haven't existed for very long. In fact, our plastic society owes its existence in part to an evening out in 1950 which went wrong. Businessman Frank McNamara was wining and dining clients at an expensive Manhattan restaurant. When the check arrived, his heart sank – he didn't have enough cash with him, not enough to pay a check that was more than he expected. He phoned his wife, who drove to the rescue. But out of that embarrassing moment came the idea for Diners Club. Why not lend money to restaurant-goers? Frank McNamara thought. And that's what he did – lend money to restaurant-goers through a credit card. In the first year, 200 cards were issued by McNamara and they were accepted at 27 restaurants. Then, in 1958, the first widely used bank credit card was introduced by Bank of America. It later became Visa. Another entrant that year was American Express. Today, there are 140 million cardholders in the U.S. alone.

Judy: 140 million! Including you and me, Jack. We couldn't live without our magic plastic.

Jack: I guess not, Judy.

3 What about you?

Aim: To discuss the advantages and disadvantages of credit cards.

- Put students in groups.
- Have them discuss the advantages and disadvantages of credit cards.
- Get feedback from the groups.

4 Mail order

Aim: To practice giving personal information and form filling.

- Elicit from students that the text of exercise 4 is a mail order form for some CDs.
- Have students complete the form with their own personal details.
- Put students in pairs to check that they understood and completed the forms appropriately.
- Get feedback on whether students would really like to order the CDs.

5 Internet

Aim: To discuss shopping on the Internet.

Helping the learner	This would be a good opportunity to work on extending the vocabulary associated with the Internet. Let students brainstorm the vocabulary and decide on categories to form word groups. Write the words on the board in groups and flag the word stress of any difficult examples. Encourage students to record the word stress when they record new vocabulary.

- Put students in groups.
- Have them discuss their experience of shopping on the Internet.
- Get feedback from the groups.

| Optional activity | Internet order forms
Ask students to bring an Internet order form to class to look at the kind of information required. Alternatively, if computers are available, let students go online and look for order forms. |
|---|---|

③

What about you?

⑤

Internet

Could you (or do you) live without "magic plastic"? Discuss the advantages and disadvantages of credit cards with your group.

Of course, you can also shop on the Internet. Does anyone have any experience of this? How has it worked out? What good advice is there?

④

Mail order

Complete the form with your own information.

20TH CENTURY TOP 50! – 2 exclusive CDs with the 50 absolute top songs of the last century. You'll never know how wonderful they still are until you hear them in this re-engineered digital version. Not sold in stores. Order by mail now! Just complete and send the form below.

20TH CENTURY TOP 50! * * * * CD EXPRESS * * * * ORDER FORM

Last name(s) .... First name(s) .... Mr ☐ Mrs ☐ Miss ☐ Ms ☐

Address (street and number) ....

.... City and country .... Zip code ....

Telephone .... Fax .... E-mail ....

Number of sets you want (each set consists of 2 CDs) ....

Form of payment: Check ☐   Money order ☐   Credit card (details below) ☐

Credit card: American Express ☐   MasterCard ☐   Visa ☐   Diners Club ☐

Expiry date: Month ☐☐ Day ☐☐ Year ☐☐   Card number ☐☐☐☐ ☐☐☐☐ ☐☐☐☐ ☐☐☐☐

Cardholder's name .... Signature ....

We would really appreciate your answers to these questions:

Are the CDs for yourself or for someone else? ....

Why are you buying these CDs? ....

Check your completed form with a partner. Have you interpreted everything the same way? Would you really like these CDs for yourself or someone else? Why or why not?

1 Learning check

1 Progress check

a **Complete the paragraph using the verbs in parentheses.**

Canada (**1**) *has existed* .... (*exist*) as a nation since 1867. Initially, it (**2**) *consisted* ....
(*consist*) of four provinces: Ontario, Quebec, New Brunswick and Nova Scotia. But at the time of
independence, immigrants (**3**) *moved* .... (*move*) fast into the west, and soon new
provinces (**4**) *were added* .... (*add*), beginning with Manitoba in 1870 and British
Columbia in 1871. Canada now has 10 provinces and three territories. Nunavut, an autonomous
Inuit or Eskimo territory, (**5**) *was established* .... (*establish*) in 1999.

b **Select appropriate completions for the conversation.**

Jill: Tell me about that article (**6**) *you read* .... about Nunavut.

    a) that read   **b)** who read   **c)** you read

Jack: Sure. Do you know what (**7**) *the population is*? Only 25,000! That's really tiny for a territory

    a) large is the population   **b)** the population is   **c)** is the population

    (**8**) *that's* .... larger than Argentina.

    a) who's   **b)** which it's   **c)** that's

Jill: Larger than Argentina? Do you really know how big (**9**) *Nunavut is*? Or Argentina?

    a) does Nunavut have   **b)** is Nunavut   **c)** Nunavut is

Jack: That's what the article says. Anyway, if I (**10**) *were* .... an Inuit, I'd feel happy about Nunavut.

    a) were   **b)** am   **c)** would be

Jill: Yes. But what's (**11**) *being done* to improve the Inuits' lives?

    a) been doing   **b)** being done   **c)** be done

Jack: I can't remember. If I find the article, (**12**) *I'll give* ..... it to you.

    a) I'll give   **b)** I give   **c)** I'd give

c **Write a compound word (e.g. *classroom* or *compact disc*) for each definition.**

13 A *post office* .... is a place to buy stamps and mail letters.

14 *Housework* .... is what you do to keep your home clean and tidy.

15 An *Internet café* .... is a place where anyone can go to use the Internet.

Learning check 1

1 Progress check

Aims: To provide an opportunity to assess students' progress and help them according to the results.
To provide an opportunity for learners to test themselves.
To allow students to evaluate their own progress and act on areas they need to improve.

Suggestions for using the *Progress check* sections
This section can be done in a variety of ways depending on how much time you have and whether you want students to do it as part of an individual assessment or as general revision.
a As a test – students work individually on the *Progress check* sections and you then check their work and record their score out of 15.
b Students work on the *Progress check* sections alone and then check their answers in pairs.
c Students work on the *Progress check* sections in pairs or groups and you later check the answers with the whole class.
d Students do the *Progress check* sections for homework.

In all cases, conduct a feedback session with the whole class to check any queries students may have and see how they did.

Explanation of answers
a
1 Present perfect for something that started in the past and continues up to the present.
2 Past simple for something that is no longer true, indicated by the use of the word *initially*.
3 Past simple for a completed action in the past.
4 Past simple passive to focus on the provinces, rather than who added them.
5 Past simple passive to focus on Nunavut, rather than who established it.

b
6 *That / which* is not needed, as another noun is the subject of the following verb.
7 Indirect question word order needed here; *what large,* in **a**, is not a possible reported question word.
8 *That* is needed after a noun referring to a thing; *which it's,* in **b**, is not possible, as it includes the subject *it*.
9 Indirect question needed here, so there is no auxiliary and statement word order is used.
10 *Were,* to complete second conditional, expressing what you would do in a hypothetical situation.
11 Present progressive passive to focus on the action, not the doer.
12 *I'll give,* to complete first conditional expressing the result of a certain action.

c
This exercise is to test students' knowledge of compound words and there is only one possible answer for each question.

2 Proficiency check

Aims: To expose students to TOEFL and UCLES-style exam formats, which will be useful for those students interested in taking such formal proficiency exams.
To develop students' exam-taking strategies.
To allow teachers and students the opportunity to evaluate students' proficiency in English.
To test students' listening and reading skills under pseudo-exam conditions.

Suggestions for taking the test

Taking language tests is not only about knowing the language. It also involves knowing how to deal with exams: how to work under pressure; how to recognize the operations of the exam; and how to apply strategies to get the best results in an exam. These *Proficiency checks* give students the opportunity to work on all of these areas.

Students could do this as a formal proficiency test where they work individually, in silence. The tests are then collected and checked by the teacher. Alternatively, students could do the test individually and then check their answers in pairs or groups.

In either case, it is recommended that students as a class have the opportunity to discuss their answers and how they arrived at them with the teacher. Explanations of the correct answers are given to facilitate the teacher's role here. In addition, the teacher can highlight the strategy that is given in every *Proficiency check*. This is very helpful in giving students the chance to work on their exam-taking strategies as well as their accuracy with the language.

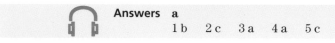

Answers a

1 b   2 c   3 a   4 a   5 c

Tapescript
Man 1: Miss ... uh ... Pérez, do you speak English?
Applicant: Yes, I do. I'm studying with *Skyline 4*, and I'm going to take TOEFL next year.
Woman: Good. So we can have the interview in English.
Applicant: Uh ... yes.
Man 2: You're applying for a scholarship in ... psychology?
Applicant: Yes, psychology.
Woman: Are you interested in research or practice?

Applicant: Both – research and practice.
Man 1: I see. And in what specific area?
Applicant: Education, educational psychology.
Man 2: OK. Now tell us why you think you deserve a scholarship.
Applicant: Why I ... uh ... deserve a scholarship?
Man 2: Yes.
Applicant: Well ... uh ... my grades at college ...

b

1 b   2 c   3 a   4 c   5 a

Exam-taking tip   Reading the questions first
Students often start reading a reading comprehension passage without reading the questions first. Reading the questions first can help to save time and to focus the reading. Encourage students to read the questions first.

2 Proficiency check

a Read sentences 1–5, below. Then listen to the interview, and select the best completion (a–c) for each sentence. You will hear the interview only once.

1 Ms. Pérez is applying for:
   a) a promotion.
   b) a scholarship.
   c) a job.

2 Her subject is:
   a) physics.
   b) sociology.
   c) psychology.

3 She is interested in:
   a) research and practice.
   b) practice.
   c) research.

4 Her area of interest is:
   a) education.
   b) industry.
   c) occupational therapy.

5 She is going to explain:
   a) her needs.
   b) her special interests.
   c) her strong points.

b Read the passage. Then read the questions and select the best answers.

You should now be able to use English reasonably well in many real situations outside the classroom, for example:

- understanding announcements or simple presentations
- talking with foreigners in your own country or abroad
- reading for study, work or general interest; writing e-mails, letters or simple reports.

Many institutions of higher education and companies require candidates for a course, scholarship or job to prove their ability to use English for real communication. This usually means taking some kind of proficiency test. These tests check not only what you have just studied, but also all the English you have accumulated – your general proficiency in the language and your ability to communicate in real situations.

The Proficiency check section of Skyline will help you begin to prepare for widely accepted proficiency tests like TOEFL and Cambridge.

1 What is the main purpose of the whole text?
   a) To encourage you to use English outside the classroom.
   b) To explain the function of the "Proficiency check" section of this book.
   c) To discuss the use of English in study and work.

2 What is the main idea of the first paragraph?
   a) Your knowledge of English grammar is now almost complete.
   b) You now have to speak English outside the classroom a lot.
   c) Your English should now be good enough for many practical purposes.

3 What is the main idea of the second paragraph?
   a) To continue your studies or to work, you may need to pass a proficiency test.
   b) Colleges, companies, etc. have to use English proficiency tests now.
   c) Proficiency tests do not test what you have just learned.

4 *Abroad* in line 4 of paragraph 1 means:
   a) in another city.
   b) outside the classroom.
   c) not in your country.

5 *This* in line 2 of paragraph 2 refers to:
   a) proving ability to really use English.
   b) a course, scholarship or job.
   c) real communication in English.

Unit 3 Keeping up with technology

1 Developing the automobile

1 Speaking

a In pairs or groups, discuss the following questions.

1 Do you have a car? If so, what do you use it for? If not, what would you like to use one for?

2 What kind of problems do cars cause in big cities?

b Which of the cars on the right would you like to own? Why?

2 Reading and speaking

a In pairs, answer these questions, guessing if necessary.

1 Have there been gasoline-powered motor vehicles for more than 100 years or less?

2 Were cars in 2000 technically very different from cars in 1970 or virtually the same?

3 Which state in the United States took the lead in moving toward non-polluting vehicles – California, Illinois or New York?

4 Will non-polluting vehicles ever be as satisfactory in general performance as gasoline-powered cars?

b Read the following magazine article and check your answers to exercise 2a.

WHY CHANGE FROM GASOLINE ENGINES?

Automobiles have come a long way since Carl Benz built the first practical gasoline-powered motor vehicle in 1885. Over the first seven decades of the 20th century they became increasingly fast, comfortable, safe and reliable. Most of them also became much less expensive, so more and more people could afford one, new or secondhand.

By 1970 little technical improvement of automobiles seemed possible. However, by the end of the century virtually any new car could cruise safely at 20 miles an hour faster, using less gasoline and producing 80% less pollution than a new 1970 car. This was the result of using new technology such as fuel injection, multi-valve cylinders, and above all, microprocessors (or minicomputers).

But even today's cars produce about 50,000 kilograms of pollutants annually, mostly carbon monoxide and ozone, and every day there are more motor vehicles. Most people realize this is leading towards an ecological and human health disaster and some governments have been pushing automobile manufacturers to produce clean alternatives to the gas engine. In California, 10% of all new cars from 2003 have to be ZEVs (Zero Emission Vehicles) and that quota will increase progressively.

The first electric ZEVs were slow, limited in range, and very expensive compared with conventional cars, but that will soon change. The automobile

Keeping up with technology

Helping the learner: giving learners responsibility

Current language teaching methodology suggests that students learn more effectively if they are given responsibility for their own learning. The following list shows how you can make learners more responsible:
- Ask students to work things out for themselves.
- Use students' input as material for the class.
- Use group and pair work.
- Expose students to different ways of learning, e.g. online courses.

In this unit, there is a lot of material which helps to give students more responsibility.

Further reading:
Scrivener, J., (1998) *Learning Teaching*, Macmillan Heinemann ELT, Ch. 2

Lesson 1   Developing the automobile

> **Aims:**   To develop students' reading and speaking skills on the topic of cars.
> Io learn about and practice contrastive stress.

1 Speaking

Aim: To introduce the topic of cars.

a • Ask a few students if they have a car and what kind they have.
   • Put students in pairs or groups.
   • Tell them to discuss questions 1–2.
   • Ask for feedback from the class.

b • Focus attention on the pictures of the cars.
   • Keep students in the same pairs / groups; have them discuss the questions in the exercise.
   • Ask for feedback from the class.

Teaching tip   Remember to ask students for reasons to justify their choice of car from exercise 1b.

2 Reading and speaking

Aim: To practice reading for specific information.

a • Put students in pairs.
   • Tell them to try to answer questions 1–4. Encourage them to share knowledge and guess the answers if necessary, without reading the article in exercise 2b at this stage.
   • Get feedback, asking students to give possible reasons for their answers.

Teaching tip   Pre-teach the term *Zero Emission Vehicle*, the abbreviation *ZEV*, and check students understand what it means – *a non-polluting vehicle*.

b • Now have students read the article in exercise 2b to check their answers.
   • Check the answers with the class.

Answers   1 For more than 100 years, since 1885.   2 Very different, as new technology such as fuel injection, multi-valve cylinders and micro-processors has been introduced.
3 California   4 ZEVs will be better than gas-engine vehicles in every way.

c • Tell students to work individually and write down three facts they learned from the article.
• Put students in pairs and have them compare what they learned.

3 Reading, listening and speaking

Aim: To practice predicting and listening to check answers.

a • Check comprehension of statements 1–5 about ZEVs.
• Get students to predict whether the statements are true or false.

b • Play the tape and have students check their predictions from exercise 3a.

Answers	1 F 2 T 3 F 4 T 5 T

c • Check comprehension of the categories in the chart.
• Play the tape again and have students complete the chart.

Answers	**Gasoline vehicles**	**ZEVs**
	gasoline	electricity, hydrogen and oxygen
	high	low
	high	low
	more expensive	cheaper
	as fast as ZEVs	as fast as gasoline vehicles

Tapescript

Interviewer: So Zero Emission Vehicles will take over, will they?
Professor: Yes. Soon they'll be better than traditional gasoline-engine vehicles in every way.
Interviewer: That means speed, range, economy.
Professor: Yes. People think the only advantage of ZEVs is that they don't pollute. But electric vehicles can already reach the same speeds as gasoline vehicles.
Interviewer: Really! But the range is limited, isn't it? I mean, the batteries need recharging every 50 or 100 miles, don't they?
Professor: That depends on the technology you use. Storing energy in batteries is a problem at present. But new smaller and lighter batteries are being developed that can store more electricity. However, the real solution is probably in fuel cells.
Interviewer: Fuel cells? What are they?

Professor: Well fuel cells actually generate electricity, so storage is no problem. In fact, with fuel-cell technology you'll be able to travel further than you can at the moment. And you won't need to stop to refuel. So you may be able to drive for a thousand miles without refueling. And the fuel is hydrogen and oxygen, two of the most common gases in nature.
Interviewer: That makes it more economical, doesn't it?
Professor: Yes. Traveling by ZEV will be cheaper, much cheaper. And the cost of the vehicles will also come down as they go into mass production. And don't forget the noise pollution of gasoline and diesel engines as well as the air pollution. Just imagine the quiet cities of the future compared with the noisy ones today.
Interviewer: Right. Thank you very much, Professor Bunsen.
Professor: My pleasure.

d • Put students in groups and have them discuss the question and the situation.
• Conduct whole class feedback session.

4 Pronunciation: contrastive stress

Aim: To practice recognition and production of contrastive stress.

Helping the learner	This exercise gives students responsibility for their own learning by getting them to work out how contrastive stress works.

a • Focus attention on sentence 1, and on the underlined words.
• Elicit why the underlined words are stressed.

Answer	Because two different types of pollution are being contrasted.

• Now get students to underline the stressed words in sentence 2.

b • Play the tape again and say why the words are stressed. Have learners check the answer.

| Answer | quiet, noisy
Because noise levels in the cities of today and the future are being contrasted. |
|---|---|

• Now ask students to practice saying the sentences with appropriate stress.

c • Put students in pairs, and elicit which words will need to be stressed when students compare the things that are contrasted.

Answers	big, small; public, private

• Have students discuss their ideas.
• Ask for feedback, encouraging students to use contrastive stress.

industry is exploring different technologies, and several breakthroughs are close. More new cars are sold in California annually than in most countries, so this will have an impact everywhere. A change in the global market will then lead to mass production and reduced cost. One day soon, your city will be a quiet, pollution-free place, and ZEVs will be better than gas-engine vehicles in every way.

c Note at least three facts you have learned from reading this article. Compare your notes with a partner.

3 Reading, listening and speaking

a Read the following statements. Mark the statements T (true) or F (false).

1 ZEVs (Zero Emission Vehicles) will never be able to go as fast as gasoline-engine vehicles. T ◯ F ◯
2 Some ZEVs will be able to go farther than gasoline-engine vehicles without refueling. T ◯ F ◯
3 The best option for the development of ZEVs is new types of electric battery. T ◯ F ◯
4 ZEVs will soon be more economical than gasoline-engine vehicles. T ◯ F ◯
5 ZEVs are expensive at present because they are not mass produced. T ◯ F ◯

b Listen to an interview about ZEVs and check your answers.

c Listen again and complete the chart.

	Gasoline vehicles	ZEVs
source of energy		
level of pollution		
amount of noise		
cost		
speed		

d What have authorities in your country done to reduce pollution from vehicles? Imagine you are responsible for reducing vehicle pollution in your city. Make a list of five ideas to attack the problem of vehicle pollution.

4 Pronunciation: contrastive stress

a Look at the two sentences below from the interview. The two words in (1) that have the strongest stress or emphasis are underlined. Why are those two words stressed? Underline the two words in (2) with the strongest stress.

1 Don't forget the noise pollution as well as the air pollution.
2 Just imagine the quiet cities of the future compared with the noisy ones today.

b Listen to these sentences, and check the stressed words in 4a. Practice saying the two sentences.

c In pairs, discuss your ideas about the following things.

1 Big cars and small ones
2 Public transportation and private cars

2 Communications systems

1 Speaking

a **Talk to the people in your class. Find people who do these things.**

- spend more than one hour on the telephone every day
- listen to the radio a lot
- spend more than two hours watching television every day
- spend more than two hours using a computer every day
- have a cellular telephone
- have an e-mail address

Check (✔) each of the statements every time a student says *yes*.

b **In groups of three or four, discuss what you found out from the questionnaire. Summarize your conclusions by writing *Everybody*, *Most people*, *Very few people* or *Nobody* beside each statement.**

Most people spend more than one hour on the telephone every day.

2 Reading and speaking

a **Read the three topic sentences below, and then read the article. Match each topic sentence with the appropriate paragraph.**

1 But in our natural excitement over this constant development of electronic media, we should not forget that most people in the world don't have a telephone, and many don't even have electricity or clean water. ○

2 Almost all households in the U.S. today have at least three pieces of electronic communications equipment: a radio, a television and a telephone. ○

3 Major electronics companies are already working on the next generation in communications technology – combining all these modes of communication. ○

> **Learning tip:**
>
> using topic sentences
>
> - When you read a text, the topic sentence gives the reader the main idea in each paragraph.
> - The topic sentence is almost always the first sentence in a paragraph. The other sentences give more details or examples.

ACCESS TO TECHNOLOGY

a)
At least one third of American households also have a computer connected to the Internet. In addition, more than one in every five adults has a cell phone, and more and more people have some kind of portable computer which connects to the Internet.

b)
There will soon be fast, functional and widely affordable mobile "media phones" that will give you telephone, television and Internet all in one. And at home your telephone (or videophone) will also have a television and computer with Internet in a single apparatus. And it won't end there.

Lesson 2 Communications systems

Aims:	To develop students' reading and speaking skills on the topic of communications systems.
	To focus on topic sentences.
	To practice using the gerund.

1 Speaking

Aim: To introduce the topic of communications systems.

a • Have students read the list of activities.
  • Elicit the questions that they should ask each other, to find the answers they need.
  • Have students move around the classroom asking each other the questions and putting a check for every person they find who says yes.

b • Put students in groups of three or four.
  • Have students summarize by writing the words *everybody, nobody, some people, most people* against the statements in the questionnaire.
  • Get feedback from the groups.

Helping the learner In this exercise, the students' answers to the questionnaire are used to produce summaries. Using students' input in this way encourages them to take responsibility for their learning.

2 Reading and speaking

Aim: To recognize topic sentences.

  • Focus attention on the Learning tip, and check students understand what is meant by a topic sentence.

a • Have students read the three topic sentences.
  • Check they understand that they need to work out which sentence goes with which paragraph.
  • Have students do the task.
  • Check the answers.

Answers **Paragraph a** – sentence 2 **Paragraph b** – sentence 3 **Paragraph c** – sentence 1

  • **Optional step:** Refer students back to the reading text in Unit 3 Lesson 1, page 24 and get them to underline the topic sentences in each paragraph.

b • Have students decide which paragraph of the article contains the writer's main point and what that point is.
 • Put them in groups of three or four.
 • Have them discuss the writer's main point.
 • Ask for feedback from the groups.

Answer The writer seems to be making the point that technology is not the most important thing in the world and is not available to everyone, so paragraph 3 expresses the main point.

c • Keep students in their groups.
 • Have students discuss their knowledge and use of technology compared with their parents'.
 • Encourage students to focus on the advantages and disadvantages of technological changes.
 • Get feedback from the groups.

3 Grammar builder: gerunds

Aim: To practice the use of gerunds.
 • Write the sentence *Smoking is bad for you* on the board.
 • Underline the gerund *Smoking* and make sure students understand that gerunds are nouns that take the *-ing* form.
 • Elicit other examples of gerunds.

a • Focus attention on the sentences, and on the underlined gerund phrase in the example.
 • Have students underline the gerund phrases in the other sentences.
 • Check the answers.

Answers 2 Traveling by ZEV   3 Using a portable computer   4 creative thinking

b • Focus attention on the sentences, and on the gerund phrase in the example given for sentence 1.

Teaching tip Highlight the change in word order in the example to help students with the other gerund phrases.

 • Tell students to substitute the underlined words with gerund phrases in the other sentences.
 • Check the answers.

Answers 2 Working at night / nights   3 Living in a city / cities   4 developing technology

Teaching tip Elicit the stress in the gerund phrases – tra**vel**ing by **sea**, **work**ing at **night** / **nights**, **liv**ing in a **cit**y, deve**lo**ping tech**nol**ogy

c • Put students in pairs.
 • Student A looks at column A, and reads the statements. Student B says whether she / he agrees or disagrees.
 • Student B looks at column B, and reads the statements. Student A says whether she / he agrees or disagrees.
 • Get feedback from the pairs.

c)

Using a cell phone or handheld computer doesn't make you an Aristotle, Galileo or Einstein, whose achievements were made without the help of computers and the Internet. Living "off-line" is still the essential human condition.

b Decide which of the three paragraphs contains the writer's main point. What is that point? Compare and discuss your ideas with two or three partners.

c Work in groups of three or four. What are the main differences in technology between your generation and your parents' when they were your age? What are the main advantages and disadvantages of these changes?

I don't have a cell phone, but I know how to use one. My parents have no idea!

3 Grammar builder: gerunds

Gerunds are nouns that take the **–ing** form.

Smoking *is bad for you.*

a Underline the gerund phrases below. The first one has been done for you.

1 <u>Storing energy in batteries</u> is a problem at present.
2 Traveling by ZEV will be cheap.
3 Using a portable computer doesn't make you an Aristotle, Galileo or Einstein.
4 Our best hope for the future is creative thinking.

b Substitute the underlined words below with gerund phrases. The first one has been done for you.

1 <u>Sea travel</u> is uncommon nowadays. Traveling by sea
2 <u>Night work</u> is usually very inconvenient. ....
3 <u>City life</u> can be dangerous. ....
4 A lot of investment goes into <u>technology development</u>. ....

c Work in pairs. Student A look at column A and student B look at column B. Read each sentence to your partner and say if you agree or disagree with the statement and why.

Using computers doesn't improve your life. *No, I don't agree. Using computers is really useful.*
For example, you can bank on the Net 24 hours a day.

Column A

Surfing the Internet is a waste of time.
Playing video games makes kids hyperactive.

Column B

Using cell phones is usually unnecessary.
Watching TV is an escape from reality.

3 Using technology

1 Listening and speaking

a Work in pairs. Identify the appliances in the pictures using the words in the list below. Put them in order of most useful to least useful. Compare your list with another pair and give the reasons for your choices.

- a microwave oven   ◯
- a dishwasher   ◯
- an airconditioning / heating unit   ◯
- an electric toothbrush   ◯
- a videocassette recorder   ◯

b An 80-year-old man and his 18-year-old granddaughter are talking in the kitchen. Listen to their conversation and answer these questions.

1 How does the grandfather feel?
2 What is his attitude toward technology?
3 How does the granddaughter feel?
4 What is her attitude toward technology?

c Listen to the conversation again and answer these questions.

1 What is the grandfather trying to do?
2 Why is he having a problem?
3 What sequence of buttons should he be pressing?
4 The final time, what does he forget to include?

d The grandfather says "The trouble with technology is that it makes life easier but more impersonal. People don't talk to each other anymore." What do you think? Discuss your ideas in groups.

2 Pronunciation: intonation – question tags

a Listen to the intonation in the following two sentences. In the first one the speaker is sure and the intonation on the question tag falls. In the second, the speaker is unsure and the intonation on the question tag rises.

1 *This soup's hot, isn't it?* (Sure)   2 *You didn't resign, did you?* (Unsure)

Lesson 3 Using technology

> **Aims:** To practice the four skills on the topic of technology.
> To focus on the intonation and grammar of question tags.

1 Listening and speaking

Aim: To introduce the topic of technology.

a • Put students in pairs.
  • Have them identify the appliances in the pictures and check they can explain what each one does.
  • Have them put the appliances in order (1 = the most useful, 5 = the least useful).
  • Ask for feedback from the pairs.

b • Ask students to read the situation described, and the questions, and to predict what the old man and granddaughter will discuss on the tape.
  • Play the tape and have students check their predictions.
  • Play the tape again and have students answer the questions.
  • Check the answers.

Answers 1 He feels frustrated and unsure of himself.   2 He finds technology frustrating. He thinks technology makes life easier but more impersonal.
3 She feels confident and sure of herself.
4 She thinks technology is good and she's looking forward to living with more technology.

c • Have students read the questions.
  • Play the tape again.
  • Have students answer the questions.
  • Check the answers.

Answers 1 He wants to heat a cup of coffee.   2 He can't get the sequence of buttons right.
3 CLEAR, TIME, number of minutes, START   4 CLEAR

d • Put students in groups.
  • Have them read what the grandfather said.
  • Have them discuss their ideas.
  • Ask for feedback from the groups.

Helping the learner This section has students working in pairs and groups, as well as individually. Collaborative pair and group work makes lessons more student-centered and helps learners take responsibility for the content and direction of the discussion.

Tapescript
Man: Why do these things never work?
Girl: The microwave? Oh, Grandpa, everyone knows how to ...
Man: You press CLEAR first, don't you? I did that. Then I pressed TWO ZERO ZERO – you know, two minutes, for a cup of coffee. Then I pressed START, but it didn't start. Is it stupid or something?
Girl: No ... you ... uh, to set the time you have to press the TIME button first, like this.
Man: So it's first CLEAR, then TIME, then the number of minutes, and finally START, is that it?
Girl: That's right.
Man: Hmm, I could do it faster on the stove, couldn't I?
Girl: Maybe. But instead of TIME and the number of minutes, try pressing BEVERAGE and START.

Man: Uh ... so it's BEV ...
Girl: ... CLEAR first ...
Man: (taking no notice) ... ERAGE, START. There you are! It hasn't started, has it? It just won't work for me, will it?
Girl: You didn't press CLEAR, did you?
Man: What? Oh, forget it, Mandy. I'm going to stop using these infernal machines.
Girl: Well, the future isn't just a few "infernal machines". It's "smart houses" – everything electronically controlled and interconnected. I'm going to live in a house like that.
Man: Huh! The trouble with technology is that it makes life easier but more impersonal. People don't talk to each other anymore.

2 Pronunciation: intonation – question tags

Aim: To focus on the intonation of question tags.

a • Write the two sentences on the board.
  • Play the tape and draw in arrows 🗘 or 🗘 to show the intonation of the question tags.
  • Check students understand that in sentence 1 the speaker is sure and in sentence 2 the speaker is unsure.

b • Have students listen to the four sentences from the conversation in exercise 1, and decide if the speaker is sure or unsure according to the intonation of the question tag.
   • Play the tape again and stop after each sentence to check.

Answers   1 U   2 S   3 S   4 S

Language help   Point out to the student that it is the verb in the grammar tag which carries the main stress. If they stress the pronoun, it does not sound natural.

3 Grammar builder: question tags

Aim: To focus on the grammar of question tags.

a • Focus attention on the examples in exercise 2b.
   • Ask students what they notice about the grammar of the question tags.

Answer   If the statement is affirmative, the question tag is negative. If the statement is negative, the question tag is affirmative. If there is no auxiliary in the statement, the auxiliary *do / does* must be used the question tag. If there is an auxiliary verb, this is also used in the question tag.

   • Now have students supply the missing question tags in the sentences.
   • Have them check their answers in pairs.
   • Play the tape and have students check their answers against the recording.

Answers   1 doesn't it?   2 didn't it?   3 won't it?   4 do you?   5 can they?   6 aren't you? 7 did you?

b • Put students in pairs.
   • Have them talk about how they express question tags in their native language.
   • Get feedback from the pairs.

4 Speaking, reading and writing

Aim: To practice giving instructions.

a • Put students in pairs or groups.
   • Have them discuss how easy or difficult it is to use the items listed. Encourage students to talk about their own experiences of using the items.
   • Ask for feedback from the class.
b • Tell students to read the text about the camera quickly, and say what the function is of each of the features shown.
   • Check the answers.

Answers   preview button – to preview pictures, select button – to print pictures, mode button – to make reprints

c • Tell students to read the text again and underline the words which show the order of the instructions.
   • Check the answers.

Answers   First, ... then ... . When you have ... . Finally, ...

d • Divide students into two groups, A and B.
   • Tell students from group A to choose an activity from the list.
   • Now tell them to find someone from group B who can explain how to do it.
   • When everyone has a partner, they sit together and group A students write down the instructions group B students give them.
   • Then have students change roles – group B students choose an activity from the list and find a new partner from group A who can give them instructions. Group B students write the instructions down.
   • Elicit instructions for each activity in the list.

b Now listen to these four sentences from the conversation in exercise 1.
Decide if the speaker is sure (S) or unsure (U).

1 You press CLEAR first, don't you? ◯

2 I could do it faster on the stove, couldn't I? ◯

3 It hasn't started, has it? ◯

4 It just won't work for me, will it? ◯

3 Grammar builder: question tags

a Notice the grammar form in the examples in exercise 2b. Write question tags
for the following sentences. Then listen and check your answers.

1 New technology makes life easier, ... ?

2 Modern technology really began in the 19th century, ... ?

3 Technology will develop faster and faster, ... ?

4 You don't use a computer much, ... ?

5 Most people can't afford the latest technology, ... ?

6 You're an electronic engineer, ... ?

7 You didn't press CLEAR, ... ?

b How do you express question tags in your language? Think about intonation
and grammar.

4 Speaking, reading and writing

a How difficult or easy is it to use each of the following items?

- a camera
- a cell phone
- a computer
- a photocopier

Talk about any experiences you have had.

b Read the text on the right quickly, and write
the function of each of the features of this
product in the picture.

c Which words from the text show the order of
the instructions? Underline each one.

d Choose one thing from the following list that
you would like to be able to do. Find someone
who can explain what to do, and write down
his or her instructions.

1 Store a telephone number on a cell phone.

2 Set the alarm on a digital watch.

3 Program a VCR to record your favorite
program.

4 Heat up some soup in a microwave oven.

It's easy. First you ...

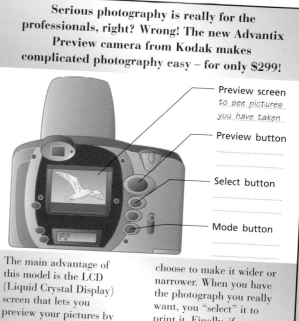

Serious photography is really for the
professionals, right? Wrong! The new Advantix
Preview camera from Kodak makes
complicated photography easy – for only $299!

Preview screen
*to see pictures
you have taken*

Preview button
....
....

Select button
....
....

Mode button
....
....

The main advantage of
this model is the LCD
(Liquid Crystal Display)
screen that lets you
preview your pictures by
pressing the preview
button. First you take your
picture, then you can
choose to make it wider or
narrower. When you have
the photograph you really
want, you "select" it to
print it. Finally, if you
want reprints, you can
copy as many as you want
by using the mode button.

LANGUAGE for life:
learning on *the Web*

① Online courses

Online courses are becoming increasingly popular. How much do you know about them? For example, how are they similar to and different from traditional courses? And what about the jargon? What do these things refer to?

Match each of the areas above to the spaces in the text below. Check your answers with another student.

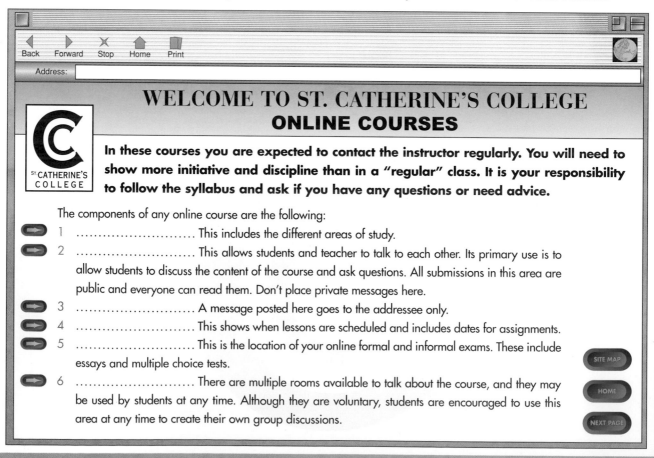

WELCOME TO ST. CATHERINE'S COLLEGE
ONLINE COURSES

In these courses you are expected to contact the instructor regularly. You will need to show more initiative and discipline than in a "regular" class. It is your responsibility to follow the syllabus and ask if you have any questions or need advice.

The components of any online course are the following:

1 .... This includes the different areas of study.

2 .... This allows students and teacher to talk to each other. Its primary use is to allow students to discuss the content of the course and ask questions. All submissions in this area are public and everyone can read them. Don't place private messages here.

3 .... A message posted here goes to the addressee only.

4 .... This shows when lessons are scheduled and includes dates for assignments.

5 .... This is the location of your online formal and informal exams. These include essays and multiple choice tests.

6 .... There are multiple rooms available to talk about the course, and they may be used by students at any time. Although they are voluntary, students are encouraged to use this area at any time to create their own group discussions.

Lesson 4 Language for life: learning on the Web

Aim:	To raise awareness of English and online learning.

Helping the learner This lesson is about online learning. Reading and talking about different ways of learning encourages students to assess how they learn and take responsibility for what they learn.

1 Online courses

Aim: To raise awareness of courses available on the Web.

- Ask students whether any of them have ever taken a course on the Web. Elicit any experiences they may have had.
- Put students in pairs.
- Ask them to discuss ideas on the similarities and differences between online and traditional courses.
- Get feedback from the pairs.
- Keep students in pairs. Have them look at the words in the buttons, and see if they know what they refer to.
- Tell them they will find the answers in the text in exercise 1b.
- Tell students to read the excerpt from a website, and to match the words from the buttons in exercise 1a to the definitions that are given.
- Put students in pairs to check their answers.
- Check the answers with the class.

Answers	1 course contents	2 discussion page	3 private mail	4 course calendar
	5 quizzes and tests	6 chat rooms		

- Have students read the text again and mark the statements *true* or *false*.
- Check the answers.

Answers	1 T 2 F 3 F 4 T 5 F 6 F

- Put students in groups.
- Tell them to discuss taking an online course.
- Ask for feedback from the groups.

Teaching tip	Recommend some good websites for English students. Please remember to check these websites before the class, as websites can change and become obsolete very quickly.

2 Distance learning

Aims: To practice listening for the main idea and note-taking.
To practice writing an e-mail.

- Tell students they are going to hear part of an interview about distance learning.

Teaching tip	Check students understand the concept of distance learning – taking a course without attending classroom-based lessons and without regular face-to-face contact with a teacher or other students.

- Have students read questions 1–3 , about the first part of the interview.
- Play the first part of the recording and have students answer the questions.
- Check the answers.

Answers	1 education 2 Head of Distance Learning 3 courses on the Internet

- Play the second part of the recording.
- Have students complete the notes.
- Check the answers.

Answers	languages, degrees, generally cheaper, time, combine, speed, slow, e-mail, online, motivation, contact

Part 1

Interviewer: You're listening to WBC and it's time for our weekly look at education on our program *Learning for Life*. Today Alan Martin, the Head of Distance Learning at Bedford College, is here to talk to us. Alan, thanks for coming.

Alan: It's nice to be here.

Interviewer: Alan, you're going to talk about courses on the Internet, aren't you?

Alan: Yes, online courses are becoming increasingly popular with students.

Part 2

Interviewer: What kind of courses can you take online?

Alan: Well, you can take almost anything online: vocational courses, languages, college degrees. Even courses on cooking or wine.

Interviewer: And what about cost? How much are these courses?

Alan: Well that depends, but in general, online courses are cheaper than paying for classroom courses. And they're more convenient.

Interviewer: In what way?

Alan: Well, you can study when you have the time and combine this with other activities. Also, you take a course at your own speed: fast or slow, it's up to you.

Interviewer: And how do these courses work?

Alan: Instruction is by e-mail, and the course is on a Web page and there's an online classroom too. Students also have access to online libraries as well as academic and technical support.

Interviewer: And are there any exams?

Alan: Unfortunately yes! But you can take exams online or off-site.

Interviewer: It sounds perfect but does online learning work?

Alan: Yes it does. But more people fail online courses than traditional classroom courses.

Interviewer: Why?

Alan: First of all, you need a high level of self-motivation on any distance learning course. Secondly, many people like to have personal contact with the teacher and with other students.

Interviewer: OK. We have a short commercial break but we'll be back with you soon for some phone in questions for Alan from our listeners.

- Have students read the e-mail from Kenny.
- Tell them to write a reply to Kenny, using the notes they have completed.
- Ask students to exchange replies in groups and to choose the best and most helpful one.
- Have one student read out the best reply in their group.

Read about online courses again. Mark the following statements T (true) or F (false).

1   In an online course you need to be responsible for organizing your own learning.   T ◯ F ◯

2   You can talk about personal problems on the discussion page.   T ◯ F ◯

3   Private mail is an open forum for all the people on your course.   T ◯ F ◯

4   To check when your assignments have to be ready, look at the course calendar.   T ◯ F ◯

5   All the writing tests are formal.   T ◯ F ◯

6   The chat room is compulsory.   T ◯ F ◯

And how about you? Would you be interested in taking an online course? Why or why not?

② Distance learning

Listen to the first part of an interview about distance learning and answer the following questions.

1   What is the topic of the radio program?

2   What does Alan Martin do at Bedford College?

3   What kind of courses is he going to talk about?

Listen to the second part of the interview and complete the notes below.

ONLINE COURSES:
Type of courses: vocational courses, ..., college ...., cooking and wine.
Cost: .... than classroom courses.
Advantages over traditional classroom courses: you can study when you have .... and .... this with other activities. You can do the course at your own ...., fast or ....
Instruction: by ...., course Web page and online classrooms.
Testing: you can take exams .... or off-site.
Reasons for failing: 1) you need a high level of self .... 2) many people like to have personal ....

Read this e-mail from Kenny to his friend, and write a reply using the notes above.

◀ Back   ▶ Forward   ✖ Stop   ⌂ Home   ▯ Print   ▭ Mail

Address: [   ]

Hi _____
I think you wrote me a month ago, didn't you? So sorry this is late. Anyway, how are things going?
I've been very busy. I finished school in July and I have a part-time job with a design studio. It's really interesting and I'm looking for a course in computer design. I don't have much money to pay for a course, or time either. You did a distance learning course, right? Can you do me a favor and give me some information and advice about online courses? Mail me with your news and the info about the course!
All the best,
Kenny

Unit 4 House and home

1 Home away from home

1 Speaking and listening

a Look at the three photographs and identify the different types of accommodations. What are the good and bad points about each place?

b Listen to a student talking with her brother on the telephone. Check (✔) the points she mentions from the list.

courses ○   music ○   apartment ○
friends ○   food ○   TV ○
parties ○   sports ○   e-mail ○

c Listen to the conversation again and answer the questions.

1 Why isn't Lilly living at home?
2 Where's she living?
3 What extra classes is she taking?
4 How is she feeling?

2 Pronunciation: intonation in questions

a Listen to these questions from the conversation in exercise 1 and notice the intonation. Why do you think the intonation changes?

1 *How are you doing?*

2 *Can you do that?*

3 *But what will Mom and Dad say?*

4 *Are they in?*

Unit 4 House and home

Helping the learner: ways of teaching and learning grammar

There are different techniques you can apply to teaching and learning grammar.
- Review the grammar students need in order to do pair work exercises.
- Give examples and ask students to work out the rules.
- Ask questions to help students to work out the rules.

Further reading:
Scrivener, J., (1994) *Learning Teaching,* Macmillan Heinemann ELT, Ch. 9

Lesson 1 Home away from home

> **Aims:** To focus on intonation in questions.
> To practice vocabulary for talking about items in the home.

1 Speaking and listening

Aims: To introduce the topic of homes, and student accommodations.
To practice listening for the main idea and specific information.

a • Have students look at the photographs, and identify the types of accommodations shown.

Answers 1 house in the suburbs   2 terraced townhouse   3 city apartment

- Establish some of the differences between the types of accommodations, e.g. *size.*
- Have students work in groups and discuss the good and bad points of each type of place.
- Get feedback from the groups.

b • Tell students they are going to hear a student, Lilly, talking to her brother.
- Play the tape and get students to check off the points Lilly mentions.

Answers courses, music, an apartment, e-mail

c • Get students to read the questions in exercise 1c.
- Play the tape again and have students answer the questions.

Answers 1 Because she's finished high school and she is away studying.   2 in an apartment with two girls   3 drama and conversational Spanish   4 Fantastic! She likes the freedom.

Tapescript

Lilly: Hi, Jack!
Jack: How are you doing?
Lilly: Great! Classes have started, I've signed up for a couple of extra courses - conversational Spanish and drama ...
Jack: Gee, I can't wait to get out of High School and away from home!
Lilly: And I've found a great place to live. Instead of moving into a residence hall, I'm sharing a rented apartment with two other girls.
Jack: Wow! Can you do that?

Lilly: Sure, no problem ...
Jack: But what will Mom and Dad say?
Lilly: Uh, I don't know. Are they in?
Jack: No, they're out until this evening.
Lilly: Well, you tell them - you know, that I'm fine, classes have started, I've signed up for a drama course and conversational Spanish classes ... and I'm sharing an apartment with two other girls. That will get the topic on the table for when I e-mail them.
Jack: How does it feel living in your own apartment?

Lilly: Fantastic! I can get up when I like, go out when I like, get home when I like. I don't have to turn my music down – all three of us like the same noisy stuff. It's just great!
Jack: Hey, you took my Mariah Carey CD!
Lilly: Yeah, sorry. I must have picked it up with mine by mistake. Don't worry, I'll take care of it.
Jack: Yeah, but ...!
Lilly: Well, I have to rush to class, Jack. I'll e-mail you tomorrow, OK? Got to go!

2 Pronunciation: intonation in questions

Aim: To recognize and practice rising and falling intonation in questions.

a • Write questions 1 and 2 on the board.
- Play the recording of the sentences and establish which have the same intonation.
- Ask students to explain why they think the intonation is different in the different questions.

Answer 1 and 3 are *wh-* questions (or information questions), 2 and 4 are *yes / no* questions.

b • Check students can recognize the difference between *wh- /* information questions and *yes / no* questions.
• Put students in pairs.
• Get them to practice the questions with their partner.
• Play the tape so they can check their answers.

Answers
1 What time are we going shopping?
2 Is this table new?
3 Where did you put the brochure?
4 Do you want to change the wallpaper?

3 Speaking and reading

Aim: To practice reading for specific information.

a • Put students in pairs or groups.
• Have them discuss the question.
• Get feedback from the class.

b • Tell students to read questions 1–7.
• Now have them read the website article to find the answers.
• Check the answers.

Answers
1 near the campus   2 no   3 not necessarily   4 full kitchens; coin operated washers and dryers   5 It depends on the availability.   6 one full academic year
7 Contact the Housing Assignment Office by mail, phone, fax or e-mail.

c • Put students in groups of three.
• Have them discuss the advantages and disadvantages of each type of accommodation for college students.
• Get feedback from the groups.

4 Word builder: interiors

Aim: To build up and practice the vocabulary of items in the home.

a • Put students into two groups, A and B.
• Have group A look at the first picture, and write the words next to the items, while group B does the same with the second picture.

Answers Group A: stove, table, chairs, washing machine, sink, toilet, computer, cups, garden fork, fruit, bowl
Group B: armchair, bed, TV, stereo, coffee table, hairdryer, shower, microwave oven, sideboard, desk, toothbrushes

b • Keep students in two groups, A and B.
• Focus attention on the example in the Students' Book. Highlight the use of *should / shouldn't* to talk about right and wrong places for the items in the pictures.
• Have students talk about which items are in the wrong places and where they should be.

c • Now put student As and student Bs together in pairs.
• Tell them they are going to exchange information about their rooms and they should talk about what is in the room, where it is and whether it is in the right place.

Helping the learner Briefly review the grammar students will need to do this exercise. This includes *there is / are*, prepositions of place, and *should / shouldn't*.

• Have students exchange information about their rooms.

Teaching tip Remind students not to look at their partner's picture, but to exchange the information verbally.

b **Work in pairs. Practice asking the following questions with the right intonation. Then listen and check your answers.**

1 What time are we going shopping?

2 Is this table new?

3 Where did you put the brochure?

4 Do you want to change the wallpaper?

3 Speaking and reading

a **In pairs or groups, discuss this question.**
Where do college students normally live in your country?

b **The University of California at Los Angeles has four apartment buildings for students. Read the students' questions below. Then read the UCLA website and answer the questions.**

1 Are the university apartment buildings on, near or some distance from the campus?

2 Do I have to buy any furniture?

3 Do I have to share an apartment with another person?

4 What kind of cooking and cleaning facilities are there?

5 If I apply for an apartment, will I get one?

6 What is the shortest period I can rent an apartment?

7 How can I get more information about the apartments?

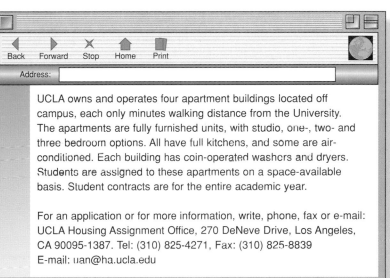

Back Forward Stop Home Print

Address:

UCLA owns and operates four apartment buildings located off campus, each only minutes walking distance from the University. The apartments are fully furnished units, with studio, one-, two- and three bedroom options. All have full kitchens, and some are air-conditioned. Each building has coin-operated washers and dryers. Students are assigned to these apartments on a space-available basis. Student contracts are for the entire academic year.

For an application or for more information, write, phone, fax or e-mail: UCLA Housing Assignment Office, 270 DeNeve Drive, Los Angeles, CA 90095-1387. Tel: (310) 825-4271, Fax: (310) 825-8839 E-mail: uan@ha.ucla.edu

c **Work in groups of three. Discuss the advantages of these different types of accommodations for college students: apartments, rooms on campus, living at home.**

4 Word builder: interiors

a **Form two groups, A and B. Group A look at picture 1 and group B look at picture 2. Write the names of the items shown in each room.**

b **Which items are in the wrong room and where should they go?**

The garden fork shouldn't be there. It should be in the ......

c **Work in pairs with a student from the other group and exchange information about your rooms.**

2 Decoration

1 Speaking and listening

a Look at this picture of a room. What would you change to make it look nicer? Discuss your ideas with another student.

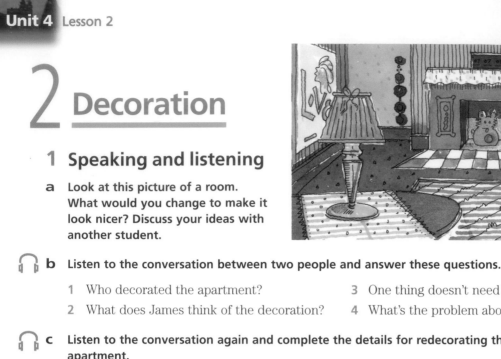

b Listen to the conversation between two people and answer these questions.

1 Who decorated the apartment?

2 What does James think of the decoration?

3 One thing doesn't need changing. What is it?

4 What's the problem about redecorating the apartment?

c Listen to the conversation again and complete the details for redecorating the apartment.

Area	Change
1 walls	....
2	Throw it out and get something to match the walls.
3 lighting	....
4	You couldn't give it away.
5 floor	....
6	Take them down and look for some posters.

2 Speaking and reading

a What are the main things that affect the decoration of a room? Discuss your ideas in groups of three. Then read the following article on interior decoration quickly to check your answers.

Three key elements in home interior decoration are the use of space, the use of light and color and the use of decorative objects of personal significance to the people who live in the home. However, personal taste and the specific use of a room or area of the house can influence decoration.

A teenager's (1) .... is usually a very private space into which few people are invited. It may be decorated in a way that horrifies the parents but thrills the youngster; the shelves covered with all sorts of objects and sentimental or shocking posters on the walls. The use of the room and the taste displayed in it are highly personal.

A (2) .... is essentially a functional space used for preparing and eating food. Many families eat there on a daily basis and use the dining room for more formal occasions. These days, they are usually colorful and designed to make life easier.

The (3) .... is a more public place, and may be carefully designed to make guests feel comfortable, and perhaps to impress them a little. The decoration, therefore, considers other people's tastes, and goes for many common denominators

rather than purely personal or idiosyncratic options. There are likely to be fairly conventional pictures, ceramic objects and ornamental lampshades.

Lesson 2 **Decoration**

> **Aims:** To develop students' speaking and listening skills on the topic of interior decoration.
> To classify different types of multi-word verbs.

1 Speaking and listening

Aim: To introduce the topic of interior decoration.

a • Have students look at the picture, and say if they like the room.
• Put them in pairs and let them discuss what they would change, e.g. *colors, furniture, pictures, objects*.
• Ask for feedback from the pairs.

b • Tell students they are going to hear two friends, James and Karen, talking about the decoration in a room in James's apartment.
• Have them read questions 1–4.
• Play the tape and get students to answer the questions.

Answers 1 James's roommate 2 He thinks it's horrible. 3 the wooden floor
4 It will cost $2,000.

c • Have students look at the table and check what information is missing.
• Play the tape again and have students complete the table.
• Check the answers.

Answers 1 Repaint them a lighter color. 2 furniture 3 Change it and buy a new lamp.
4 rug 5 Keep it and don't put a rug on it. 6 pictures

Teaching tip Compare Karen's suggestions for redecorating the room with what the students said in exercise 1a.

Tapescript
Woman: Thanks for the meal James.
Man: It's my pleasure. Coffee?
Woman: Thanks. Er James. Did you decorate this room?
Man: No. Carol, my roommate, did, but she moved out. Horrible, isn't it?
Woman: Yes, it certainly is but why don't you change it?
Man: Hmm, any ideas?
Woman: Yes, repaint the walls a lighter color. Then, throw out the furniture and get something which matches the walls – maybe use beige or white.

Man: Sounds good. I think I'll change the lighting and buy a new lamp.
Woman: Definitely. That rug is awful. You couldn't give it away.
Man: Yes, it's a really revolting color, isn't it? The floor is nice – parquet. It doesn't need a rug.
Woman: Mmm, I love wooden floors, and it's in good condition too. Those pictures aren't very nice. I'd take them down and look for some movie or art posters. Something more decorative.
Man: Right. Only problem is we're talking about a couple of thousand dollars here.

2 Speaking and reading

Aims: To practice identifying the main idea when reading a text.
To analyze the structure and content of a text.

a • Put students in groups of three.
• Have them discuss the question.
• Ask for feedback from the groups.
• Write their ideas on the board.
• Let students read through the article quickly, and check which things affect the decoration of a room.

Teaching tip The key information comes early in the article so ask the students to stop reading when they have found the answer.

Answers The three key elements are use of space, use of light and color, and the use of decorative objects.

b • Now have students read the article again and fill in the three missing words.
   • Check the answers.

Answers	1 bedroom 2 kitchen 3 living room

c • Focus students' attention on the diagram.
   • Explain that it shows the structure and content of the article.
   • Have students complete the diagram, working individually.
   • Put students in pairs or groups.
   • Have them compare their completed diagrams.
   • Check the answers with the class.

Answers	1 space 3 decorative objects Example 1: teenager's bedroom Example 2: kitchen Typical features: functional space for preparing and eating food colorful and designed to make life easier Example 3: living room more public, carefully designed, considers other people's tastes, conventional decorative objects

d • Put students in pairs.
   • Have students discuss a room they really like.
   • Ask for feedback, asking students to nominate the most interesting / unusual rooms.

3 Grammar builder: multi-word verbs

Aim: To focus on and classify multi-word verbs.

   • Write the two examples from the Students' Book on the board.
   • Elicit other examples of verbs that take an object and those that don't,
     e.g. *She turned off the lights.* (object); *The plane took off.* (no object)

a • Have students look at the verbs in sentences 1–8, and underline and circle appropriately.
   • Check the answers.

Answers	4 <u>put them away</u> 5 <u>gave away their old car</u> 6 <u>take down that old bathroom mirror</u> 7 <u>turned the water off</u> 8 (went out)

Helping the learner	In this exercise, students are given examples and then have to classify the multi-word verbs. This helps them to understand how the verbs work in terms of structure as well as meaning.

b • Focus attention on the table.
   • Check comprehension of the categories in the table and focus on the examples.
   • Ask students to classify the verbs from exercise 3a.
   • Check the answers.

Answers	Type 1: the two parts of the verb cannot be separated – look after Type 2: no object – go down, went out Type 3: the two parts can be separated – turn down, put away, give away, take down, turn off

   • Get students to find other examples of multi-word verbs and classify them accordingly.
   • Have them make sentences which illustrate the meaning of the verbs and how the grammar works.

b Read the article again and fill in the spaces with the name of the correct room.

c Complete the diagram of the article's structure and content. Compare your completed diagrams in pairs or groups.

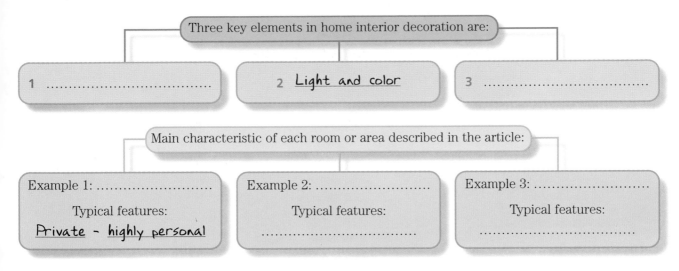

Three key elements in home interior decoration are:

1 ....

2 _Light and color_

3 ....

Main characteristic of each room or area described in the article:

Example 1: ....
Typical features:
Private – _highly personal_

Example 2: ....
Typical features:
....

Example 3: ....
Typical features:
....

d In pairs, describe and discuss a room you really like in your own house or a relative or friend's house. What makes it so special?

3 **Grammar builder:** multi-word verbs

Some multi-word verbs have an object:

Throw out _the furniture_.

Others don't:

He ***moved out***.

a Look at the multi-word verbs in italics in the sentences below. Underline the verbs with an object, and put a circle round those without an object. The first three have been done for you.

1 I'll _look after_ the dog while you're away.

2 Prices of houses and apartments do not often _go down_.

3 I wish the neighbors would _turn_ their TV _down_.

4 There are tools all over the floor. _Put_ them _away_ before you go to bed.

5 They _gave away_ their old car.

6 We should _take down_ that old bathroom mirror.

7 I've _turned_ the water _off_.

8 The candle went _out_.

b Classify the multi-word verbs used above according to type.

Type 1: two parts, with a final object	Type 2: two parts, without an object	Type 3: two parts, with a middle or final object
look after (the dog)	go down	turn (the TV) down / down (the TV)
....	....	....

35

3 Street scenes

1 Listening and speaking

a In pairs or groups, compare the two scenes on the right. What are the similarities and the differences between them?

b Listen to two people talking about where they live. Look at the scenes on the right, and list the things in the scenes they mention. Compare your answers in pairs.

c Listen to the conversation again, and check (✔) points about the neighborhood you hear mentioned.

1 The elevator sometimes breaks down.

2 Children played on the street when there were houses.

3 There's a lot of vandalism in the apartments.

4 You don't meet many people in the apartment building.

5 There were lots of parties on the old street.

6 The old houses had small yards.

7 The play area at the apartments isn't very clean.

8 The apartments only have one bedroom each.

d Problem solving. Work in groups of three. Look again at the second street scene. How would you improve things? Imagine you have a budget of $120,000. Decide how you would use it to make conditions better for the residents.

2 Grammar builder: *used to* and *would*

a Look at examples 1–3 from the conversation in exercise 1. Match the questions with the examples.

1 *I **used to see** my neighbors almost every day.*

2 *The kids **would play** on the street except in winter.*

3 *You know I **used to have** a dog.*

a Which examples talk about habits in the past? ....

b Which example talks about a state in the past? ....

c In which example (1 or 3) is it **not** possible to use *would*? ....

b Decide, in each of the sentences below, if it is possible to use both *would* and *used to* or only *used to*.

1 At my grandma's house we *used to / would* eat a lot of cake.

2 We *used to / would* live in an apartment.

3 When we were children we *used to / would* go swimming every weekend.

4 Tim *used to / would* smoke a lot at college.

5 The Simpsons *used to / would* play on a football team at college.

Lesson 3 Street scenes

Aim: To practice the four skills on the topic of neighborhoods.

1 Listening and speaking

Aims: To introduce the topic of changes to a neighborhood.
To practice listening for the main idea of a conversation.

a • Have students work in groups, look at the pictures, and discuss the similarities and differences of the streets shown, e.g. *style of houses, local stores and services.*
• Ask for feedback from the class.

b • Tell students they are going to hear two people talking about where they live.
• Tell them to note the things the speakers mention which are also in the pictures.
• Play the recording and get students to note their answers.
• Put students in pairs to check their answers, then check with the whole class.

Answers They mention the gardens, the apartments, the houses, seeing neighbors, kids playing, the play area, the supermarket.

c • Have students read statements 1–8.
• Play the tape again and let them check the statements as they are mentioned in the conversation.

Answers 1   2   4   6   7 (statements 3–5 are not made on the tape)

d • Put students in groups of three and focus attention on the second picture of the street.
• Get students to decide how they would improve things for the residents.
• Get feedback from the groups.

• **Optional step:** Get the whole class to decide which group has the best plans.

Tapescript

Sandra: Morning Mr. Solano. How are you today?
Mr Solano: Oh hi Sandra. OK, but the elevator's not working again.
Sandra: Oh no! And I have a load of shopping. Let's sit outside for a while.
Mr. Solano. It's nice here but I miss my yard. You know I used to have a dog.
Sandra: A dog! Really! So you lived here before they built the apartments?
Mr. Solano. Yeah. Look here's a photo of the street before they developed it. The houses were small but there was more contact with people.
Sandra: I know what you mean. I've lived in my apartment three years and I've only met two people.
Mr. Solano: I used to see my neighbors almost every day. The kids would always play on the street except in winter.

Sandra: Really? Well we have the play area but it's always full of garbage and graffiti.
Mr. Solano: You're so right! The apartments are very functional but for older people it's quite lonely sometimes.
Sandra: I can imagine. Well, I like it here but I've always lived in apartments. They're easy to keep clean and they're cheaper than houses. The supermarket is really convenient too. Still, I'd love to have a yard.
Mr. Solano: Yes, we used to have a small yard and we had some nice flowers and an apple tree.
Sandra: OK, let's see if the elevator is working and you can come up and have a cup of coffee.
Mr. Solano. Thanks. I'd love to.

2 Grammar builder: *used to* and *would*

Aim: To understand and practice the difference and similarity between *used to* and *would*.

Helping the learner In this exercise students answer the questions to work out the rules of the target grammar.

a • Tell students to look at examples 1–3.
• Have them match the examples with the questions. Check the answers.

Answers a 1 and 2   b 3   c 3

b • Have students look at sentences 1–5, and decide whether they can use both *would* and *used to*, or only *used to*.
• Check the answers.

Answers 1 both   2 only *used to*   3 both   4 both   5 only *used to*

c • Focus attention on the instructions and examples.

Teaching tip   Demonstrate the game by giving different statements about the past, and getting students to guess which is *true* and which is *false*.

- Tell students to write two true and two false statements about their past.
- Put them in pairs.
- Have students tell each other their statements and guess which are true and which are false.
- Have some students say their sentences aloud, for the whole class to guess.

d • Have students work in groups and discuss how things have changed where they live.
- Have them read the sentences in exercise 1b to help them with ideas.

3 Speaking, reading and writing

Aims: To practice reading for the main idea of a text.
To practice writing a short description of a street.

a • Put students in groups of three.
- Have them describe the photograph, and guess where it is.

b • Have students read the article, and match one of the paragraphs to the photograph.
- Have them guess the names of the places described in the other paragraphs.
- Check the answers.

Answers   **paragraph 1** – The photo (Rome),   **paragraph 2** – Venice,   **paragraph 3** – India,
paragraph 4 – New York

c • Have the students read the article again, and identify in which paragraphs the items listed occur.
- Check the answers.

Answers   2 paragraph 2   3 paragraph 3   4 paragraph 1   5 paragraph 4
6 paragraph 2   7 paragraph 3   8 paragraph 4

d • Put students in pairs.
- Have them brainstorm ideas about typical streets in their town or country.
- Have each pair write a description of a typical street.
- Have some pairs read out their paragraphs or exchange them with another pair for comparison.

c Write two true and two false statements about your past, using *used to* and *would*. Work with a partner and guess which are true and which are false.

> *A: I used to work in a movie studio.*   *B: Really! I don't believe you.*

d Work in groups. Talk about how things have changed where you live.

3 Speaking, reading and writing

a Work in groups of three. Look at the photograph below and describe it.

b Read the article and match the photograph to a paragraph. Guess the names of the other three places.

STREET SCENES

Every country has its street life which is influenced by factors such as climate, culture, the economy and urban development.

1 In some countries street cafés are a common feature where, especially in summer, people sit outside to drink coffee, chat, eat and watch the world go by. In some cases you pay more for food and drinks if you sit down than if you stand up at the bar.

2 In this famous city the streets are canals and people move from place to place by boat or gondola. This situation is due to the city being built on a lagoon with 400 bridges linking 118 separate islands. Boats of all shapes and sizes transport people and goods, and even act as ambulances.

3 Because of religious beliefs, cows are a common feature of street life in this country. As they are sacred they can walk where they want and even eat the vegetables from market stalls without the owners doing anything. Streets are normally crowded with buses, rickshaws and bicycles.

4 This city has such tall buildings that the sun is blocked out from the streets. The Empire State

Building has 102 stories and can house 14,000 workers. Although there are lots of stores and places where you can buy newspapers and flowers, most activity is inside or underground because of the extremely cold winters.

c Read the following list of items, and identify in which paragraphs in the article above they appear. Some appear in more than one paragraph.

1 forms of transport: 2 ↓ 3
2 bridges:
3 sacred animals:
4 outdoor cafés:
5 big buildings with thousands of workers:
6 boats:
7 markets:
8 underground areas to avoid the cold weather:

d In pairs, write a short description of a typical street in your town or country. Look at exercise 3c for ideas.

LANGUAGE for life:
places to *stay*

① Vacation choices

Match the different types of vacation, a–d, with descriptions 1–4.

A ecological vacation   **C** cruise

B package tour   **D** adventure vacation

1 Italia Mia. Eight days all inclusive. Visit Milan, Venice, Florence and Rome. Price includes airfare, food and accommodations (4-star hotels). ○

2 The Florida Everglades offer a vast natural space full of plants, birds and wildlife. Ideal for nature lovers, you can canoe or travel by boat to remote areas where civilization is a long way away. ○

If you like playing around with boats, Sail Away is the vacation for you. Our experienced instructors will teach you to sail and take you along the California coast to visit wonderful beaches and towns. Water skiing and diving are available. ○

The Andrea Doria is waiting for you. Passengers have 5-star accommodations and nine restaurants to choose from. There are also swimming pools, gymnasiums, a movie theater, a full social program plus visits to some of the most beautiful places in the Caribbean. ○

In groups, decide on one vacation that you will all take.

② Timesharing

Ever heard of timesharing vacations? Yes? No? What do you know about them? Discuss the question then read the text quickly and check your answer.

Lesson 4 Language for life: places to stay

| **Aim:** | To raise awareness of the use of English for planning a vacation. |

1 Vacation choices

Aim: To talk about types of vacation.

- Ask students to look at the photograph, and describe what it shows.
- Elicit which places students would like to go to on vacation.
- Check comprehension of the types of vacation, A–D.
- Tell students to read descriptions 1–4 quickly and match them to the types of vacation.
- Check the answers.

Answers 1 B   2 A   3 D   4 C

- Put students in groups.

Helping the learner Briefly review the structures students will need to decide on one vacation. This includes *would like, should / shouldn't,* first and second conditional, and comparatives.

- Students decide on one vacation for the whole group based on what they read.
- Ask students which vacation the groups decided on, and why.

2 Timesharing

Aim: To practice reading for specific information.

- Write the words *timesharing vacations* on the board.
- Put students in pairs or groups.
- Have students discuss what they know about timesharing vacations.
- Tell them to read the text quickly to check their ideas.
- Ask for feedback from the class.

Answers Timesharing is a system for sharing ownership of a vacation home, where each "owner" occupies the building for a specific time each year.

• Have students read the text again, and decide whether the statements are *true* or *false*.

Answers 1 T   2 F   3 T   4 F   5 T   6 F

• Have students read the Learning tip, about how to work out the meaning of words, and highlight the strategies a–d.
• Ask students to underline any words in the text that they needed to work out from context.
• Elicit how students worked out the meaning by getting them to refer to the strategies a–d.

3 Clinching a sale

Aim: To practice listening for specific information.

a • Tell students they are going to hear a conversation between a travel agent, Angie, and a client, Mr. Turner.
• Ask them to read questions 1–2, about a timeshare sale.
• Play the tape and have students answer the questions.
• Check the answers.

Answers 1 the company brochure   2 a representative from the company

b • Focus attention on the form and check comprehension of the categories.
• Play the tape again and have students complete the form.
• Check the answers.

Answers

Last name: Turner
First name(s): Carl
Street: Station Road
Number: 337
City: Chicago
State: Illinois
Zip code: 60803
Telephone: (645) 387 4596
E-mail: cturner@hotmail.com

Resort: Cancún
Country: Mexico
Week: first week of September
Total cost: $18,000
Maintenance: $150
Form of payment: American Express
Expiration date: 4/04

c • Put students in groups of three.
• Have them discuss the questions.
• Ask for feedback from the groups.

Tapescript

Angie: Worldwide Vacations. Angie speaking.
Carl: Good morning. I'm calling about a timeshare in Cancún.
Angie: Oh yes. The Cancún Flexivilla. Did you receive our brochure?
Carl: Yes, I did and one of your reps visited us. We talked it over and we've decided to go ahead.
Angie: Great. Just let me get a form on the screen and fill it in. Here we are. Could I have your name please?
Carl: Carl Turner. That's Carl with a C. Turner, T-U-R-N-E-R.
Angie: Carl with a C, OK. And your address?
Carl: 337 Station Road, Chicago, Illinois. Zip code 60803.
Angie: 337 Station Road, Chicago. And your phone number, please, Mr Turner.
Carl: My area code is 645 and the number is 387 4596.

Angie: Okay, that's 387 4596. And do you have an e-mail address?
Carl: Yes, it's carl@turner.com.
Angie: Okay, and the resort you chose is Cancún, Mexico.
Carl: Yes, the Flexivilla. And we'd like the first week of September.
Angie: Let me check that. Hmm, that's fine. The cost is 18,000 plus $150 maintenance. And how would you like to pay?
Carl: American Express. The number is 3789 2378 2874 3289, expiration date: 04/04.
Angie: 3789 2378 2874 3289. Expires 04/04. OK. I'll mail you the details and we'll charge your card and send you a receipt.
Carl: Thank you very much.
Angie: Thank you, Mr. Turner.

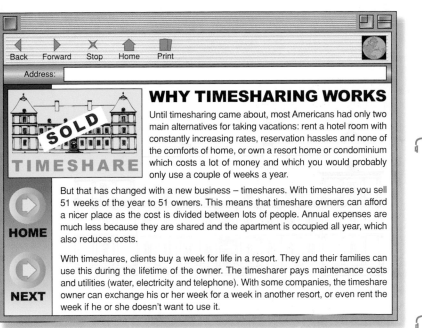

WHY TIMESHARING WORKS

Until timesharing came about, most Americans had only two main alternatives for taking vacations: rent a hotel room with constantly increasing rates, reservation hassles and none of the comforts of home, or own a resort home or condominium which costs a lot of money and which you would probably only use a couple of weeks a year.

But that has changed with a new business – timeshares. With timeshares you sell 51 weeks of the year to 51 owners. This means that timeshare owners can afford a nicer place as the cost is divided between lots of people. Annual expenses are much less because they are shared and the apartment is occupied all year, which also reduces costs.

With timeshares, clients buy a week for life in a resort. They and their families can use this during the lifetime of the owner. The timesharer pays maintenance costs and utilities (water, electricity and telephone). With some companies, the timeshare owner can exchange his or her week for a week in another resort, or even rent the week if he or she doesn't want to use it.

Read the text again and answer T (true) or F (false) to the following statements.

1 The article suggests the two normal vacation alternatives are unsatisfactory. T ◯ F ◯

2 People who own vacation homes use them intensively. T ◯ F ◯

3 Timeshare companies rent every week of the year to different people. T ◯ F ◯

4 Timeshare owners don't pay for anything except the cost of the week they buy. T ◯ F ◯

5 You buy a timeshare for a number of years. T ◯ F ◯

6 You can always change your week for a different week if you want. T ◯ F ◯

Learning tip: working out meaning of new words

- When you read a text quickly for general understanding (as in exercise 2a), don't worry about individual words you don't understand. When you read more carefully (as in exercise 2b), you will need to guess some words because they are important for understanding the text.

- In these cases, try to work out:
  a) the type of word it is – adjective, noun, adverb, verb;
  b) how it fits in with the rest of the sentence, especially the theme or topic;
  c) if it is similar to a word in your own language;
  d) what kind of word you could put in its place.

---

③ **Clinching a sale**

Listen to the conversation between Angie Brown of Worldwide Vacations and Mr. Turner, a client, and answer the following questions.

1 Where did the client see the information about the timeshare?

2 Who have the Turners talked to?

Listen to the conversation again and complete the form.

WORLDWIDE VACATIONS

Timesharing information card

Rep.: Angie Brown   Date: 8/17/01

Client: Carl

Last name: ....

First name(s): ....

Address: ....

Street: .... Number: ....

City: .... State: Illinois ....

Zip code: ....

Telephone: (645) ....

E-mail: ....

Resort: .... Town: ....

Country: .... Week: ....

Total cost: US$ ....

Maintenance cost: US$ ....

Form of payment: Check ☐

Credit card: Visa ☐   Diners ☐

American Express ☐

Card details: ....

Card number: 3789 2378 2874 3289

Expiration date: ....

Work in groups of three and answer the following questions.

1 Where would you like to have a timeshare?

2 Are timeshares common in your country?

2 Learning check

1 Progress check

a **Rewrite each of the sentences replacing the underlined verbs with the correct form of one of the multi-word verbs in the box.**

1 Prices for computers have <u>fallen</u>.

gone down   *Prices for computers have gone down.*

2 Production of microchips is <u>increasing</u>.

going up   *Production of microchips is going up.*

3 She's <u>managing</u> very well in her new job.

getting along   *She's getting along very well in her new job.*

4 I need to <u>learn</u> more about word processing.

find out   *I need to find out more about word processing.*

5 They had to <u>lower</u> the volume of the microphone.

turn down   *They had to turn down the volume of the microphone.*

get along
go down
turn down
find out
go up

b **Complete the instructions using a suitable word from the lists below.**

To use a CD player, first you have to (**6**) *turn* it on. (**7**) *Then* you select "CD" from the controls and (**8**) *press* "OPEN." After (**9**) *choosing* a CD, you put it in the tray and press "CLOSE." (**10**) *Finally* , you push "PLAY" and listen to the music.

6 a) connect   **b)** find   c) turn   d) move
7 a) After   **b)** Then   c) Finally   d) Before
8 a) pull   **b)** lift   c) take   d) press
9 a) cleaning   **b)** choosing   c) deciding   d) looking
10 a) Last   **b)** Finally   c) Second   d) After

c **Read the text below and look carefully at each line. Some of the lines are correct and some have a word that should not be there. Check (✔) the correct lines or write the words that should not be there.**

Sony has introduced the world's first only robot pet.   *only*
AIBO (Artificial Intelligence Robot) costs $2000   ✔

11 and is the first of a whole complete menagerie of   *complete*
12 artificial pets. The robot has only modest abilities.   ✔
13 For example, it can bark itself for attention   *itself*
14 and sit up or lie down. It can't no understand   *no*
15 orders or bring you the newspaper in the morning.   ✔

Learning check 2

1 Progress check

Aims: To provide an opportunity to assess students' progress and help them according to the results.
To provide an opportunity for learners to test themselves.
To allow students to evaluate their own progress and act on areas they need to improve.

Suggestions for using the *Progress check* sections
This section can be done in a variety of ways depending on how much time you have and whether you want students to do it as part of an individual assessment or as general revision.
a As a test – students work individually on the *Progress check* sections and you then check their work and record their score out of 15.
b Students work on the *Progress check* sections alone and then check their answers in pairs.
c Students work on the *Progress check* sections in pairs or groups and you later check the answers with the whole class.
d Students do the *Progress check* sections for homework.
In all cases, conduct a feedback session with the whole class to check any queries students may have and see how they did.

Explanation of answers

a
1 two-part verb with no object.
2 two-part verb with no object.
3 two-part verb with no object.
4 two-part verb with middle or final object.
5 two-part verb with middle or final object.

b
6 *turn* is the only verb that goes with *on* and makes sense in the context.
7 *before* and *finally* don't fit with the sequence of instructions; *after* won't work with the structure of the sentence.
8 *press* is the only verb that expresses the direction of the action.
9 *cleaning* and *looking* don't fit the context; *deciding* won't work without the preposition *on*.
10 *Finally* is the only word that will fit the sequence of instructions and the structure of the sentence.

c
11 It's unnecessary to write both *whole* and *complete*.
12 The line is correct.
13 The verb *bark* is not reflexive.
14 This is ungrammatical as the negative is expressed by *can't*.
15 The line is correct.

2 Proficiency check

Aims: To expose students to TOEFL and UCLES-style exam formats, which will be useful for those students interested in taking such formal proficiency exams.
To develop students' exam-taking strategies.
To allow teachers and students the opportunity to evaluate students' proficiency in English.
To test students' listening and reading skills under pseudo-exam conditions.

Suggestions for taking the test

Taking language tests is not only about knowing the language. It also involves knowing how to deal with exams: how to work under pressure; how to recognize the operations of the exam; and how to apply strategies to get the best results in an exam. These *Proficiency checks* give students the opportunity to work on all of these areas.

Students could do this as a formal proficiency test where they work individually, in silence. The tests are then collected and checked by the teacher. Alternatively, students could do the test individually and then check their answers in pairs or groups.

In either case, it is recommended that students as a class have the opportunity to discuss their answers and how they arrived at them with the teacher. Explanations of the correct answers are given to facilitate the teacher's role here. In addition, the teacher can highlight the strategy that is given in every *Proficiency check*. This is very helpful in giving students the chance to work on their exam-taking strategies as well as their accuracy with the language.

Exam-taking tip Reading the questions first
Before starting a listening comprehension exercise it is essential that students read all the questions and options first. This will help them to predict what they are going to be hear and to be familiarized with the layout of the exercise and where they need to note the information. Encourage them to read all information before they start the exercise and to predict what kind of information is expected in each space.

Answers **a**

Last name: Sinclair
Number of nights: two
Dates: November 9 and 10

Type of room: single
Cost per night: $ 120.00
Price includes: (continental) breakfast
Form of payment: credit card (Visa)

Tapescript
Receptionist: Sotwell Inn Hotel. Can I help you?
Alex: Yes, I'd like to book a single room please.
Receptionist: Can I have your name?
Alex: Yes, it's Alex Sinclair. That's S-I-N-C-L-A-I-R.
Receptionist: S-I-N-C-L-A-I-R. When would you like the room, Mr. Sinclair?
Alex: For November 9 and 10.

Receptionist: November 9 and 10. Okay. I can do a single room with bathroom for $120.00 a night.
Alex. That's fine. Does that include breakfast?
Receptionist: Yes, that includes a continental breakfast. How would you like to pay, Mr. Sinclair?
Alex: Um ... credit card. Visa. Can I just get the card?

b
1 c - this is summed up in the title
2 d - key sentence: the second biggest holiday, in terms of dollars spent, after Christmas
3 b - key sentence: 20% of all confectionery bought in the United States is purchased in the two months before November 10.
4 a - key sentence: the Halloween Association estimates $6 billion will be spent this year – up from $5 billion last year.
5 d - key sentence: ... because of a general fascination with the different elements of Halloween ... .

2 Proficiency check

a Look at the booking form about the Sotwell Inn Hotel. Then listen to the telephone conversation and complete the information.

SOTWELL INN HOTEL
BOOKING FORM

Name of customer: First: ALEX .... Last: ....

Number of nights: .... Dates: ....

Type of room: single ☐ double ☐ suite ☐

Cost per night: U.S.$ .... Price includes: ....

Form of payment: cash ☐ credit card ☐ (American Express Visa MasterCard)

---

b Read the passage. Then read the questions and statements and select the best answers.

Americans Spend a Scary Amount on Halloween

Halloween is a huge celebration in America and this year is expected to be bigger than most. The statistics themselves are scary. The average American adult is expected to spend $43 on celebrating October 31, making Halloween the second biggest holiday after Christmas in terms of dollars spent.

Most of the money (an estimated $1.9 billion) will be spent on candy. In a survey carried out by American Demographics last year, seven out of ten Americans said they would be handing out treats to ward off tricks. The demand is so great that 20% of all confectionery bought in the United States is purchased in the two months before October 31.

An estimated $1.5 billion is also expected to be spent on costumes. If you include candy, costumes, decorations and cards, the Halloween Association estimates $6 billion will be spent this year, up from $5 billion last year. Hallmark sells about 23 million Halloween cards every year.

What is the fascination with Halloween? Partly it is because of economic prosperity and partly because of a general fascination with the different elements of Halloween: witches, ghosts, monsters and pagan rituals. And it's not just limited to children. Between 40% and 60% of all adults between the ages of 18 and 44 said they intended to dress up for Halloween; 8% said they intended to dress their pets as well!

1 What is the main theme of the text?
a) Halloween customs in the United States.
b) The popularity of Halloween.
c) The amount of money spent on Halloween in the United States.
d) The activities of the Halloween Association.

2 The article says that Halloween:
a) is more popular than any other holiday.
b) is a big holiday for children.
c) is an official government holiday.
d) is a holiday where people spend less than at Christmas.

3 During the Halloween period:
a) most money is spent on cards and costumes.
b) the U.S. confectionery industry sells a fifth of its annual sales.
c) people spend too much.
d) everyone sends Halloween cards.

4 For this year's Halloween, people:
a) will spend 20% more than last year.
b) will spend $1.5 billion on costumes.
c) will buy all their cards from Hallmark.
d) will pay a lot more for decorations.

5 People are fascinated with Halloween because:
a) they want to escape from economic problems.
b) they like dressing their pets in costumes.
c) adults are less mature these days.
d) they like the different elements involved in Halloween.

Unit 5 Crime and law

1 Unsolved crimes

1 Speaking and reading

a What do you know about this person?

b Before reading, check you know what these words mean. Use a dictionary to help you if you want.

> gunshots wounded bullet witnesses unidentified rifle motorcade karate chop

John F. Kennedy
(1917–63)

c Read questions 1–5, then read the following text and answer the questions.

1 How many people were killed or wounded at or near the assassination of Kennedy?
2 Who was accused of the assassination, and what happened to him?
3 What was the official interpretation of the events?
4 What did witnesses report?
5 What suspicious things happened after the deaths of Kennedy and Oswald?

THE JFK ASSASSINATION

At 12:30 p.m. on November 22, 1963, the limousine carrying President Kennedy, Governor Connally and their wives through Dallas, Texas, turned out of Dealey Plaza past the Schoolbook Depository Building. There were a number of gunshots. The President received bullets in the neck and the head, and Governor Connally a bullet in his back. A man some distance away was wounded by a passing bullet.

Forty-five minutes later, the police arrested Lee Harvey Oswald on a charge of murdering police officer Tippit, who had died of gunshot wounds in the vicinity of the assassination. After the police had interrogated Oswald for several hours without a lawyer present, they accused him of murdering the President.

On November 24, 1963, the police were handing Oswald over to State Prison officers in the garage of the police building, when he was shot dead by Jack Ruby in front of hundreds of journalists and millions of TV watchers.

After several months, investigators declared that Oswald was the only assassin, had acted on his own, and had shot from the 6th floor of the Schoolbook Depository Building. Witnesses in Dealey Plaza saw things differently, however. Many reported that shots had been fired from a nearby park, and a cloud of smoke had been visible there. There are also photographs of two unidentified men behind the fence at the park, one with a rifle. Before the motorcade arrived, people had seen men with rifles in downtown Dallas.

In the three-year period following the assassination of President Kennedy and the "silencing" of Oswald, 18 important witnesses died, including six by gunshot, two by suicide, one from a cut throat, and one from a karate chop to the neck. All this supports the theory of a conspiracy and cover-up. Oliver Stone's movie *JFK* asks questions about what exactly happened and who was responsible.

d Does the writer tend to support the official version of events or the conspiracy theory? Give reasons.

Unit 5 Crime and law

Helping the learner: strategies for listening and reading

When we ask students to read or listen to a text for the first time, we usually want them to get a general idea of what the text is about (often called *skimming*). We sometimes want students to find some specific information (often called *scanning*) or to check their predictions about the content of the text. The second time students read or listen, we want them to process the information in some way in order to get a better / deeper understanding of the content. In some listening exercises, e.g. note-taking, students listen to a text more than once in order to complete or check their answers.

Further reading:
Gower, R., Phillips, D., Walters, S., (1995) *Teaching Practice Handbook,* Macmillan Heinemann ELT, Ch.5

Lesson 1 Unsolved crimes

> **Aims:** To develop students' speaking and reading skills on the topic of crime.
> To practice reading for the main idea and specific information.
> To build up and practice crime vocabulary.

1 Speaking and reading

Aim: To practice reading a text for specific information and to understand the writer's opinion.

a • Focus attention on the photograph and caption.
  • Ask students what they know about John F. Kennedy.
  • Write students' ideas on the board.

b • Have students check the words in the box, using a dictionary if appropriate.
  • Let them check in pairs or groups.
  • Check the meaning of the words with the class.

c • Tell students to read questions 1–5.
  • Now have them read the text about the JFK assassination, to find the answers.
  • Check the answers.

Answers
1 4 – President Kennedy, Governor Connally, a man, a police officer
2 Lee Harvey Oswald. He was killed by Jack Ruby.
3 Lee Harvey Oswald killed President Kennedy, acting alone, from the Schoolbook Depository Building.
4 They had seen shots from the park and they had seen other men with rifles.
5 18 important witnesses died.

d • Put students in pairs or groups.
  • Have students read the questions about the writer's opinion.
  • Get them to read the text again and discuss the question in pairs or groups.
  • Get feedback from the class.

Answer The writer seems to support the conspiracy theory as she / he says the deaths of 18 important witnesses support the theory of a conspiracy and a cover-up.

2 Speaking and listening

Aim: To practice listening for the main idea and specific information.
- Ask students what problems they have with listening to and understanding spoken English.
- Have students read the Learning tip, about listening skills, and elicit other suggestions for help with listening from the class.

a • Put students in pairs. Tell them to look at the pictures, and answer questions 1–3.
- Get feedback from the pairs.

b • Play the tape and get students to check their answers to questions 2 and 3.
- Check the answers with the class.

Answer	The paintings are connected to crime because the interview is about art theft.

Helping the learner	Ask students if the prediction activity helped them cope with the first listening. Encourage them always to think about the topic of a listening or reading *before* they listen or read.

c • Have students read questions 1–5.
- Play the tape again and get students to answer the questions.
- Check the answers.

Answers	1 Decreasing because it's more difficult to sell stolen art. 2 more than a century 3 nine 4 all of them 5 January 1st 2001 at 1:30 a.m.

Tapescript

Woman: Our topic today is art theft, and I have Mark White of Interpol with me. Mark, how big a business – if you can call it that – is the theft of art works?
Man: Very big indeed – it's a multi-billion dollar business.
Woman: Is it on the increase?
Man: Well, it's getting more and more difficult to sell stolen art, so thefts are actually declining a little. But there are still many old cases and new cases to solve.
Woman: How old?
Man: Well, there are famous works of art that were stolen a century ago or more and are still missing. But, for example, on November

12, 1972, nine impressionist paintings worth millions of dollars were stolen from the town hall of Bagnols sur Cèze, France. They included a Bonnard, two Dufys, a Matisse, two Renoirs, and a Vuillard. None of them has yet been recovered.
Woman: And recent cases?
Man: Well, the 21st century began with the theft of a $4.5 million Cézanne landscape from Oxford's Ashmolean Museum at 1:30 on New Year's Day morning. Thieves broke in through a glass skylight in the roof while the streets were full of people celebrating the new millennium.
Woman: That was certainly a bad start to the century.

3 Word builder: crime vocabulary

Aim: To build up and practice crime vocabulary.

a • Have students match verbs 1–4 with the correct definitions a–d.
- Check the answers with the class.

Answers	1 c 2 d 3 a 4 b

b • Have students fill in the table.

c • Have them check their answers in pairs.
- Check the answers with the class.

Answers	robbery	robber	to rob
	murder	murderer	to murder / kill
	assassination	assassin	to assassinate

Optional activity	What's the crime? Have students write a short account of a crime without naming it. Students work in groups and read their account to the group members. The other group members have to name the crime(s).

Preparation:
Bring a map of the world to the next lesson.

2 Speaking and listening

a Look at the pictures on this page, and discuss questions 1–3 in pairs.

1 What do you think of each painting?
2 How could they be connected with crime?
3 What do you think is the topic of the interview you are going to hear?

> **Learning tip**
>
> Listening is often difficult because we do not usually hear every word, not even in our own language! To develop your listening skills:
> - before or when you begin listening, think about what you know about the topic
> - while listening, try to understand the general idea without worrying about each word
> - in a conversation, ask for clarification or repetition if you need to.

b Listen to the radio interview and check your answers to questions 2 and 3 above.

c Listen again, and answer the following questions.

1 Is art theft increasing or decreasing?
2 What is the longest time works of art have been missing?
3 How many paintings were stolen in Bagnols sur Cèze in 1972?
4 How many are still missing?
5 What was the time and date of the theft of the Cézanne painting from the Ashmolean Museum?

3 Word builder: crime vocabulary

a Match the verb with the correct definition.

1 to rob   a) to kill someone for political reasons
2 to murder   b) to take something which is not yours
3 to assassinate c) to take something illegally from a person or a place
4 to steal   d) to kill someone intentionally, not usually for political reasons

b Fill in the table. The first one has been done for you.

Crime	Criminal	Verb
theft	thief	rob / steal
robbery		
murder		
assassination		

c Check your answers in pairs.

2 Crime and punishment

1 Speaking and reading

a In groups, discuss what you know about Australia.

b Read the book extract about Australia, below, and write the correct dates in statements 1–4.

1 .... : America gains its independence from Britain.
2 .... : first British settlement in Australia, Port Jackson.
3 .... : arrival of the last convicts in Australia.
4 .... : full independence of Australia.

THE BEGINNINGS OF MODERN AUSTRALIA

The first humans to settle in Australia came from south-eastern Asia and are called Aborigines, which means "the first people who lived in any country." Now the word is used mainly for native Australians.

The next big influx came thousands of years later when the British began to colonize Australia. This colonization was based on convict labor (work done by people who had previously been in prison). There were two reasons why convicts were deported to Australia: one was that Britain wanted to colonize Australia before the French did. The other reason was that America, where convicts used to be sent, was no longer a colony of Britain. (America gained its independence in 1776.)

The first place convicts were sent to was Port Jackson, which was established in 1788 and later became Sydney. Deportation, also called "transportation," to Sydney, only stopped in 1837 when a Parliamentary Committee Report strongly condemned the practice. However, it wasn't until 30 years later that the practice had stopped completely in Australia.

Many of the convicts had committed what would now be considered minor crimes, such as stealing food for a hungry family. Australia, which was at first their prison, later became for them a land of opportunity. It became a fully independent nation in 1901, only 34 years after the last convicts had arrived to serve their sentences.

Lesson 2 Crime and punishment

Aims: To practice reading for specific information.
To practice the past perfect.
To practice the pronunciation of past tense forms.

1 Speaking and reading

Aim: To practice reading for specific information.

Helping the learner Encourage students to decide what they want from a text *before* they listen or read. If they know *what* they want, it will help them to decide *how* to read / listen, i.e. for gist or for specific information.

a • Show students the map of the world you have brought to class and have students point out Australia.
• Put students in groups and have them discuss what they know about Australia.
• Get feedback, writing the main points on the board.

b • Get students to read the book excerpt quickly, and find the dates.
• Check the answers.

Answers 1 1776   2 1788   3 1867   4 1901

c • Have students read the text again.
   • Now ask students to discuss and answer questions 1–3 in groups.
   • Get feedback from the groups.

Answers 1 Britain could no longer send convicts to America and they wanted to colonize
         Australia before the French did.
         2 A Parliamentary Committee Report condemned it.
         3 Minor crimes like stealing food.

2 Grammar builder: past perfect

Aim: To practice the past perfect.

a • Tell students to look at the two sentences and answer the questions.
   • Check the answers.

Answers The tenses used are the past simple and the past perfect. The past perfect is used for the
         action that happened first and the past simple for the later action.

   • Have students read the Language assistant box, and highlight that the simple past can be
     used for both past actions or events, e.g. *Australia became a fully independent nation only
     34 years after the last convicts arrived.*

b • Tell students to read the first sentence of each pair of sentences 1–3, and decide what
     happened first.
   • Check the answers.

Answers 1 The French considered colonizing Australia   2 Britain lost American colonies
         3 convicts committed minor crimes

   • Now have students complete the second sentence of each pair, using the past perfect and
     the past simple.
   • Check the answers.

Answers 1 had considered colonizing, established settlements   2 had lost, began to send convicts
         3 had committed minor crimes, were convicted

3 Pronunciation: past tense forms

Aim: To practice the pronunciation of past tense forms.

a • Focus attention on the past tense forms in the box and on the examples.

Language help Check students understand that a sound can have different spellings, and that words that
              look the same may have different pronunciations.

   • Elicit an example of two past tense forms that rhyme, e.g. *went – sent*.
   • Put students in pairs.
   • Have them put the rest of the verbs into rhyming pairs.
   • Check the answers.

Answers went – sent, drank – sank, met – let, flew – grew, bought – caught, read – said,
         made – paid

   • Now have students try to think of more words that rhyme with each pair, e.g. *went – sent*
     and *lent*.

b • Tell students to check the infinitive and past participle of each verb in exercise 3a.
   • Have them check in dictionaries or in the irregular verb table at the back of the Students' Book.

c **Read the text again. Discuss these questions.**

1 Why were convicts taken all the way to Australia at the end of the 18th century?

2 Why did Port Jackson stop transportation?

3 What kind of crimes had most of the convicts committed?

2 **Grammar builder:** past perfect

a **Look at the following two sentences. Which two tenses are used? Which tense is used for the action / event that happened first, and which for the one that happened later?**

1 Parts of Australia still <u>received</u> convicts 30 years after the Committee <u>had presented</u> its report.

2 Australia <u>became</u> a fully independent nation only 34 years after the last convicts <u>had arrived</u>.

b **Read the first sentence of each pair and complete the second sentence of each pair, making sure it has the same meaning. Use the past perfect.**

1 The French considered colonizing Australia, but then the British established settlements there.

The French .... Australia before the British .... there.

2 Britain lost its American colonies, and then it began to send convicts to Australia.

After Britain .... its American colonies, it .... to Australia.

3 Many of the convicts committed minor crimes and then they were convicted.

Many of the convicts .... before they ....

Language assistant

In these kinds of examples, the past simple is often used for both past actions or events, but the past perfect emphasizes which one happened first.

3 **Pronunciation:** past tense forms

a **Look at the following past tense forms. Write them out as rhyming pairs.**

went	sent	drank	met	flew	bought	read
said	grew	made	sank	caught	let	paid

Notice that the spelling for the same sound is sometimes the same and sometimes different:

/e/ went met said

Notice also that the same spelling may represent more than one sound:

said /e/ paid /eɪ/

b **Check that you know the infinitive and the past participle for each of these verbs, and also the pronunciation of each form. Use a dictionary or the verb table at the back of the book to help you.**

3 Crime knows no borders

1 Speaking and reading

a In pairs, discuss the following five statements and decide if you think they are T (true) or F (false).

1 INTERPOL is an international police force.   T ○   F ○
2 It is more than 100 years old.   T ○   F ○
3 It is based in the United States.   T ○   F ○
4 More than 150 countries are members.   T ○   F ○
5 It investigates international criminal cases.   T ○   F ○

b Read the text below, and check your ideas about INTERPOL.

INTERPOL is an international organization which has coordinated cooperation between the police forces of different countries since 1923. There were 177 member countries in 1997. The headquarters or General Secretariat is located in Lyon, France. INTERPOL is not itself a police force, and it does not conduct investigations. Cases are investigated by the national police forces of the member countries under their own laws, but INTERPOL plays a very important role in supplying criminal information from one country's police force to another.

2 Grammar builder: review of past tenses

Complete the text with an appropriate verb or verb phrase from the box.
Use each one only once.

| lived | has lived | has been living | was living | had lived | used to live |

INTERPOL gets its man

Melvin Patterson (1) .... in luxurious rented apartments in different parts of the world but since November 15, 2000, he (2) .... in a prison near Toronto. He (3) .... in almost all the capitals of Europe and Latin America as well as New York, and now Toronto.

   He appeared to be a respectable businessman, but he was really a swindler, who tricked people into investing in companies which did not exist. From March to October, 2000, he (4) .... in a penthouse in Toronto. What he did not know was that a policeman (5) .... in the building across the street. In his computer he had a collection of photographs and descriptions of Patterson from the INTERPOL database collected from all the countries he (6) .... and swindled in. It was the end of the road for one more international criminal.

Lesson 3 Crime knows no borders

> **Aims:** To practice the four skills on the topic of crime.
> To review past tenses.

1 Speaking and reading

Aim: To practice reading to check information.
To practice predicting the content of a text.

Helping the learner Point out to students that the aim of this exercise is to develop their prediction skills. Tell them very briefly how using prediction can help them become better readers and listeners.

a • Write the word *INTERPOL* on the board.
• Ask if anyone remembers what it is (used in Unit 5 lesson 1, exercise 2).
• Put students in pairs.
• Have them discuss statements 1–5, and decide if they are true or false.

b • Now have students read the text about INTERPOL, and check their predictions.
• Check the answers.

Answers 1 F   2 F   3 F   4 T   5 F

2 Grammar builder: review of past tenses

Aim: To review and practice past tenses.

• Tell students they are going to find out about an international criminal who was caught with the help of information from INTERPOL, and they are also going to review past tenses

Language help Pre-teach the meaning of *swindler* (noun) and *trick* (verb).

• Tell students to look at the text, and to complete it with the appropriate forms of the verbs in the box.
• Let them check in pairs or groups.
• Check the answers with the class. Discuss the different uses of the tenses.

Answers 1 used to live (*used to* for a past action that is no longer true)
2 has been living (present perfect progressive for an action that started in the past and continues into the present)
3 has lived (present perfect for past experiences at an indefinite time in the past)
4 lived (past simple for a past action at a definite time)
5 was living (past progressive for an action in progress in the past)
6 had lived (past perfect for an action which happened before another action in the past)

Optional activity Writing follow-up
Students write a paragraph about a criminal and what she / he did, to illustrate the different uses of the tenses.

3 Speaking, writing and reading

Aims: To practice asking questions in a range of tenses.
To practice writing a short newspaper article.

a • Tell students to imagine they are going to interview the criminal Melvin Patterson.
• Put students in pairs and have them write questions, using prompts 1–7.

b • Have students change partners.
• Assign a role to each student, either the reporter or Melvin Patterson, and get the pairs to conduct the interview.
• Remind the students in the role of the reporter to take notes.

c • Keep students in the same pairs.
• Have them write a short article about the interview.

d • Have each pair show their article to another pair and compare the content.
• Get feedback on the similarities and differences between the articles.

4 Speaking, reading and listening

Aims: To discuss international crimes.
To practice listening for specific information.
To practice giving a brief presentation.

a • Put students in groups.
• Have them discuss the questions.
• Get feedback from the class, checking they understand the terms *drug trafficking* and *money laundering,* and how the two are connected.

Answers *drug trafficking* – buying and selling illegal drugs; m*oney laundering* – putting money which is obtained illegally into legal businesses or bank accounts. The two crimes are often connected, as drug traffickers need to launder the money they get from drugs, to make it look legitimate.

b • Tell students they are going to hear a radio talk about international crime.
• Have students read the statements and options and predict which are correct.
• Play the tape and let them check their answers.

Answers 1 c 2 c 3 a 4 b

Tapescript

Interviewer: Today I have an expert on international crime with me, Pierre Laporte. Hello, Pierre.
Pierre: Good morning, and thank you for inviting me to the program.
Interviewer: Thank you for coming. Now I suppose the international crime that makes the headlines most is drug trafficking. Which countries are most involved?
Pierre: Well, essentially all countries are involved or potentially involved. International crime is very agile these days and it moves from country to country at its own convenience.
Interviewer: Could you be more specific, give us some examples?
Pierre: Yes. In relation to drug production, we tend to think of Thailand, Afghanistan, Colombia ... but enormous quantities of synthetic drugs are now made in laboratories in countries like Holland and the United States. In fact, drug production today involves many countries and moves from one to another.
Interviewer: And the same applies to drug trafficking, I suppose.

Pierre: That's right. There are some traditional routes – from Asia and Latin America to Europe and North America, for example – but there are also new routes all the time.
Interviewer: And what about drug consumption?
Pierre: It's definitely greatest in rich parts of the world – North America and Europe. They now both import naturally-based drugs and produce synthetic drugs as I've said.
Interviewer: Let's shift to another, related area of international crime – money laundering. Is Switzerland the big place for that as most of us think?
Pierre: Well, the Swiss laws on banking confidentiality did tend to make it that way, but those laws are being changed. I think you could say that small rich countries and dependencies are used most – Switzerland, Luxembourg, the Cayman Islands ...
Interviewer: Finally, I'm curious about whether American and European criminals ...

Language help Check comprehension of *extradite* – to send someone who may be guilty of a crime back to the country where the crime happened.

c • Put students in groups.
• Have students discuss one of the crime problems listed, and make notes in preparation for making a short presentation to the class.

d • Have each group make a presentation about crime problems to the class.
• Ask students to make comments and ask questions about what other groups said.

Preparation:
Bring a world map
to the next class.

3 Speaking, writing and reading

a Imagine you are going to interview Melvin Patterson. In pairs, prepare some questions to ask the international criminal. Use the ideas below to help you.

1 How long have you .... ?
2 Have you ever .... ?
3 Before you were arrested had you .... ?
4 What was the biggest .... ?
5 When you were a boy did you use to .... ?
6 When was the first time you .... ?
7 Do you have any regrets?

b In pairs, conduct the interview. One of you is the reporter and one of you is Melvin Patterson. The reporter needs to take notes to write a newspaper article after the interview.

c In pairs, write a brief newspaper article of no more than 120 words based on the interview with Melvin Patterson.

d Read another article, written by another two students. How many similarities and how many differences can you find between the two articles?

4 Speaking, reading and listening

a What are drug trafficking and money laundering? What is the connection between the two crimes?

b Read the options listed below and predict which ones are correct. Then listen to a radio-talk and check your answers.

1 Drugs are produced in:
a) a few specific countries.   **b)** every country in the world.   **c)** many varying countries.

2 Drug trafficking routes:
a) are all well established.   **b)** include old and new ones.   **c)** are changing all the time.

3 Drug consumption is highest in:
a) rich countries.   **b)** poor countries.   **c)** countries that don't produce drugs.

4 Most money laundering is done through banks in:
a) large, poor countries.   **b)** small, rich countries.   **c)** large, rich countries.

c In groups, discuss one of the following international crime problems.

1 Drug trafficking.
2 The use of foreign banks to launder money – that is, to apparently "legalize" illegal money.
3 The escape of criminals to a country from which they cannot be extradited.

d When you are ready, each group should make a brief presentation of their ideas to the class.

LANGUAGE for life:
understanding *nations*

① Belonging

② Vive la différence!

They say we all need to belong. We usually begin by "belonging" with our mother, our father and our brothers and sisters. Then we belong with relatives and friends. Next, institutions invite us to belong too, our schools first. And at some point we realize that we belong to a much larger community – the nation. We feel loyalty toward it, and sometimes, unfortunately, hostility toward other nations.

What most makes you feel you belong to your nation? Is it:

- *the language, or even the accent or dialect?*
- *other cultural things like music, dance, food, festivals, religion?*
- *the physical appearance of the people or the way they behave?*
- *simply the fact that you were raised in your country and have many memories of it?*

Ask your friends in class what makes them feel they belong to their national community. How strongly do they feel about their region within their country?

Look at this picture of a suburb in Brisbane, Australia. What similarities and differences can you see between this scene and a similar scene in your own country?

What things do you find most attractive and most unattractive about this Australian city scene and a similar scene in your country?

Lesson 4 Language for life: understanding nations

Aim: To raise awareness of differences and similarities between nations.

Glossary *Down under* is an informal way of referring to Australia and New Zealand.

1 Belonging

Aim: To read and talk about belonging to a community.

- Write the word *belonging* on the board.
- Explain what makes you feel a sense of belonging to your community or nation.
- Ask students to read the text, and find other examples of what creates a sense of belonging.
- Focus attention on the question.
- Have students answer it for themselves.
- Have students move around the classroom asking their classmates what makes them feel they belong to their nation and their region.
- Get feedback from the class, eliciting what creates the biggest sense of belonging.

2 Vive la différence!

Aim: To develop students' speaking skills.

- Remind students of the location and size of Australia by referring to the world map you brought to class.
- Elicit similarities / differences between Australia and the students' country.

a
- Tell students to look at the picture, and elicit one or two examples of the things that are different from their own country.
- Put them in pairs or groups to discuss other differences, e.g. *people, housing, stores, trees* and *vegetation*.
- Get feedback from the class.

b
- Keep the students in the same pairs or groups.
- Now have them discuss the things they find attractive and unattractive in the picture of the Australian suburb, and in a typical city scene in their own country.
- Get feedback from the class.

3 Rules and regulations down under

Aim: To find out more information about Australia.

- Ask students what they remember about the Sydney Olympics in 2000.
- Tell them to read the paragraph about Sydney, to find out more.

- Have students answer the quiz about Australia.
- Put students in pairs to compare their answers.
- Get feedback on any answers that students disagree on.

- Have students check the answers to the quiz (shown upside down, under the quiz).
- Elicit examples of things that surprised them.

4 Advice for a visitor

Aims: To practice listening and note-taking.
To write advice for a visitor to your country.

- Tell students they are going to hear an Australian man giving advice to an American woman who is going to visit Australia.
- Have the students read sentences 1–4.

Teaching tip	Pre-teach the spelling of *Ayers Rock* – a huge mass of rock in Northern Territory, Australia.

- Play the tape and get students to complete sentences 1–4.

Helping the learner	Be prepared to play the tape a second time to allow students to complete / check their answers.

- Check the answers.

Answers	1 look right 2 plan your travel arrangements 3 Sydney, the Snowy Mountains, Ayers Rock 4 light and warm clothes

- Put students in pairs or groups.
- Have them discuss the question.
- Get feedback from the class.

- Get students to make notes for a visitor about their own home, city, or region, referring to points 1–3.
- Ask them to expand their notes into three paragraphs.
- Have them read out their advice for the class.
- Have them vote for the most useful pieces of advice.

Tapescript

Woman: I imagine the only big difference between Australia and the U.S. is driving on the left.
Man: Well, not really, but don't forget that. Several foreigners, including one athlete, were killed during the Olympics because they didn't look right before crossing the street.
Woman: Yes, I remember.
Man: So, always look right before you cross the street!
Woman: Right! Any other advice?
Man: Well, Australia's a big country with a small population and vast open spaces. You won't see much staying in one city, not like in Europe. You need to plan your travel arrangements so that you visit interesting places a long way apart.
Woman: You mean actually plan with a travel agent?

Man: Yes.
Woman: OK. What places do you recommend me to visit?
Man: Well, I'd go to at least three different places, a long way apart. First Sydney, of course – a bit of history, the Opera House, Bondi Beach and all that. Then somewhere up in the mountains for the scenery and the wildlife – the Snowy Mountains. And finally right into the desert heart of the continent – Ayers Rock – for the magic of it, and to see the aborigines, even if only as a passing tourist.
Woman: It sounds good – Sydney, the mountains, and the desert around Ayers Rock. And clothes, the weather?
Man: Well, informal – Australians are mostly informal. But you will need light clothes and warm ones for April – it's fall, and the nights can be cool.

③ Rules and regulations down under

The 2000 Summer Olympics drew enormous numbers of visitors to Sydney, Australia, from all round the world. Although it was the "summer" Olympics, it was still winter, or perhaps early spring, in Australia, the equivalent of March in the Northern Hemisphere. Other things were different for most of the visitors too.

What do you know about Australia? Answer this quiz.

VISAS

1   Which is the only country whose passport holders do not require a visa to visit Australia?

LANGUAGE – English, of course, but ...

2   What does "G'day" mean in Australian English?

3   What are the second and third most widely spoken languages in Australia?

4   What language do "boomerang" and "didgeridoo" come from, and what do they mean?

DRIVING

5   Do vehicles drive on the right or the left?

6   Is it compulsory to wear a seatbelt or not?

SMOKING

7   In which of the following places is smoking prohibited: government buildings, public transportation, airports?

GEOGRAPHY

8   What is the capital of Australia?

9   Where do most Australians live?

10   What type of land covers most of Australia?

Check your answers with the key below.

Answers: 1 New Zealand. 2 Good day (i.e. Good morning / afternoon, or simply Hello). 3 Second biggest language is Italian. Third biggest language is Greek. 4 Both words come from the Aborigines. A "boomerang" is a hunting weapon and a "didgeridoo" is a musical instrument. 5 Left. 6 Compulsory. 7 All of them. 8 Canberra. 9 Most people live on the coast. 10 Much of Australia is flat, dry desert.

④ Advice for a visitor

Listen to an Australian giving advice to an American who is going to visit Australia. Complete sentences 1–4, below, and discuss them with a friend.

1   Before crossing a street in Australia always

....

2   Before you make your trip to Australia ....

.

3   Visit different places a long way apart, for example:

a) ....

b) ....

c) ....

4   For April, take

.... clothes.

Would you like to visit Australia? If yes, why? If no, why not?

Imagine a friend from Australia is going to visit your city or region next month. Make brief notes and then write three short paragraphs about the following.

1   The weather, clothes, etc.

2   Places to visit and things to see and do.

3   Any customs that you think might be different, for example how people say hello to each other.

Unit 6 Mass media

1 Sensationalism

1 Reading and speaking

a Read the headlines on this page. What do you think each story is about? Compare your ideas in groups.

HUSBAND'S BODY IN ROSE GARDEN!

MISSING MILLIONS IN DIRECTOR'S SWISS BANK ACCOUNT!

EX-PRESIDENT CONFESSES SECRET LIFE!

KILLER HURRICANE COMING!

b In pairs, list all the sensationalist newspapers, magazines and TV programs in your country. Decide which one strays farthest from the truth. Compare your choice and reasons with other pairs.

2 Word builder: nouns as adjectives (noun-noun phrases)

a Look at the following noun-noun phrases. What does each mean?

1 bank account   2 rose garden   3 killer hurricane

b Write phrases using one noun from box 1, below, with another noun from box 2. In pairs, discuss the phrases you have written – describe who or what they are.

1			
bank	corruption	crime	drug
earthquake	kidnap	passport	plane
car	sex	tax	terrorist

2			
accident	attack	crash	damage
evasion	forgery	fiend	robbery
scandal	scene	trafficking	victim

Learning tip

Try to learn common word groups (e.g. noun-noun phrases like *bank account,* multi-word verbs like *put up with* and expressions like *out of order*) as single vocabulary items, which they really are. Here is one way to work on new vocabulary items.

• Write the items on cards. Stick the cards in a place you will see every day, e.g. around the mirror in your bathroom. Say sentences including the new items every time you see them.

Unit 6 Mass media

Helping the learner: developing competence in speaking

In order to develop competence in speaking, it is important to understand the focus of each speaking exercise that students do. This can include:
• Speaking to practice key features of pronunciation.
• Speaking as part of grammar practice.
• Speaking to express ideas and exchange information.
The focus of the speaking exercise also links to feedback and correction. It's important to correct mistakes in exercises that focus on accuracy, but not to over-correct in exercises that focus on fluency.

Further reading:
Scrivener, J., (1998) *Learning Teaching*, Macmillan Heinemann ELT, Ch. 6

Lesson 1 Sensationalism

> **Aims:** To develop students' reading and speaking skills on the topic of newspapers.
> To raise awareness of writing style.
> To practice noun-noun phrases.

Glossary   *Hara-kiri* is a way of committing suicide used in former times in Japan.

1 Reading and speaking

Aim: To introduce the topic of sensationalism.

a • Put students in groups.
  • Have them look at the headlines, and decide what the stories are about.
  • Get feedback from the groups.

b • Divide students into pairs.
  • Elicit some names of sensationalist papers, magazines and TV programs in the students' country.
  • Get students to list and discuss all the examples they know in pairs.
  • Tell students to decide which publication or program strays farthest from the truth.
  • Get feedback from the class.

2 Word builder: nouns as adjectives (noun-noun phrases)

Aim: To practice the use of nouns as adjectives.

a • Write the noun-noun phrases on the board.
  • Elicit from students what each one means.

Answers   1 bank account – money kept in a bank that you can add to or take back
2 rose garden – a piece of land on which roses are grown
3 killer hurricane – a violent storm with circular winds that causes death and destruction

b • Put students in pairs.
  • Have them make as many noun-noun phrases as they can, combining words from boxes 1 and 2, and describe what they mean.
  • Get feedback, writing the possible combinations on the board.

Possible answers   bank robbery, car accident, car crash, corruption scandal, crime scandal, crime scene, crime victim, drug trafficking, kidnap scene, kidnap victim, passport forgery, sex attack, sex fiend, sex scandal, tax evasion, terrorist attack

• Decide which are the common collocations and underline them on the board.
• Focus attention on the Learning tip. Ask students if they have tried the vocabulary learning technique and if it worked. Elicit other techniques, e.g. recording lexical sets, word maps.

3 Pronunciation: word stress

Aim: To practice the word stress in noun-noun phrases.

a • Play the tape and ask students which nouns in the noun-noun phrases are stressed.

Answer	the first word

b • Put students in pairs.
• Have them practice the words in exercise 3a and the ones from exercise 2.

Helping the learner Giving students pronunciation rules helps them with their overall competence in speaking. Monitor and check for accurate word stress in exercise 3b.

4 Reading and speaking

Aims: To practice reading for specific information.
To raise awareness of writing style.

a • Check that students know the names Marc Antony and Cleopatra.
• Focus the students on the headline and photograph of the article.
• Put them in pairs to discuss what they know about the two characters.
• Get feedback from the pairs.

Teaching tip Ask if students have seen the Elizabeth Taylor and Richard Burton movie *Antony and Cleopatra*.

b • Now ask the students to read the article and discuss questions 1–5.
• Check the answers.

Answers 1 Queen Cleopatra VII killed herself.
2 The stock market was affected and a state of emergency was called.
3 The people went out into the streets.
4 Antony with a sword and Cleopatra with a poisonous snake.
5 By having a relationship with Julius Caesar and Marc Antony.

• Check students understand that this is a modern sensationalist report of an ancient event in history.
• Get them to underline the language that characterizes sensationalist writing – the use of abbreviated names, e.g. *Cleo*, the use of informal language, e.g. *Latin lover*, emotive language, e.g. *shock, chaos, drama*.

Optional activity Story writing
Students choose their own historical event and write a sensationalist story about it.

5 Writing, reading and speaking

Aims: To practice writing a short newspaper article.
To practice comparing writing styles.

a • Put students in pairs.
• Have them read the headline and opening paragraph.
• Students continue the story, to write their own article, including the information listed.

b • Students read and compare the articles and vote for the article with the best story and the article with the best writing.

Teaching tip This is a discussion of style *vs.* content. Make sure students understand that the article on Antony and Cleopatra is sensationalist in style, while the beginning of the rose garden article is more factual.

3 Pronunciation: word stress

a Listen to the following noun-noun phrases. Is the main stress on the first or the second noun?

bank account   crime scene   tax evasion   terrorist attack

b In pairs, practice saying these and other noun-noun phrases.

4 Reading and speaking

a Look at the newspaper headline and the photograph. In pairs, discuss what you know about this famous sensational story.

b Read the article about Queen Cleopatra, and discuss these questions in pairs.

1 What happened in Egypt in November, 30 BC?

2 What was the effect of these events in Rome?

3 How did people in Egypt react?

4 How did Marc Antony and Cleopatra each commit suicide?

5 How did Cleopatra keep Egypt "more or less independent"?

THE ATHENS POST

Athens

Friday, November 13, 30 BC

QUEEN CLEO FOLLOWS LATIN LOVER INTO NEXT WORLD!

Only a day after the shock of Marc Antony's Roman hara-kiri comes a new shock – Queen Cleopatra VII also took her own life yesterday! Both Rome and Egypt are in chaos because of the double drama. Reliable sources in Rome said that confidence in the stock market had declined dramatically and a state of emergency had been declared. Throughout Egypt crowds have filled the streets day and night. A violent reaction against the Roman army of occupation is expected.

Though exotic and eccentric, Queen Cleo was notoriously astute in politics. And she had never spoken of suicide, a close aide told our reporter. While Marc Antony fell on his Roman sword, Queen Cleo chose a deadly poisonous African snake to do the job!

So, after almost 22 years of what has been called "bedroom politics," Cleo has gone. She kept Egypt more or less independent by her relationships, first with Julius Caesar and then with Marc Antony. A high-ranking Egyptian official said yesterday that Egypt's love affair with Rome had finished and ...

5 Writing, reading and speaking

a In pairs, write a short article for the headline: HUSBAND'S BODY IN ROSE GARDEN! Begin:

Yesterday police found a man's body in the rose garden behind Mrs. Barbara Thorn's house in Sanderstone. It was identified as the body of Mrs. Thorn's husband, Eric Thorn. Forensic experts said he had been dead for about one month. The police are holding Mrs. Thorn for questioning.

Neighbors told the police ...

Continue with paragraphs about the following.

• What neighbors told the police and the newspaper reporter.
• How the police discovered the body.
• The statement that Mrs. Thorn has made to the police.

b Read all the articles, discuss them, and vote for the following.

• The article with the best story.
• The article with the best writing.

2 Investigative journalism

1 Speaking and reading

a Do you know the answers to the following questions? If you don't, try to find someone in the group who does. Then read the article about Watergate, below, and check the answers.

1 What are the names of the two big political parties in the United States?

2 Who is the only U.S. president ever to resign – Richard Nixon, Ronald Reagan or Bill Clinton?

3 Why did this president resign?

THE **WATERGATE** STORY

Watergate is still the biggest political scandal in American history. It is also one of the biggest newspaper stories of all time – a classic example of investigative journalism.

The basic facts are well known, and have been told in two movies, *All the President's Men* starring Robert Redford and Dustin Hoffman, and *Nixon* starring Anthony Hopkins and James Woods.

In June 1972, five men were arrested during a break-in at the Democratic Party's headquarters in the Watergate Building. Two young reporters of the Washington Post newspaper heard about these arrests, apparently insignificant, and published an article two days later. Republican President, Richard Nixon,

insisted that he knew nothing about the break-in. But the reporters followed the story closer and closer to the White House.

Their big break was when an anonymous informant telephoned one of them, Bob Woodward, and told him that Nixon had directly ordered the break-in to spy on the opposition Democratic Party, and had tried to cover it up. He also said that Nixon kept recordings of all his meetings. The Investigating Committee demanded the tapes. Nixon said he would never hand them over, but was finally obliged to do so. They revealed that he was indeed behind the Watergate break-in and the cover-up.

In 1974, Nixon resigned, and Bob Woodward, the reporter, was famous.

Bob Woodward, the reporter who trapped a dishonest President

b Read the article again and answer these questions.

1 Which two movies are about the Watergate scandal?

2 What was the first indication that political spying was taking place?

3 What position did the President take about it?

4 Who began to investigate the story?

5 What was the big opening in their investigation?

6 How was the President's involvement confirmed?

7 What happened in 1974 as a consequence of the scandal?

c Have any big scandals been revealed by the media in your country?

Lesson 2 Investigative journalism

> **Aims:** To develop students' reading and speaking skills.
> To practice reporting statements.

1 Speaking and reading

Aims: To introduce the topic of political scandals.
To practice reading for specific information.

a • Put students in groups.
• Have them try to answer the three questions about the Watergate story, working individually.
• Then have them discuss the questions in groups and exchange any information they know.
• Students then read the article to check their answers.
• Check the answers with the class.

Answers 1 The Republican Party and the Democratic Party.   2 Richard Nixon
3 Because of the Watergate scandal.

b • Have students read questions 1–7.
• Now tell students to read the article again and to answer the questions.
• Let them check in their groups, and then check the answers with the class.

Answers 1 *All the President's Men* and *Nixon*
2 Five men were arrested at the Democratic Party's headquarters.
3 He said he knew nothing about it.
4 Two young reporters at the *Washington Post*.
5 An anonymous informant said that Nixon had ordered the break-in.
6 The tape-recordings of his meetings confirmed it.
7 Nixon resigned and the reporter became famous.

Optional activity Movie-watching
If possible, and if students are interested in the topic, it would be good to watch *All the President's Men* or *Nixon* as a follow-up to this lesson.

c • Elicit any examples of scandals revealed by the media in the students' own country.
• Get students to discuss the scandals in groups.

2 Grammar builder: past reported speech – statements

Aim: To practice reporting statements.

a • Focus attention on the reported statements 1–4, and the original versions.
  • Put students in pairs.
  • Have them discuss how the verbs differ in the original and reported versions.
  • Check the answers.

Answers 1 *will* changes to *would* 2 present simple changes to past simple
3 past simple changes to past perfect 4 present perfect changes to past perfect

b • Elicit other changes when reporting statements – pronouns, e.g. *I* to *he / she*;
    time expressions, e.g. *today* to *that day*; possessives, e.g. *my* to *his / her*; also *this* to *that* or
    the, and *here* to *there*.
  • Now tell students to report the statements.
  • Check the answers.

Answers 1 ... had told no lies about that / the matter
2 ... would resign there ... following
3 ... his family understood
4 ... could be proud of his achievements as President

  • Focus attention on the Language assistant box, and highlight the omission of *that,* and the
    use of the original tense, in speech.

3 Speaking, writing and reading

Aim: To practice reporting speech.

a • Tell students to think of something terrible they did when they were younger.
  • Have them move around the class telling their story to at least three classmates.

Teaching tip If students are unable to think of a story, suggest that they invent one.

Helping the learner In order for students to practice past reported speech in the writing phase, students need to
be accurate in the use of past forms in the speaking phase. Monitor and check as students
tell their story, and feedback on any common errors in the past forms.

  • Each student then writes the worst story they heard, using reported speech.

Language help Highlight the use of *tell* + object and *say* + that.

b • Put students in groups.
  • Tell them to read each other's reports and discuss them.

2 **Grammar builder:** past reported speech – statements

a Look at the reported statements below, and compare them with the original statements. How have the verbs changed in the two versions? Are there similar changes in your language?

1 Nixon said he would never hand over the tapes.

"I will never hand over the tapes."

2 He insisted that he knew nothing about the break-in.

"I know nothing about the break-in. Nothing!"

3 An informant told Woodward that Nixon had ordered the break-in.

"Nixon ordered the break-in, Mr. Woodward."

4 He also said Nixon had tried to cover it up.

"Nixon has tried to cover it up."

b Read the first part of the pairs of sentences below, and complete the second part using reported speech.

1a) "I have told no lies about this matter," he said.

 b) He said he ....

2a) "I will resign here in the Oval Office tomorrow," he announced.

 b) He announced that he .... in the Oval Office the .... day.

3a) "My family understands," he told reporters.

 b) He told reporters that ....

4a) "I can be proud of my achievements as President," he insisted.

 b) He insisted he ....

Language assistant

- It is common to omit *that*, especially in speech:
  He said (that) he would never hand over the tapes.

- In speech, we often use the original tense, especially when the situation is still happening:
  She said she studies English (instead of: She said she studied English.)

3 **Speaking, writing and reading**

a Think of something terrible you did when you were younger. Share stories with at least three people. Write a brief report about the worst story you heard in your investigation.

Samantha told me she ...   She said that ...

b Read one another's reports in groups, and discuss them.

3 Ethical issues

1 Speaking, listening and reading

a In pairs, look at the photograph. What do you think about the paparazzi?

b Listen to a TV discussion program about news photographers. Who is closest to your opinions, the woman or the man?

c From your memory of the discussion, mark the following opinions as **W** (the woman's) or **M** (the man's). Listen again and check.

1 Most celebrities want attention at first, and should not complain later. ○
2 Everyone has the right to privacy, especially at home. ○
3 Celebrities should accept that fame means loss of privacy. ○
4 Laws that try to protect privacy are hard to enforce. ○
5 Censorship can interfere with serious investigative journalism. ○
6 There have to be laws against the invasion of privacy. ○

2 Grammar builder: past reported speech – questions

a Read the conversation below. Then look at the reported questions that follow and compare them with the original questions underlined. How many changes can you see?

Woman: There should be a law against taking photographs through private windows.

Man: Well, <u>have you ever taken a photograph through someone else's window</u>?

Woman: Uh … well, maybe … but it was a friend's house …

Man: Ah, but <u>how can you prove your friend's consent</u>? Your friend might protest later.

He asked her if she had ever taken a photograph through someone else's window.

He asked her how she could prove her friend's consent.

b Read the first sentence of each pair, and complete the second sentence of each pair using the correct form of the verb for reported questions.

1 "Where do you live?" she asked him.
   She asked him where ……………

2 "Can you stop photographing me?" she asked him.
   She asked him if ……………

3 "What have you done to protect your privacy?" he asked her.
   He asked her what ……………

4 "Will you let me take some photographs?" he asked her.
   He asked her if ……………

Lesson 3 Ethical issues

Aims: To develop students' listening and speaking skills.
To practice reporting questions.
To practice useful expressions for discussion.

Glossary The term *paparazzi* refers to a group of journalists and photographers who follow famous people around.

1 Speaking, listening and reading

Aims: To introduce the topic of the paparazzi.
To practice listening for the main idea and for specific information.

a • Write the word *paparazzi* on the board and ask students if they know what it means.
• Have them discuss the photograph in pairs or groups.

b • Tell students they are going to hear a TV discussion program about news photographers.
• Have them think about who shares their opinion of the paparazzi – the man or the woman.
• Play the tape and get students to compare their opinions with the speakers'.
• Check students understand the general opinions expressed.

Answers The man thinks that famous people don't have a right to privacy, but the woman thinks all people should be protected from the paparazzi.

• Elicit if students share the man's or the woman's opinion.

c • Tell students to read statements 1–6, and to decide if they show what the man or what the woman thinks.
• Play the tape again and have the students check their answers.

Answers 1 M   2 W   3 M   4 M   5 M   6 W

Tapescript
Woman: One thing that's being talked about again is the harassment of celebrities by photographers, paparazzi.
Man: Well, I think many celebrities complain too much. Most of them want as much publicity as they can get at first. They want photographers to follow them everywhere. Then, when they're rich and famous, they suddenly want to stop photographers from following them.
Woman: But don't you think there should be a limit? Don't you think everyone has the right to some privacy?
Man: I agree up to a point. But in my opinion, people who want fame should accept that they'll have to sacrifice their privacy.
Woman: I don't agree at all. Privacy in one's own home, for instance, should be an absolute right for everyone. There should be a law against taking photographs through the windows of private houses, or on private property.
Man: Well, according to legal experts, laws like that are very hard to enforce. It's often impossible to prove whether a photo was taken accidentally or intentionally, or even whether it was taken with or without the celebrity's consent at the time.
Woman: Yes, I see the problems, but …
Man: Also, any censorship of that kind could affect the freedom of journalists to investigate serious stories.
Woman: I'm not sure about that. I think there just have to be some laws against the invasion of privacy.
Man: Well, there are, of course, but …

2 Grammar builder: past reported speech – questions

Aim: To practice reporting questions.

a • Elicit the rules for tense changes in reported statements from lesson 2.
• Have students look at the reported questions under the conversation, and note the changes in word order.
• Have students check how the verb changes and discuss what they notice with a partner.

Answer Reported questions use statement word order, i.e. subject verb. Verbs go "one step back", e.g. present perfect changes to past perfect, *can* changes to *could*. *Yes / no* questions are reported with *if*, and *wh-* questions repeat the question word.

b • Now tell students to change questions 1–4 to reported questions. Check the answers.

Answers 1 …. he lived.   2 he could stop photographing her.
3 she had done to protect her privacy   4 she would let him take some photographs.

3 Word builder: useful expressions for discussions

Aim: To practice language used in discussions.

- Tell students to read the discussion, and complete it with words from the box.
- Check the answers.

Answers 1 I think   2 don't you think   3 I agree   4 in my opinion   5 I don't agree
6 I don't think

4 Speaking and reading

Aims: To develop students' reading and speaking skills.
To consolidate language used in discussions.

Helping the learner In exercises 4a and 4d students are given the opportunity to practice the expressions from exercise 2 in personalized discussion. The focus is on fluency in these exercises, so do not over-correct students' mistakes.

a
- Put students in groups.
- Tell them to discuss questions 1–3, encouraging them to use the expressions from exercise 3.
- Get feedback from the groups.

b
- Tell students they are going to read an article about censorship on the Internet.
- Check that they understand the terms *concerned parents* and *smart kids*.
- Now have the students read the article and decide whose side they are on.
- Get feedback, establishing who most students agree with – the concerned parents or the smart kids.

c
- Put students in pairs.
- Tell them to complete the table from the point of view of parents with children under 15.
- Check the answers.

Answers **Advantages:** The Internet is one of the keys to success. There's a lot of information children can benefit from. Children can have a lot of fun.
Disadvantages: It's hard to control what children see. Young people can come across virtual "red light" districts and crime zones and access extreme violence, pornography and racist propaganda.

d
- Now join the pairs to make groups of four and let them compare what they wrote.
- Ask how many students know children who have access to the Internet.
- Students then discuss the question of Internet filters and whether they should be used and whether children should be helped to get past them.

Teaching tip Encourage students to use the expressions from exercise 3.

- Get feedback from the groups.

Preparation:
Ask students to find the answers to the three questions in lesson 4 exercise 1a.

3 Word builder: useful expressions for discussions

Complete the discussion below with appropriate expressions from the box.

I think	I don't think	don't you think	I agree	I don't agree	in my opinion

Woman: What about the harassment of celebrities by paparazzi?

Man: Well, (1) .... many celebrities complain too much. They want attention at first, then, when they're famous, they want it to stop.

Woman: But (2) .... everyone has the right to some privacy?

Man: Yes, (3) .... up to a point. But (4) .... , people who want fame should accept the sacrifice.

Woman: (5) .... at all. Privacy in one's own home should be an absolute right. There should be a law against taking photographs through private windows.

Man: Well, (6) .... it's possible to enforce a law like that.

4 Speaking and reading

a In groups, discuss these questions.

1 Do you think there should be censorship of violent or other material in the media?

2 Why or why not?

3 What do you think the kids are looking at in the picture below?

b Read the article below about censorship on the Internet. In general, whose side are you on – the smart kids or the concerned parents?

A VIRTUAL BATTLEGROUND

Most parents would like their children to succeed in life, and recognize that the Internet is one of the keys to success in the 21st century. So parents that are able to get a computer and Internet connection at home usually do. But most parents also realize that the Internet is a world of unrestricted information, communication and entertainment – including extreme violence, pornography and racist propaganda. They want their child to benefit from the information and fun, but they do not want them to wander into virtual "red-light" or crime zones any more than they would like them to wander into real red-light or crime zones in a city.

To help concerned parents control their children's access to the wide world of the Internet, software companies are offering many filter or "blocking programs" – family filters, "under-10 blocks," and so on. However, other groups, some supporting "freedom of speech," are working against such blocks and filters. One of these, *Peacefire*, offers children ways around their parents' filter or blocking programs. Their motto is: "It's not a crime to be smarter than your parents." They comment as follows: "An Associated Press story reports that 'only one in 20 children can evade computer filtering technology.' Good, let's keep the adults thinking that."

c In pairs, list advantages and disadvantages of free access to the Internet from the point of view of parents with children under the age of 15.

Advantages	Disadvantages

d Compare your list with another pair's, and discuss them. Then discuss this question.

Do you think it should be illegal to assist minors (under-18-year-olds) to get past Internet filters or blocks imposed by their parents?

LANGUAGE for life:
doing *research*

① When you desperately need to know

When was Abraham Lincoln President of the United States? Is the population of Nigeria greater or smaller than the population of Mexico? How many automobiles does Brazil export to the European Union? In study and work, we often need to know the answers to questions like these. How would you find the answers to the three questions above? Compare your research strategies with those of other people.

For the next time you meet, find the answers to the three questions, and compare them with other people's answers. Who found the answers quickly and easily?

② Researching Nigeria

What do you already know about Nigeria? What can you guess? What can you find out quickly?

Official name: The .... of Nigeria
Location: West ....
Area (km²): ....
Climate: .... in the south, and .... in the north.
Capital: ....
Population: ....
Languages: official – .... ; unofficial – Hausa, Fulani, Yoruba and Arabic
Main exports: ....

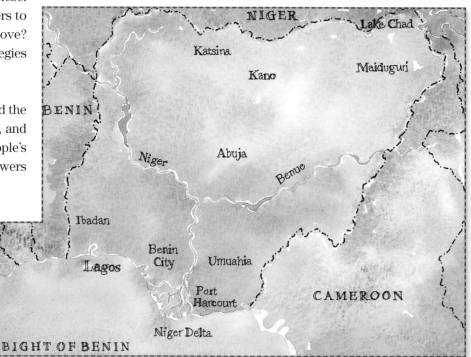

Lesson 4 Language for life: doing research

Aim: To discover ways of finding information for research in English.

1 When you desperately need to know

Aim: To discuss ways of finding information.
- Have students read the questions, and think of how they could find out the answers.
- Have them compare their research strategies in pairs or groups.
- Check the answers with the class.

Possible answers The Internet, CD-ROMS, the library, TV, radio, newspapers or magazines, a person who has knowledge on the topics of the questions

- Get students to exchange the information they found as preparation to this lesson.
- Have them discuss which research strategies they used to find the information.
- Establish which strategies were fastest and easiest.

Helping the learner In the speaking stages of this exercise, students exchange facts and information and also compare research strategies. The main focus here is on the exchange of facts and ideas so do not over-correct students' mistakes.

2 Researching Nigeria

Aim: To practice listening for specific information.
- Focus attention on the chart.
- Check comprehension of the categories.
- Ask students to fill in as much information as they can.
- Elicit where they could find the rest of the information.

- Have students read the introductory paragraph.
- Tell students that the rest of the information they need to complete the chart is on the tape.

Teaching tip Tell students that the information on tape is not in the same order as on the chart.

- Play the tape and let students complete the chart.
- Check the answers.

Answers The Republic of Nigeria; West Africa; 924,000; wet; dry; Abuja; 12 million; English; oil, minerals, agricultural products

Tapescript

The official name is the Republic of Nigeria. The capital is Abuja – that's A-B-U-J-A. It used to be Lagos, but it is now Abuja. Nigeria is not the largest country in Africa, nor even in West Africa, though it is large – 924,000 square kilometers. It is, however, the most populous African nation – almost 120 million in 2000 – and that gives it great importance, of course. It also has great international importance as a major exporter of oil. Apart from oil, Nigeria exports various mineral products and tropical agricultural produce. The climate is of course tropical, dry in the north and wet in the south, often very dry and very wet.

OK, I'd like to speak briefly about the cultural, ethnic, linguistic and religious variety of my country. Culturally, Nigeria is extremely varied, and that has been a source of problems, unfortunately, as well as great cultural wealth and tourism potential. There are many different ethnic groups with different languages – Hausa, Fulani, Yoruba and Arabic being the main ones – and religious affiliations – Muslim, Christian, animistic. For convenience and to avoid conflict, English was established as the only official national language. We have great problems, but I am confident that Nigeria's future is bright.

3 The Internet

Aims: To practice the language used when searching the Internet.
To discuss the Internet as a research tool.

- Have students read the paragraph.
- Now have them match the notes to the section number.
- Check the answers.

Answers 1 Write your search topic here.
2 Click here to begin the search.
3 Click on a specific topic area for a new search if you wish.
4 Click on one of these if you want to explore another site ...
5 Click on one of these if you want to visit a recommended site.
6 Click here if you want to see more options.

- Put students in pairs or groups to discuss the questions.
- Get feedback from the class.

Teaching tip If you have access to computers, it would be a good idea to go online to practice how to run a search.

Like most nations, especially young ones, Nigeria has its problems, but most Nigerians are proud of their nation and optimistic about the future.

Listen to a Nigerian college lecturer giving a short talk about her country. See if you can complete the information on page 56.

The Internet

The Internet is the most powerful research machine in human history – and you ain't seen nothing yet, earthling! To use it, all you need is a few basic notions and then just explore!

How are you on the basic notions? See if you can match the notes to the search page – write the appropriate section number (in red) beside each note.

Have you done any research on the Internet? What was your experience? Compare your experience with that of your friends.

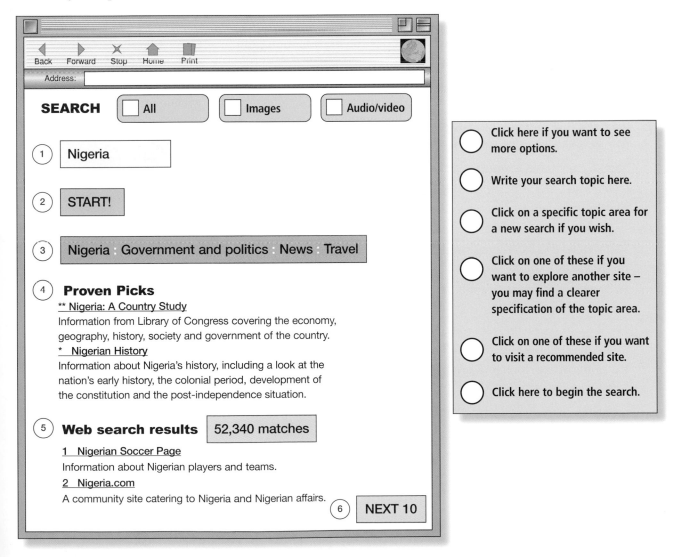

3 Learning check

1 Progress check

a Complete the sentences with the correct past tense of the verbs in parentheses.

1 Elena *lived* (live) in Houston when she was a kid.

2 The train *had* already *left* (leave) when we arrived at the station.

3 We *were driving* (drive) to the airport when Philip called to say he would be late.

4 Monica and Peter *have traveled* (travel) to Japan three times this year!

5 Sandra *went* (go) to the same college as me.

6 I *have been working* (work) on this report all morning and I still haven't finished.

7 *Have* you *seen* (see) the new Bruce Willis movie?

8 What *did* Amanda *do* (do) last night?

9 She *did* (not pass) *not pass* her driving test the first time.

b Read the first sentence of each pair. Complete the second sentence of each pair so it has the same meaning.

10 "I haven't seen Mandy for ages," he said.
He said *he hadn't seen Mandy for ages.*

11 "We can't come to the party on Saturday," they told me.
They told me *they couldn't come to the party on Saturday.*

12 "You have to call the office immediately," he insisted.
He insisted we *had to call the office immediately.*

13 "I will meet you in front of the drugstore," he told us.
He told us *he would meet us in front of the drugstore.*

14 "We can repair the car today," he insisted.
He insisted they *could repair the car that day.*

15 "You can save money if you travel by bus," he suggested.
He suggested I *could save money if I traveled by bus.*

Learning check 3

1 Progress check

Aims: To provide an opportunity to assess students' progress and help them according to the results.
To provide an opportunity for learners to test themselves.
To allow students to evaluate their own progress and act on areas they need to improve.

Suggestions for using the *Progress check* sections
This section can be done in a variety of ways depending on how much time you have and whether you want students to do it as part of an individual assessment or as general revision.

a As a test – students work individually on the *Progress check* sections and you then check their work and record their score out of 15.

b Students work on the *Progress check* sections alone and then check their answers in pairs.

c Students work on the *Progress check* sections in pairs or groups and you later check the answers with the whole class.

d Students do the *Progress check* sections for homework.

In all cases, conduct a feedback session with the whole class to check any queries students may have and see how they did.

Explanation of answers

a

1 Past simple for a completed action in the past.
2 Past perfect for an action which happened before another action in the past.
3 Past progressive for an action in progress in the past.
4 Present perfect simple for experiences in the past in an unfinished time period – we do not know exactly when they went and they may go again.
5 Past simple for a completed action in the past.
6 Present perfect progressive for an activity that began in the past and continues up to the present. The emphasis is on the activity, which is unfinished.
7 Present perfect to talk about general experience.
8 Past simple for a completed action at a specific time in the past.
9 Past simple for a completed action at a specific time in the past.

b

10 Present perfect changes to past perfect.
11 *Can* changes to *could*.
12 Present simple changes to past simple.
13 *Will* changes to *would*.
14 *Can* changes to *could*; *today* changes to *that day*.
15 *Can* changes to *could*; *travel* changes to *traveled*.

2 Proficiency check

Aims: To expose students to TOEFL and UCLES-style exam formats, which will be useful for those students interested in taking such formal proficiency exams.
To develop students' exam-taking strategies.
To allow teachers and students the opportunity to evaluate students' proficiency in English.
To test students' listening and reading skills under pseudo-exam conditions.

Suggestions for taking the test

Taking language tests is not only about knowing the language. It also involves knowing how to deal with exams: how to work under pressure; how to recognize the operations of the exam; and how to apply strategies to get the best results in an exam. These *Proficiency checks* give students the opportunity to work on all of these areas.

Students could do this as a formal proficiency test where they work individually, in silence. The tests are then collected and checked by the teacher. Alternatively, students could do the test individually and then check their answers in pairs or groups.

In either case, it is recommended that students as a class have the opportunity to discuss their answers and how they arrived at them with the teacher. Explanations of the correct answers are given to facilitate the teacher's role here. In addition, the teacher can highlight the strategy that is given in every *Proficiency check*. This is very helpful in giving students the chance to work on their exam-taking strategies as well as their accuracy with the language.

Exam-taking tip   Timing yourself carefully
It is very important when taking a test that the student is aware of the amount of time available to do the tasks and consequently how much time she / he has for each question. In this test, help students to divide up the time available for each task and remind them of the remaining time so that they get used to always timing themselves carefully.

Answers   **a**
1 c   2 a   3 d   4 b   5 c   6 b

Tapescript

This is the Richmond Festival Information Center. We cannot take your call but here is some information about the main events of the festival.

The Festival runs from August 17 to August 30.

In the Kennedy Center, there is a series of classical music concerts by the Richmond Philharmonic Orchestra starting with a performance of Beethoven's 9th symphony on Saturday August 18. Other composers featured are Rossini, Mozart and Tchaikovsky.

The Richmond Movie Society is offering a short season of Latin American movies with samples from Brazil, Mexico and Argentina.

In the Civic Theater, the Royal Shakespeare Company is performing *A Midsummer Night's Dream* from August 19 through the 21. There will also be two lectures by Dr. Barbara Morrison of Harvard University on "Shakespeare and his World" at 8:00 p.m. on August 22 and the 23 in the Community College.

The Riverside Center is offering a series of lunchtime jazz and blues concerts every day from 1:00 to 3:00 p.m. There will also be a permanent exhibition of paintings and photographs in the center.

If you would like information about accommodations, press 1; if you want to order tickets for any event, press 2; if you want information about other events, press 3; if you want information about excursions, press 4.

b
1   C – He is 40 now and it has just been published.
2   C – He was born in a shanty town, lived in one room, had only one pair of trousers.
3   C – From 4 a.m. to 3 p.m.
4   I – He made his professional debut at the age of 15.
5   C – He was part of the Argentina team which won the World Cup.
6   C – He was one of the highest paid players in the world.
7   I – He has had problems with drugs.

2 Proficiency check

a Look at the questions. Then listen to the recorded message about the festival and check (✔) the correct box for each one.

1 The Richmond Festival takes place from:
   a) August 7 to 30. ◯
   b) August 17 to 13. ◯
   c) August 17 to 30. ◯
   d) August 7 to 13. ◯

2 Which composer's work is being performed at the Kennedy Center on August 18?
   a) Beethoven ◯
   b) Rossini ◯
   c) Mozart ◯
   d) Tchaikovsky ◯

3 The Movie Society is showing movies from:
   a) Colombia, Brazil and Chile. ◯
   b) Brazil, Paraguay and Mexico. ◯
   c) Brazil, Mexico and Panama. ◯
   d) Brazil, Mexico and Argentina. ◯

4 Dr. Barbara Morrison is:
   a) giving a lecture on Shakespeare at Harvard University. ◯
   b) giving two lectures in the Community College. ◯
   c) acting in *A Midsummer Night's Dream.* ◯
   d) a member of the Royal Shakespeare Company. ◯

5 The jazz and blues concerts are every day:
   a) between 1:00 and 2:00 p.m. ◯
   b) between 12:00 and 3:00 p.m. ◯
   c) between 1:00 and 3:00 p.m. ◯
   d) between 2:00 and 3:00 p.m. ◯

6 You press 2 if you want:
   a) information about accommodations ◯
   b) to buy tickets. ◯
   c) information about other events. ◯
   d) information about excursions. ◯

b Read the statements below about the soccer player, Diego Maradona. Then read the text and decide if they are correct (C) or incorrect (I).

1 Diego Maradona wrote his autobiography before he was 40. C ◯ I ◯
2 He was very poor when he was a boy. C ◯ I ◯
3 His father worked 11 hours a day. C ◯ I ◯
4 He became a professional soccer player when he was 16. C ◯ I ◯
5 In 1986 Argentina won the World Cup. C ◯ I ◯
6 He made a lot of money playing for big teams. C ◯ I ◯
7 He has had problems with alcohol. C ◯ I ◯

Diego Maradona is one of the world's most famous soccer players. Although he is only 40, he has just published his autobiography. One hundred and fifty thousand copies have been printed and will be sold in 80 countries. Maradona was born in the shanty town of Villa Fiorito in Argentina. He was one of eight children and the family lived in one room. He only had one pair of pants and his father worked from four in the morning until three in the afternoon.

Diego was such a talented soccer player he made his professional debut at the age of 15. He played for Argentina for the first time when he was 16, and by the age of 19 he had already scored 100 league goals. His first World Cup game in 1982 was a disappointment and he played badly. But in 1986 in Mexico he was part of the Argentina team which won the World Cup. In the game against England, he scored two goals: the first with his hand, and a fantastic second goal. Maradona said the first goal was "the hand of God."

Later he played for famous teams such as Barcelona and Naples and was one of the highest paid players in the world. Sadly, he has had problems with drugs which he hasn't been able to solve. However, in Argentina he is still a hero and people remember the poor boy from Villa Fiorito.

Unit 7 Trends

1 My generation

1 Speaking

a Work in pairs. When was this photograph taken? What clues are there?

b How are people from your generation different?

2 Listening and speaking

a Listen to Joanne Michaels talking about her life in the 1980s. Check (✔) the topics she mentions from the list.

1	music	3	politics	5	family	7	rock groups	9	events
2	clothes	4	movies	6	games	8	magazines	10	TV programs

b Listen again and complete the information about Joanne.

	Games	Music	TV programs	Movies	Clothes	Memorable events
Joanne	....	Duran Duran &	"Scooby Doo" &	.... & *Indiana Jones*	....	Challenger explosion & ....
You						

c Now complete the row for your generation and compare your choices with two other students.

3 Pronunciation: linking

a Listen to the examples of linking 1–4 below, and match the linked words to the descriptions a–d.

1 I was born in 1967.
2 He's too old to play soccer.
3 Are you French? Yes, I am.
4 She's a member of generation X.

a) /r/ to vowel
b) consonant to vowel
c) a 'back' vowel (as in *so, now, too*) is joined to another vowel by /w/
d) a 'front' vowel (as in *tea, be, see*) is joined to another vowel by /j/ (*She is French!*)

60

Trends

Helping the learner: pronunciation – connected speech

Learners need practice in aspects of connected speech. These include:
• linking   • sentence stress / rhythm   • intonation

Further reading:
Underhill, A., (1994) *Sound Foundations,* Macmillan Heinemann ELT, Levels 1 & 2, part 3

Lesson 1 My generation

> **Aims:** To practice speaking about generation differences and pop music groups.
> To focus on linking words in pronunciation.

1 Speaking

Aim: To introduce the topic of generation differences.

a • Put students in pairs.
   • Focus attention on the photograph and have students discuss the question.

Answer The picture is from the 1980s. The clues are the clothes, hairstyles and the posters.

b • Let students discuss the question in pairs.

2 Listening and speaking

Aim: To practice listening for the main idea and specific information.

Cultural note *Generation X* refers to people born between 1965 and 1980. They were usually dissatisfied with their lives and were pessimistic.

a • Tell students they are going to hear a woman called Joanne talking about the 1980s.
   • Play the tape and get students to check the topics Joanne mentions against the list.

Answers music, clothes, movies, games, events, TV programs

b • Focus attention on the table. Play the tape again and have students complete it.

Answers Nintendo, Michael Jackson, *Casper, ET*, jeans, sneakers and T-shirts, the Berlin Wall coming down

c • Have students complete the table with answers about their generation.
   • Put students in groups of three and have them compare their answers.

Tapescript

Reporter: Today in our series on culture Joanne Michaels is here to talk about growing up in the 1980s. Joanne, what was it like being a member of *Generation X*?
Joanne: Great! I was born in 1967 so I was a teenager in the 1980s. I loved being a kid in the 1980s. I remember the first time Nintendo came out. What a great game!
Reporter: What other things do you remember? For example, music from the 80s?
Joanne: Oh I loved Duran Duran. And Michael Jackson too. Everyone I knew bought the *Thriller* album and the video was a classic.
Reporter: What about TV programs?
Joanne: I was really into cartoons. I remember watching stuff like *Scooby Doo* and *Casper.*
Reporter: And which movies did you like?

Joanne: I thought *ET* was great and *Indiana Jones* too.
Reporter: Yes, *Indiana Jones.* Remember *Raiders of the Lost Ark?*
Joanne: Yeah, now that was a great movie!
Reporter: Yeah, I really enjoyed it too. Now how about clothes, Joanne? What did you wear?
Joanne: Um, jeans of course. And, um, sneakers, T-shirts, that kind of thing.
Reporter: Okay, and finally, do you remember any special events?
Joanne: Hmm, let me think. Why, yes, 1987 ... the Challenger exploding. I still remember that like it was yesterday. I was completely shocked. Everyone was. I also remember the Berlin Wall coming down in 1988.
Reporter: 1988? It was 1989, wasn't it?
Joanne: Yeah, you're right. The wall came down in '89. It still seems incredible ... like living history!

• See page T61 for notes on exercise 3.

3 Pronunciation: linking

Aim: To practice linking words to improve connected speech.

Helping the learner	This exercise highlights typical links between words in connected speech. Explain to students that by becoming aware of and practicing linking their spoken English will sound more natural.

a • Write sentence 1 on the board; highlight the linking between *born* and *in*.
 • Play the tape and get students to focus on the linking between words.
 • Play the tape again and have them decide what kind of linking it is.

Answers	1 b, b, a, b, d 2 b, b, b

b • Put students in pairs.
 • Tell them to read the sentences and try to identify the type of linking.
 • Play the tape and stop after each one to check.

Answers	1 b, b, a, d 2 b, b, b

 • Have students practice the pronunciation.

Teaching tip	Play the tape again if students have difficulty with the pronunciation.

 • Focus attention on the Learning tip, and check students appreciate the importance of linking in understanding spoken English.
 • **Optional step:** Have students write and practice their own sentences with the different types of linking.

4 Reading, speaking and writing

Aims: To develop students' reading and speaking skills.
 To practice understanding text structure.
 To practice writing a short article.

a • Put students in groups.
 • Have them identify the two pop groups (The Corrs and The Backstreet Boys).
 • Now tell them to think about the differences between them.
 • Get feedback, writing the main ideas on the board.

b • Now have students read the paragraphs, identify which paragraphs are about which group, and put them in the right order.
 • Check the answers.

Answers	The Backstreet Boys: 1 e 2 a 3 d The Corrs: 1 c 2 b 3 f

Teaching tip	You could ask students which key words in the text gave them the answers, e.g. The Backstreet Boys' incredible story began ... After forming in 1991 ...

 • Refer students back to the notes on the board and check them against the information in the texts.

c • Check comprehension of the categories in the table in exercise 4d.
 • Ask students to read the articles again to complete the first two columns of the table.
 • Check the answers.

Answers	**Backstreet Boys:** the USA, pop and Rhythm and Blues, *Black and Blue*, *I'll never break your heart*. **The Corrs:** Ireland, pop and traditional Irish music, *In Blue*, *What can I do?*, *So Young* and *Breathless*.

d • Have students complete the final column of the table, about their favorite group or singer.
 • Have them write an article about the group / singer, using the texts in exercise 4b as a model.
 • Have students exchange and read each other's articles.

b Work in pairs. Read sentences 1 and 2 and identify the type of linking (a, b, c or d from exercise 3a). Then listen and check your pronunciation.

1 Whe**n I** wa**s a** teenage**r I** didn't have m**y o**wn room.
2 Thi**s apple is a**bsolutely delicious.

4 Reading, speaking and writing

a Work in groups. Do you know the two groups shown above? What do you think are the main differences between them? Discuss your ideas.

b The texts below are from two newspaper articles about the two groups. Identify the three paragraphs that belong to each article and put them in the correct order. Check your ideas from exercise 4a with the texts.

The Backstreet Boys: Paragraphs   1 ◯   2 ◯   3 ◯
The Corrs: Paragraphs   1 ◯   2 ◯   3 ◯

a) The vocal quintet sing a mixture of pop and Rhythm and Blues. Six months after forming they were one of Florida's hottest live acts and signed with Jive Records. In 1995, their second single *I'll Never Break Your Heart* was a huge success and in April 1996 they released their first full-length album.

b) Their first album *Forgiven, Not Forgotten* in 1995 was a mixture of traditional Irish music and pop. The group toured non-stop and lead singer Andrea appeared in the movie *Evita*.

c) One of Ireland's most successful pop exports of the 90s, the family group the Corrs consists of Jim on guitar and keyboards, sisters Sharon, violin and vocals, Caroline, drums and vocals and Andrea, lead vocalist. After forming in 1991, they played locally in Dublin and signed with Atlantic Records in 1994.

d) A very popular group, by 2001 they had sold 28 million albums worldwide and had scored five Top Ten singles. Their album *Millennium*, released in 1999, has sold over 10 million copies. *Black and Blue*, another album, released in 2001, will probably be just as successful.

e) The Backstreet Boys' incredible story began in Orlando, Florida in 1993. High school students A.J. McLean, Howie Dorough and Nick Carter met each other at local acting auditions and formed a singing group. The trio then decided to expand by two, adding Kevin Richardson and his cousin Brian Littrell.

f) The next album *Talk on Corners* was a more pop-oriented album and included several hot singles: *What Can I Do?* and *So Young*. The album eventually sold one million copies. Their third album *In Blue* was a hit and the single *Breathless* was an international success.

c Read the articles again and complete the table below.

d Complete the final column of the table, writing about your favorite group or singer.

	The Backstreet Boys	The Corrs	Your favorite group / singer
country of origin			
type of music			
name of latest album			
best-known songs			

2 Looking good

1 Word builder: clothing

a Look at the photograph and then match each article of clothing with the correct word from the list below.

baseball cap	jeans
tie	T-shirt
mini skirt	suit
sweater	sandals
leather jacket	boots
tank top	coat
pants	dress
hat	jacket
sneakers	anorak
blouse	shirt
socks	tights
shoes	

b Which clothing articles are not included in the photograph? Can you find examples of these words in your class?

c Work in pairs. Imagine you could each pick two items of clothing to wear. Which would you choose? Compare ideas with your partner.

2 Grammar builder: order of adjectives

a Look at the examples.

- *a blue cotton shirt*
- *a large khaki bag*

Based on these examples, decide the usual order for adjectives.

material ◯ color ◯ size ◯ + noun

Language assistant

Notice that opinion adjectives – great, nice, beautiful, ugly – come first:
*I got a **great** leather jacket.*

b Put these sentences in the correct order.

1 ugly / red / an / sweater / wool
2 large / a / brown / of / leather / boots / pair
3 gold / round / a / watch / small
4 plastic / black / long / raincoat / a

Lesson 2 Looking good

Aims: To practice using clothing vocabulary.
To discuss clothing and image.
To practice the order of adjectives by describing clothes.

1 Word builder: clothing

Aim: To practice and expand students' clothing vocabulary.

a • Tell students to look at the photograph, and to match the words from the box with the articles of clothing.
  • Now have them check in pairs.
  • Check the answers with the class.

Answers 1 dress 2 boots 3 sweater 4 sneakers 5 pants 6 baseball cap 7 shirt 8 shoes
9 hat 10 T-shirt 11 mini skirt

b • Students now decide which are the items of clothing not included in the photograph.
  • Check the answers.

Answers tie, leather jacket, tank top, blouse, socks, jeans, suit, sandals, coat, jacket, anorak, tights

  • Tell students to look for examples of the clothing in the classroom.

c • Put students in pairs.
  • Get them to choose two items of clothing they would like to wear.
  • Have students compare their ideas.
  • Get feedback from the students with reasons for their choice.

2 Grammar builder: order of adjectives

Aim: To practice order of adjectives.

a • Check comprehension of the categories *material, color* and *size,* and of adjectives of fact – adjectives which give factual information.
  • Write the examples on the board.
  • Have students decide the usual order of adjectives.
  • Check the answers.

Answers size, color, material + noun

b • Focus attention on the Language assistant box and check students understand that opinion adjectives come before adjectives of fact.
  • Have students put sentences 1–4 in the right order.
  • Have them check in pairs.
  • Check the answers with the class.

Answers 1 an ugly red wool sweater   2 a large pair of brown leather boots
3 a small round gold watch   4 a long black plastic raincoat

Helping the learner Help students with sentence stress and rhythm by asking them to identify the stressed words in the sentences, e.g. *an **ugly** red wool sweater.* Also highlight the effect of changing the stress on the meaning, e.g. *an ugly **red** wool sweater* (focus on the color), *an ugly red **wool** sweater* (focus on the material).

c • Put students in pairs.
  • Tell students they have 30 seconds to look at what their partner is wearing and memorize it (without writing).
  • Have students sit back to back and try to describe their partner's clothes in as much detail as possible.
  • Have students change roles so that the student who described first, now listens.

3 Speaking and reading

Aim: To practice predicting and reading for specific information.

a • Tell students to look at the photograph.
  • Put students in pairs and make a list of at least five things they know about Barbie dolls.
  • Get feedback from the pairs.
  • Now have the students read the article quickly to check their answers.

b • Have the students read the article again, and mark the statements 1–6 true or false.
  • Check the answers.

Answers   1 F   2 T   3 F   4 T   5 T   6 T

c • Check comprehension of the items in the box.
  • Put students in groups of three.
  • Have them discuss the two questions.
  • Get feedback from the groups, eliciting which fashion is most popular with the whole class.

c Work in pairs. Look at what your partner is wearing for 30 seconds. Then sit back to back and describe your partner's clothes.

You're wearing a pair of black jeans, a blue wool sweater, ...

3 Speaking and reading

a In pairs, look at the photograph and make a list of at least five things you know about Barbie dolls.

Barbie dolls are sold all over the world.

TATTOO BARBIE GETS THE CHOP

Barbie dolls have been part of American culture since they were first sold in 1959. Aimed at 6 to 9-year-old girls, Mattel, the maker of Barbie, has sold more than one billion dolls worldwide. The Barbie range includes Malibu Barbie, Babysitter Barbie and Wedding Barbie. Every year a new Barbie arrives on the market.

However, anyone can make a mistake, as Mattel showed. The company introduced a version of Barbie which they said would be "every mother's nightmare." Butterfly Art Barbie came with a butterfly tattoo on its stomach and a set of temporary transfer tattoos for the owner. A Mattel spokesperson said:

"Nowadays tattoos are classed as art."

Although the firm acknowledged that the new toy might inspire young girls to want a real tattoo, it argued it was only keeping up with fashion. The spokesperson said: "Ask any cool chick and she'll tell you that tattoos are one of the latest fashion crazes."

Mattel was right about one thing. Parents were outraged and the company took Butterfly Art Barbie off the market.

b Now read the article and mark the statements T (true) or F (false).

1 Barbie dolls have been sold for over 50 years.   T ◯   F ◯
2 Over a billion Barbies have been sold in North America.   T ◯   F ◯
3 Butterfly Art Barbie had a butterfly tattoo on its shoulder.   T ◯   F ◯
4 The company thought the doll would definitely make lots of girls want real tattoos.   T ◯   F ◯
5 The spokesperson for Mattel said that tattoos for girls are fashionable.   T ◯   F ◯
6 Mattel withdrew Butterfly Art Barbie because parents were angry.   T ◯   F ◯

c Discuss these questions in groups of three.

1 Which of the following do you think are fashionable?
2 Would you personally have any of these?

| streaked or dyed hair | tattoos | studs in any part of the body | earrings for men | a woolen hat |

3 Shop till you drop

1 Word builder: shopping items

a Put the following list of items into one of these four categories.

1 men's toiletries   2 makeup   3 computers   4 sports

razor blades	racket	monitor	tennis balls
mouse pad	aftershave	lipstick	face cream
deodorant	keyboard	baseball bat	running suit
eye shadow	shaving cream	laptop	mascara

b Work in groups of three. What are the six most important items in your everyday life? Talk about them in your groups.

2 Listening

a Listen to interviews with four shoppers, and write down the articles each person bought.

Name	Articles
Sandra	
Jim	
Tony	
Kate	

b Who do you think spent most, and least? Why?

3 Grammar builder: quantifiers

a Look at the words in the box below. What do they have in common?

a few	a little	many	much	a lot of	most
both	neither	all	none	half	

b Put the quantifiers from the box into the correct columns below. Be careful, in some cases like *a lot of* you can use a quantifier with both types of noun!

Countable nouns (*cars*)	Uncountable nouns (*sugar*)
many a lot of	much a lot of

Lesson 3 Shop till you drop

> **Aims:** To develop students' speaking and reading skills on the subject of shopping.
> To practice using quantifiers.

1 Word builder: shopping items

Aim: To develop students' vocabulary of shopping items.

a • Tell students to read the words in the box, and put them into the four categories.
 • Check the answers by writing the categories on the board with the correct items in each list.

Answers
1 razor blades, deodorant, aftershave, shaving cream
2 eye shadow, lipstick, face cream, mascara
3 mouse pad, keyboard, monitor, laptop
4 tennis balls, racket, baseball bat, running suit

b • Put students in groups of three.
 • Have them talk about the six most important items in their everyday life.
 • Get feedback from the groups, eliciting which are the most important items for the class.

2 Listening

Aim: To practice listening for specific information.

a • Pre-teach *bathing suit*, *joystick* (for a computer game) *soccer cleats, Kleenex* (brand name for paper tissues), and *leotard*.
 • Tell students they will hear four shoppers talking about their purchases.
 • Play the tape and have students complete the table.
 • Let them check in pairs, and then check the answers with the class.

Answers
Sandra: face cream, eye shadow, bathing suit, diskettes
Jim: Nintendo game, joystick, soccer cleats, Manchester United shirt
Tony: cell phone, perfume, shaving cream and Kleenex
Kate: lipstick, leotard, laptop

b • Now have students work out which shopper spent the most and the least amount of money.
 • Check the answers with the class, asking students to give reasons for their answers.

Possible answers There is no fixed answer here, but Jim and Kate bought the most expensive items.

Tapescript

Reporter: I asked four people in a shopping mall about the kind of things they bought. First I talked to Sandra. Well, Sandra. What do you have in those bags?
Sandra: Well, I didn't buy much. Um, some face cream and eye shadow.
Reporter: Okay, cosmetics. Anything else?
Sandra: Oh yes. A bathing suit, oh, and some diskettes for my computer.
Reporter: Thank you. Then I talked to Jim.
Jim: I bought a lot beacuse it's my son's birthday on Saturday. A Nintendo game, and I also had to buy a joystick which was really expensive.

Reporter: Yes, but kids love computer games, don't they?
Jim: Oh yes. I do too.
Reporter: Did you get anything else?
Jim: Yes. Some soccer cleats and a Manchester United shirt.
Reporter: After that I spoke to Tony.
Tony: Well I bought a new cell phone.
Reporter: Anything else?
Tony: Yes, it's my girlfriend's birthday so I got her some perfume.
Reporter: That's a nice present ... is that all?

Tony: Um, no, I got some shaving cream and Kleenex.
Reporter: Finally, I spoke to Kate. Have you been shopping?
Kate: Well, yes. I spent more than I meant to as usual.
Reporter: What did you buy?
Kate: Well, some lipstick and an outfit for aerobics.
Reporter: Oh, you mean a kind of leotard?
Kate: Right. And there was an offer in the computer center so I finally bought a laptop. 40% off!
Reporter: Wow! That's a real bargain for a laptop.

3 Grammar builder: quantifiers

Aim: To practice quantifiers.

a • Ask students to look at the words in the box and decide what they all have in common.
 • Check the answer and establish that all the words express quantities.

b • Now tell students to put the quantifiers from the box in the correct column in the table.
 • Check the answers.

Answers Countable nouns: a few, many, a lot (of), most, both, neither, all, none, half
Uncountable nouns: a little, much, a lot (of), most, all

c • Now have students write the quantifiers on the scale.
   • Check the answers.

Answers 0% ⟶ 100%

none	a few	half	a lot of	most	all
neither	a little		many		both
			much		

d • Focus attention on the Language assistant box in the Students' Book, and elicit other sentences to illustrate the use of *lots of* and *many / much*, and the position of quantifiers before a noun or noun phrase.
   • Now ask students to complete the sentences with an appropriate quantifier. Point out that sometimes more than one answer is possible.
   • Check the answers.

Answers 1 most, many, a lot of, all   2 both   3 a lot of   4 a few
5 most, all, a few, many, a lot of   6 none, both, all   7 half

   • **Optional step:** Students make up sentences for their classmates about people in the class, leaving out the quantifier. They give them to another student, who completes the sentence.

4 Reading and speaking

Aim: To develop students' reading and speaking skills.

a • Focus attention on the questionnaire.
   • Have students answer the questions and check the key.

Helping the learner Remind students of the intonation of *wh-* and *yes / no* questions (rise-fall and fall-rise). This will help them when discussing their answers.

   • Now get them to compare their answers with two other students.
   • Get feedback from the groups.

b • Focus attention on the statements 1–4 in the questionnaire.
   • Have the students discuss them with the class, and decide whether the statements are true or false for the group.

c Write the quantifiers on the scale from 0% to 100%.

0% ⟶ 100%

.....none..... .... .a lot of. ....

....

....

d Complete sentences 1–7, below, with an appropriate quantifier.

1 .... children like candy.

2 My cousin and I were born in Hong Kong, but we
.... live in Australia now.

3 Yes, I'm ambitious. I want to get a good job and make
.... money.

4 Can you help me? It will only take .... minutes.

5 .... of the people in my class speak at least
two languages.

6 .... of us can speak Mandarin Chinese.

7 Only 50% of the class passed the math test. Yes, only
...............!

> **Language assistant**
>
> In affirmative sentences use *a lot (of)*. If the style is formal, use *many* or *much*.
> - *A lot (of)* and *Lots (of)* are basically the same.
> - Quantifiers always come before a noun, or a noun phrase:
>
> *Could I speak to you for **a few** <u>minutes</u>, please?*
>
> *Could **all** of <u>the parents who are waiting</u> speak to me later, please?*

4 Reading and speaking

a Answer the questionnaire and check the key. Compare your answers with two other students.

Are you a shopaholic?

1 You have a free Saturday morning. Would you rather:
a) buy a plant for your apartment?
b) go straight to the local shopping mall?
c) read the newspaper?

2 A clothing store in the mall has a sale and is full of people. Would you:
a) go in but only buy what you really need?
b) rush in to look for bargains?
c) find a nice quiet place for coffee?

3 One of your friends is getting married next weekend. Do you:
a) try to use existing clothes and maybe buy one or two new items?
b) go straight out to buy a new outfit?
c) find something to wear in your closet?

4 You're in your local supermarket and notice the imported cookies have an offer of buy one package and get one free. Do you:
a) buy one because it's a good offer?
b) buy two packages and get two free ones?
c) ignore it because cookies are fattening?

5 You have to buy a jacket for work. Do you:
a) think about what you want and go to a couple of stores to compare prices?
b) spend a happy morning trying on jackets in every clothes store you can find?
c) go to the nearest clothes store and buy the first jacket that looks all right?

6 You feel really depressed. To feel better would you:
a) go and have a coffee in your favorite coffee shop?
b) go and buy something you really wanted?
c) go to bed early with a good book?

Answer key:
Mostly As – You like shopping but you can control it most of the time.
Mostly Bs – You are a real shopaholic. You are never happier than when you are in a department store or mall.
Mostly Cs – Shopping isn't your cup of tea. You'd rather be doing anything else!

b Discuss the questionnaire with the class. Find out which of the statements 1–4 are T (true) or F (false).

1 Half of the class hates shopping. ○

2 Most people think that clothes aren't important. ○

3 A few people buy clothes every week. ○

4 A lot of people shop in malls. ○

LANGUAGE for life:

getting the *idea*

① Types of music

How much do you know about music? Can you recognize different types of music? Listen to the six different pieces of music and see if you can classify them correctly.

rock 'n' roll ◯   classical ◯   heavy metal ◯
jazz ◯   rap ◯   latin ◯

Can you match the names of the well-known people to the photographs / pictures above, and identify the type of music they are famous for?

1) Shakira   **3)** Duke Ellington   **5)** Def Leppard
2) U2   **4)** Beethoven   **6)** Snoop Dogg

What kind of music do you listen to:
to relax?   to dance?   while you're working / studying?
first thing in the morning?   at parties?

Lesson 4 Language for life: getting the idea

Aim: To raise awareness of the use of English in music and songs.

1 Types of music

Aim: To introduce the topic of music.
- Focus attention on the photograph and ask students what type of music it represents.
- Ask students what types of music they like.
- Play the tape and have them identify the types of music.
- Check the answers.

Answers jazz, rap, heavy metal, latin, classical, rock 'n' roll

- Focus attention on the photographs / pictures of the musicians.
- Get students to match the names in the list of musicians to the photographs / pictures.
- Then have students identify the type of music that each musician is famous for.
- Check the answers.

Answers a Beethoven – classical   b Snoop Dogg – rap   c Shakira – latin pop
d U2 – rock / pop   e Duke Ellington – jazz   f Deff Leppard – rock 'n' roll / heavy metal

- Put students in groups.
- Get them to talk about the kind of music they listen to.
- Get feedback from the groups.

2 The Mozart effect

Aim: To practice reading an article for specific information.

- Have students read the article, and underline the four different effects of music that are described.
- Check the answers.

Answers	The music of Mozart can cause a temporary increase in IQ. Music can be used to heal the body, strengthen the mind and unlock the creative spirit. Children learn more at school and are likely to be nicer to each other if they are played pleasant, calming music. If children listen to exciting, aggressive music, their performance goes down and they become more anti-social.

- Elicit students' reactions to the points in the article.
- Ask students if they have any examples of the positive or negative effects of music.

3 Lyrics

Aim: To think and talk about song lyrics.

- Tell students they are going to read some song lyrics.
- Have them read questions 1–3, then read the lyrics to answer the questions.
- Have students compare their ideas in pairs.
- Check the answers to question 1.

Answer	*The Logical Song* is about losing identity in the modern world; *Oops! I did it again* is about a girl making a boy believe she is in love with him.

- Play the tape of the songs and ask students to change their answers to questions 2 and 3 if they want.
- Get feedback from the class.

Helping the learner	Song lyrics are excellent for highlighting that English is stress-timed, i.e. the stressed syllables are produced at roughly regular intervals of time. Get students to identify the stressed syllables in the song lyrics and how this goes with the beat of the music.

- Have students now look at the magazine quiz, and answer the questions.
- Have them compare their answers in pairs or groups.
- Get feedback from the class.

Optional activity	Music profiles Ask students to bring in information about different types of music and musicians. Have students form groups of four and discuss their information.

② The Mozart effect

Read the article below and underline the points where they talk about the positive and negative effects of music. There are four points.

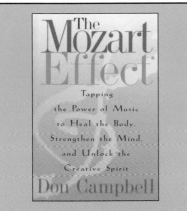

This week in our books section, we review *The Mozart Effect*.

"The nervous system is like a symphony orchestra with different rhythms, melodies and instruments," Don Campbell writes in *The Mozart Effect*. The title refers to studies showing that the music of Mozart can cause a temporary increase in IQ, but the book covers the entire range of effects music can have on us. Music is not just entertainment. It can be used to heal the body, strengthen the mind and unlock the creative spirit.

Music can also influence the early development of children. Studies have shown that children learn more at school and are likely to be nicer to each other if they are played pleasant, calming music such as Albinoni's Adagio in G minor. On the other hand, if they listen to exciting, aggressive music, their performance goes down and they become more antisocial.

③ Lyrics

How much can lyrics tell you about a song? Look at the excerpts from two songs shown here and answer the following questions.

1 What is the theme of each song?
2 What kind of music do you think goes with each song? (fast, slow, loud, soft, country and western, rock 'n' roll, blues, pop, etc.)
3 When do you think you would listen to each song?

Now listen to each excerpt and check your answers. Which excerpt do you like the best?

A

*When I was young, it seemed that
    life was so wonderful
a miracle, oh it was beautiful,
    magical
And all the birds in the trees, well
    they'd be singing so happily
Joyfully, playfully watching me
But then they sent me away to
    teach me how to be sensible
Logical, responsible, practical
And they showed me a world
    where I could be so dependable
Clinical, intellectual, cynical
There are times when all the
    world's asleep
The questions run too deep
For such a simple man.
Won't you please, please tell me
    what we've learned
I know it sounds absurd
But please tell me who I am*
The Logical Song – Supertramp

B

*Yeah yeah yeah yeah yeah
Yeah yeah yeah yeah yeah
I think I did it again
I made you believe we're more
    than friends
Oh baby
It might seem like a crush
But it doesn't mean that I'm
    serious
'Cause to lose all my senses
That is just so typically me
Oh baby, baby
Oops! … I did it again
I played with your heart, got lost
    in the game
Oh baby, baby
Oops! … You think I'm in love
That I'm sent from above
I'm not that innocent*
Oops! I did it again – Britney Spears

In pairs, look at the music magazine quiz below, and answer the questions.

> **Win a pair of free tickets to the Westlife concert. Just answer these questions and send them in:**
>
> **1 What's your favorite type of music?**
>
> **2 What singer or group do you hate the most?**
>
> **3 What's your all time favorite song?**
>
> **Finally, write in 20 words why you think music is important in life.**

Unit 8 Big moments

1 Personal firsts

1 Speaking

Work in pairs and talk about what's happening in the photograph. Complete your sections of the table below, and interview another student to complete their sections. Use the examples to help you make up your questions.

When did you go to your first party?
What did you do there?
How did you feel the first time you went to a night club?
Who did you go to the night club with?

First	You When / who / what	You How you felt	Partner When / who / what	Partner How you felt
party / night club				
time driving a car				
day at school				
girlfriend / boyfriend				
money earned				

2 Listening

a Listen to two people talking about firsts and identify the topics they are talking about.

b Listen to the people talking again and answer the questions below. Check your answers in groups of three.

Steve

1 What was Jane like?
2 What was she really good at?
3 Why couldn't Steve talk to her?

Wendy

1 What was Wendy's job?
2 How much did she earn?
3 What didn't she like about the job?

c How did each of these people feel about their firsts?

Unit 8 Big moments

Helping the learner: collocation

Recent methodology highlights the importance of getting students to focus on how words fit together. Students can be encouraged to focus on the following collocations and chunks of language: verbs like *have, go, take, make* + nouns that go together; fixed phrases; lexico-grammatical categories like prepositions of time and place; topic-specific collocations and word pairings.

Lesson 1 Personal firsts

> **Aims:** To develop students' speaking and reading skills.
> To practice listening for the main idea and specific information.

1 Speaking

Aim: To introduce the topic of important first events in people's lives.

- Put students in pairs and have them discuss what's happening in the photograph.

Answer The photograph shows two people in love, perhaps for the first time.

- Elicit examples of how students think the people in the picture are feeling.
- Focus attention on the table, and have students complete the *You* columns.
- Focus attention on the example questions at the start of the exercise.
- Get students to interview each other and complete the *Partner* columns of the table.
- Get feedback from the pairs.

2 Listening

Aim: To practice listening for the main idea and specific information.

a • Play the tape and let students identify the topics from the table in exercise 1.

Answers 1 Steve – first girlfriend   2 Wendy – first money earned

b • Play the tape again and get students to answer the questions.
- Have students check their answers in groups of three.
- Play the tape again to check the answers, pausing after the answer to each question.

Answers **Steve** 1 She was really cute. She had short hair and a small nose. She used to wear sweaters and sandals.   2 She was really good at soccer and running.
3 He was too embarrassed to talk to her.
Wendy 1 She had a paper route.   2 $20 a week.
3 It was very tiring and in the winter it was cold and wet.

c • Now have students discuss how they think these people felt about their firsts.

Tapescript

Announcer: Now it's time for Sonia Allen's weekly report.
Sonia: Hello. Memories are an important part of our lives. I'm always remembering things that happened to me. This week, I'm looking at memories of the first time we did something. I asked two different people to talk about "firsts" that were significant for them. First Steve.
Steve: Uh, my first girlfriend was when I was in elementary school. Her name was Jane and she was really cute.
Sonia: Was she? What did she look like?
Steve: I remember she had short hair and a small nose. She used to wear sweaters and sandals. Oh yeah, she was really good at soccer and she was the fastest runner in class. Faster than all the boys!
Sonia: Really! And did she like you?
Steve: I think so. Anyway, I really liked her but I always felt embarrassed to talk to her so she talked to me. She said, "Why don't we sit together at lunch?" After elementary school, we went to different schools and I never saw her again!
Sonia: Later, I asked Wendy.
Wendy: Well, the first money I earned was when I was 15. I had a paper route.

Sonia: A paper route. What did that involve?
Wendy: Well, it meant getting up really early to deliver newspapers to people's houses. Lots of kids at my school did this. I used to ride about 4 miles a day.
Sonia: Did you? Was it a well paying job?
Wendy: Not really. Although I was really happy because I was earning $20 a week, it was very tiring and in winter it was really cold and wet.
Sonia: The interesting thing about firsts is that most of them happen when we are teenagers. Experts say that ...

3 Speaking and reading

Aims: To talk about extreme sports.
To practice reading a text to identify the main idea.

a • Put students in pairs.
• Have them look at the photograph and discuss the questions about sport.
• Check the answers.

Answers The sport shown is surfing.

b • Have students read the text and identify which sport is being described and why the person wanted to do it.
• Check the answers.

Answers Parachuting. The writer and his friend discovered they had both always wanted to do it.

c • Have the students read the text again and put the events listed in order.
• Check the answers.

Answers 7   3   4   6   1   2   5

Helping the learner Ask students which common infinitive will fit with the extreme sports in exercise 3a to form verb phrases – *go* (*bungee jumping*, *surfing* etc). Have the students brainstorm other sports collocations with *do* and *play*, e.g. *do judo*, *play basketball*.

4 Pronunciation: intonation – showing interest

Aim: To practice using intonation to show interest.

a • Play the tape and get students to focus on the intonation of the questions.

Teaching tip You may need to play the tape more than once to help students focus on the intonation.

• Establish that the intonation pattern (rise-fall) is a way of showing interest and indicating that you want the other person to tell you more.
• Let students practice the intonation pattern.

b • Put students in pairs.
• Get them to write two appropriate short questions in the spaces shown.
• Get students to practice the intonation of the interview questions.
• Check the answers with the class.

Answers 1 Did you?   2 Was it?

c • Tell students to change partners.
• Have them discuss their firsts from exercise 1. Encourage them to use short questions and intonation to show interest.

3 Speaking and reading

a In pairs, look at the photograph and identify the sport. Has anyone you know ever done any extreme sports? Which? Would you like to do any of these sports? Why / why not?

b Read the text and identify the sport that is being described and the reason the person wanted to do it.

At the end of a party, when our minds weren't too clear, my friend Barry and I discovered we had both always wanted to jump out of an airplane. Before we had a chance to think about it, we'd checked the Yellow Pages, found a "drop zone," chosen a date and signed the "I accept I may die horribly" form. After a day's course the plane took off with four "first-timers" plus the jumpmaster Mick and the pilot.

When the plane reached three thousand five hundred feet we were ready to go. Mick shouted "in the door" and Barry sat in the open door with his legs hanging outside. Mick shouted "Go" and he jumped out and disappeared. Then it was my turn. I was apprehensive but not terrified. On the word "Go!" I threw myself out and spread my arms and legs and kept my eyes open as I shouted, "One thousand,

two thousand, three thousand, four thousand check canopy!" Thankfully, the main parachute was open and I could relax and admire the view.

I landed perfectly near the drop zone but suddenly fell over and discovered I was dizzy. I waited for the world to stabilize and walked back to the airport.

The first thing I did was to buy two more jump tickets!

c Read the text again and put the following list of events in the right order.

1 When he jumped his parachute opened safely.
2 He landed safely but didn't feel completely well.
3 The writer and Barry took a day's course in parachuting.
4 Barry jumped out of the plane first.
5 He decided to do another parachute jump.
6 He jumped out of the plane and looked around him.
7 The writer and Barry found details about parachuting in the Yellow Pages.

4 Pronunciation: intonation – showing interest

a Listen to these two excerpts from the interviews in exercise 2. What do you notice about the intonation of the phrases in italics?

1 **Steve:** Her name was Jane and she was really cute.   2 **Wendy:** I used to ride about 4 miles a day.

Sonia: *Was she?*   **Sonia:** *Did you?*

b Work in pairs. Write a short question in the spaces, and practice reading it out loud.

1 **A:** I found $100 in the street.   2 **A:** My first day at school was horrible.

   B: ....? Lucky you!   **B:** ....? Why?

c Change pairs and talk to another person about your firsts in exercise 1.

2 Your first date

1 Speaking and listening

a Look at the photographs above and guess what the two people are talking about. How are these people feeling? What do you think is the reason for the phone call?

b Listen to the conversation and check your ideas.

c Work in pairs. Read the conversation below and try to put it in the correct order. The first three have been done for you. Then listen again to check your answers.

Tania:	Oh, I remember. How are you?	○
Alan:	Oh wow! Is 7:30 OK? I can pick you up at your place.	○
Tania:	This is Tania speaking.	③
Alan:	See you Friday!	○
Tania:	Hmm, OK. Why not? What time?	○
Alan:	Oh, um, hi. Could I speak to Tania?	②
Tania:	On a date?	○
Alan:	Oh, hi Tania. It's Alan Turnsberry. We're in biology class together.	○
Tania:	Hello.	①
Alan:	Fine. Look. Um, I was wondering Tania, if ... um, would you like to go out with me.	○
Tania:	Fine. Thanks for calling, Alan. Bye.	○
Alan:	Yes. How about Friday? We could have coffee or go bowling. Whatever you like.	○

2 Speaking and reading

a What are the important things to think about when you go on a first date? Work in groups of three and make a list of points for her and him.

b You are going to read some advice on what to do on a first date. Read the texts on the next page quickly to compare your ideas.

Lesson 2 Your first date

Aims: To talk about dating and first dates.
To focus on the grammar of obligations and necessity using *must* and *have to*.

1 Speaking and listening

Aim: To introduce the topic of first dates.

a • Tell students to look at the photographs.
• Put them in groups to discuss the questions.
• Get feedback from the groups.

b • Tell students they are going to listen to a phone call.
• Play the tape and have students check if their ideas about the boy and the girl were correct.
• Check the answers with the class.

Answer The boy is nervous but the girl is quite calm. The boy is asking the girl out.

c • Put students in pairs.

Teaching tip Check students understand that Tania is the girl's name and Alan is the boy's name.

• Get students to put the sentences from the conversation in order.
• Play the tape again and let them check their answers.

Answers 5   10   3   12   9   2   7   4   1   6   11   8

Tapescript

Tania: Hello.
Alan: Oh, um, hi. Could I speak to Tania?
Tania: This is Tania speaking.
Alan: Oh, hi Tania. It's Alan Turnsberry. We're in biology class together.
Tania: Oh, I remember. How are you?
Alan: Fine. Look. Um, I was wondering Tania, if ... um, you ... would you like to go out with me?

Tania: On a date?
Alan: Yes. How about Friday? We could have coffee or go bowling. Whatever you like.
Tania: Hmm, OK. Why not? What time?
Alan: Oh wow! Is 7:30 OK? I can pick you up at your place.
Tania: Fine. Thanks for calling, Alan. Bye.
Alan: See you Friday!

2 Speaking and reading

Aim: To develop students' speaking and reading skills.

a • Elicit a couple of examples of important things for a girl and a boy on a first date.
• Put students in groups of three.
• Have them write down more important points for a first date.
• Get feedback and list the points on the board under the headings *Her* and *Him*.

b • Tell students to read the text quickly and compare the group's ideas on the board with the advice in the text.

c • Put students in groups of three.
    • Have them answer the questions about how dating has changed.
    • Get feedback from the groups.

Helping the learner	Get students to look back at exercises 1 and 2 and note collocations with *go*, *have*, *make* and *take*, e.g. *go bowling*, *have coffee*.

3 Grammar builder: obligation and necessity

Aim: To practice *must* and *have to*.

Language help	The main problem for students is the difference between *mustn't* (which is used for prohibition) and *don't have to* (which is used to express that there is no obligation to do something).

a • Tell students to look at the examples and answer the questions.
    • Check the answers.

Answers	1 a and c 2 b, d and e

    • Tell students to read the Language assistant box. Elicit examples which illustrate the points made in the notes.

b • Have students read the sentences, and decide if they are true or false, for them or their country.
    • Have them change the sentences they think are not true.
    • Put students in groups to compare answers.
    • Get feedback from the groups.

c • Now tell students to write a paragraph about the main obligations in their school or workplace.

Language help	Remind students of the difference between *wear* (for clothes you have on your body) and *carry* (for objects you have with you).

    • Have students compare what they have written in groups.

Helping the learner	Highlight the examples of fixed phrases in this lesson – say *please and thank you* (**not** thank you and please), *a nice touch* (**not** a good touch), *drink and drive* (**not** drive and drink).

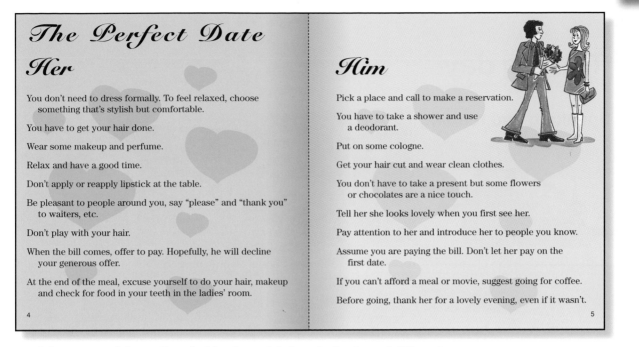

The Perfect Date

Her

You don't need to dress formally. To feel relaxed, choose something that's stylish but comfortable.

You have to get your hair done.

Wear some makeup and perfume.

Relax and have a good time.

Don't apply or reapply lipstick at the table.

Be pleasant to people around you, say "please" and "thank you" to waiters, etc.

Don't play with your hair.

When the bill comes, offer to pay. Hopefully, he will decline your generous offer.

At the end of the meal, excuse yourself to do your hair, makeup and check for food in your teeth in the ladies' room.

4

Him

Pick a place and call to make a reservation.

You have to take a shower and use a deodorant.

Put on some cologne.

Get your hair cut and wear clean clothes.

You don't have to take a present but some flowers or chocolates are a nice touch.

Tell her she looks lovely when you first see her.

Pay attention to her and introduce her to people you know.

Assume you are paying the bill. Don't let her pay on the first date.

If you can't afford a meal or movie, suggest going for coffee.

Before going, thank her for a lovely evening, even if it wasn't.

5

c Work in groups of three. How is this view of dating similar to and different from going out with people nowadays? How was dating in your parents' generation different from your generation?

3 Grammar builder: obligation and necessity

a Look at the following examples and answer these questions.

1 Which of the sentences talk about something being unnecessary?

2 Which sentences talk about obligations?

a) You don't need to dress formally.

b) You have to get your hair done.

c) You don't have to go to the meeting.

d) You must make a tax declaration every year.

e) You mustn't smoke in the building.

b Change these sentences if they are not true for you or your country.

1 I don't need to tell my parents if I'm coming home late.

2 We don't have to serve in the military.

3 You must carry an ID card at all times.

4 Boys have to help with housework.

5 You have to drink and drive.

6 I need to study every evening after class.

7 18-year-olds must ask their parents' permission if they want to marry.

c A foreign student is coming to your school or workplace for one term. Write a short paragraph explaining the main obligations and needs for people in your school or workplace.

You don't have to wear uniform. You mustn't smoke in the offices.

> ### Language assistant
>
> The opposite of *have to* is **not** *don't have to*. *Don't have to* means that you are free from obligation.
>
> *Do I **have to** wear a suit at the wedding? No, you **don't have to,** but you can if you want to.*
>
> • The opposite of *must / have to* is *mustn't*.
>
> • Imperatives can be used as orders: *Don't touch that! It's hot!*
>
> • Imperatives can also be suggestions: *Pay attention to her.*

3 The big day

1 Speaking and reading

a Look at the photographs above. Identify the occasions and talk about what is happening.

b Match the invitations below to three of the occasions in the photographs.

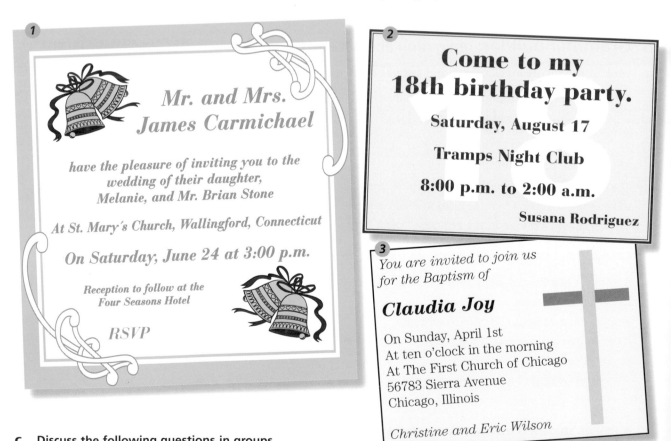

1

*Mr. and Mrs.
James Carmichael*

*have the pleasure of inviting you to the
wedding of their daughter,
Melanie, and Mr. Brian Stone*

At St. Mary's Church, Wallingford, Connecticut

On Saturday, June 24 at 3:00 p.m.

*Reception to follow at the
Four Seasons Hotel*

RSVP

2

**Come to my
18th birthday party.**

Saturday, August 17

Tramps Night Club

8:00 p.m. to 2:00 a.m.

Susana Rodriguez

3

*You are invited to join us
for the Baptism of*

Claudia Joy

On Sunday, April 1st
At ten o'clock in the morning
At The First Church of Chicago
56783 Sierra Avenue
Chicago, Illinois

Christine and Eric Wilson

c Discuss the following questions in groups.

1 Which of these occasions have you experienced?

2 What are the best and worst occasions that you remember?

Lesson 3 The big day

Aims: To practice the four skills on the topic of special occasions.
To build up vocabulary on the topic of special occasions.

1 Speaking and reading

Aim: To introduce the topic of special occasions.

a • Tell students to look at the photographs.
  • Put them in pairs and let them identify the occasions shown in the photographs.
  • Check the answers.

Answers A college graduation   B wedding   C 18th birthday party   D baptism

b • Now have students read the invitations and match them to the occasions in the photographs.
  • Check the answers.

Answers 1 B   2 C   3 D

c • Put students in groups.
  • Have them discuss the questions.
  • Get feedback from the groups, eliciting the most interesting accounts.

2 Word builder: weddings and graduations

Aim: To practice vocabulary associated with weddings and graduations.

a • Have students look at the words in the box, and write them under the correct headings.

Answers **Weddings:** ceremony, honeymoon, bride, champagne, bachelors, ring, reception, groom, engagement, marry, best man
Graduations: ceremony, examination, college, bachelors, generation, graduate, degree

b • Now have students add two more words to each list.
• Check the answers by writing the words on the board.

Possible answers **Weddings:** church, bridesmaid, marriage, wedding present, guest, wedding dress
Graduations: diploma, university, speech, education, qualifications

3 Reading and listening

Aims: To consolidate wedding vocabulary.
To practice listening to a conversation to identify specific information.

a • Have students look at the advertisement and elicit the answer to the question.

Answers The company organizes weddings and provides all you need for the service / reception.

b • Tell students that they are going to hear people talking about arrangements for a wedding.
• Play the tape and have students check the things on the advertisement that are mentioned.

Answers churches, limousines, invitations, flowers, photographers, videographers, ceremony, catering, gifts

Tapescript

Mother: Right. Now you two love birds. Let's check the wedding arrangements.
Jennie: OK Mom, but remember we want a quiet wedding. Nothing fancy. Right Charlie?
Charlie: Oh yes.
Mother: Yes, well I've booked the church and the priest for 3:00 p.m. on Saturday October 17. Oh and there's a rehearsal on Friday at 5:00 p.m.
Jennie: Father Tom?

Mother: Yes. We'll go to the church at 2:30 by limousine. We want to be on time.
Jennifer: A limousine!
Mother: Of course. I've got the guest list and the invitations.
Charlie: How many people are you inviting?
Mother: Oh, um, 130.
Jennie: Mom, that's far too many!
Mother: Of course it isn't. It's only relatives and friends. Oh, I've arranged flowers for the church and the photographer.

Charlie: OK. We want some photographs.
Mother: And a video of the ceremony, and the reception's going to be at the Rochester Hotel.
Jennifer: A video. I don't want a video.
Mother: But you can show it to your children ... when you have some!
Jennifer: Is that it?
Mother: No, there's the list of wedding presents. Look.
Charlie: Now, this is important.

4 Grammar builder: prepositions of time

Aim: To practice prepositions of time.

Helping the learner This exercise highlights common collocations with prepositions of time.

a • Tell students to look at the examples. Elicit other examples and write them on the board.
b • Students look at the dates, days and times in the box and write them under the appropriate column.

Answers **In:** January, the afternoon, the summer
On: Saturday morning, my birthday, the weekend, Monday, Independence day, August 26
At: 3 o'clock, Christmas, 5:50pm, lunchtime, midnight, Easter

• Get students to work out the rules of when each proposition is used:
in – months, parts of the day, seasons
on – particular days, dates, particular days + parts of the day, the weekend
at – times or periods of time

c • Have students complete sentences 1–5 with the correct prepositions.

Answers 1 at   2 on   3 on   4 at   5 in / in

d • Put students in pairs and have them ask and answer all the questions in 4c.
• Get feedback from the pairs.

2 **Word builder:** weddings and graduations

a Which of the following words do you associate with weddings and which with graduations? Write them under the appropriate headings.

Weddings   **Graduations**

| ceremony | examination | honeymoon | bride | champagne | college | bachelors | ring |
| reception | generation | groom | engagement | marry | graduate | best man | degree |

b Can you think of any other words for these occasions? Write two more under each heading.

3 **Reading and listening**

a Look at the advertisement. What kind of a company is this and what do they organize for you?

b Listen to the conversation about wedding arrangements, and check (✔) the items on the advertisement that you hear mentioned.

WEDDINGS UNLIMITED
We help create beautiful wedding memories!
Let us make your special day more special.
50 years of experience count!

*Audiovisual equipment   Balloons   Catering   Ceremony
Musicians   Churches   Disc jockeys   Flowers   Gifts
Hair salons   Invitations   Live bands   Limousines
Photographers   Transportation   Videographers*

Contact us on tollfree 1-0800-387-4936 or e-mail us at
weddings@weddingsunlimited.com

4 **Grammar builder:** prepositions of time

a Look at the following examples. Notice the prepositions.

On Saturday, October 17.

We'll go to the church at 2:30.

They're getting married in October.

b Put the following list of dates, days and times in the appropriate column.
When do we use *in, on* and *at*?

in	on	at

January	3 o'clock	Saturday morning	the afternoon	my birthday	Christmas
the weekend	the summer	Monday	5:50 p.m.	lunchtime	Independence Day
midnight	August 26	Easter			

c Complete the following questions with the correct preposition.

1 Where do you usually go .... Easter?

2 What do you usually do .... weekends?

3 What did you do .... your last birthday?

4 What were you doing .... 7:30 yesterday evening?

5 Do you have your longest vacation .... the summer
   or .... the winter?

d In pairs, ask and answer the questions in exercise 4c above.

LANGUAGE for life:

job *hunting*

① Job hunting

Look at the job advertisement below and answer these questions.

1 Which of the qualifications or skills do you have?
2 Would this job interest you? Why? Why not?
3 What information about the company would you want before going to an interview for this job?
4 Where is the company located?
5 What would I take to the interview?
6 What should I wear?

Norton & Martin, one of the leaders in marketing, are recruiting a Personnel Manager.

Suitable candidates will have

● A college degree
● Advanced training in the area of personnel management
● Excellent PR skills
● 5 years' experience in personnel
● Preferably experience in the marketing area
● Computer skills

Competitive salary and benefits package.
Candidates should send a letter of application with details of current salary and a current résumé to Ms. T. Lopez at tlopez@norton&martin.com not later than Wednesday, October 19.

Listen to an expert talking about preparation for an interview. Complete the notes for each heading.

Company key information –

Common questions – Practice answers to common questions.

Rehearse interview with a friend –

Prepare interview material –

Clothes –

② Résumés

OK, you've found a job you like. Now all you need to do is to send in your résumé. Let's look at a sample. Read the résumé and fill in the spaces with information from the box under it.

Lesson 4 Language for life: job hunting

Aim: To raise awareness of the importance and use of English for getting a job.

1 Job hunting

Aims: To develop students' reading and speaking skills.
To practice listening and note-taking.

- Focus attention on the job advertisement.

Language help	Check students understand that PR stands for *public relations*.
	• Check students understand what type of job the advertisement is for. • Tell them to answer the questions about themselves. • Let them compare answers in pairs. • Get feedback by seeing whether there is anyone in the class who is ideal for the job.
Helping the learner	The job advertisement contains examples of noun-noun and adjective-noun collocations, e.g. *computer skills*, *suitable candidates*. Have students underline the collocations and record them in their vocabulary notebook.
Optional activity	Real job advertisements Have students bring in job advertisements from English newspapers or the Internet. Have them add other common collocations to their vocabulary notebook.
	• Focus attention on the notes and the headings. • Tell students they are going to hear an expert talking about preparing for a job interview. • Play the tape and get students to complete the notes for each heading. • Check the answers.
Answers	Company key information: products, customers, talk to people who work there, look at the website Rehearse interview with a friend: about 15 minutes Prepare interview material: résumé, up-to-date references Clothes: professional and comfortable

Tapescript

Fiona: Tim Benyon is here to give us some advice about preparing for a job interview. Tim, do people prepare for interviews?

Tim: No, Fiona. Surprisingly they don't usually do any homework before interviews and this can make a difference.

Fiona: OK. What do you advise?

Tim: Well, first it's a good idea to research the company and the position. The more you know, the better you will appear at the interview.

Fiona: What kind of things do you have in mind?

Tim: Key information about the company, its products and customers. If possible, talk to people who work at the company. The company may have a website you can check.

Fiona: That all makes sense. Anything else?

Tim: Yes. Practice your answers to common questions. Also prepare a list of questions to ask the employer. Most interviews follow a pattern: first you answer questions about your experience and qualifications, then you ask questions about the job.

Fiona: Is it worth rehearsing the interview with someone?

Tim: Definitely. Fifteen minutes should be about right for you to give the most relevant information.

Fiona: What about on the day?

Tim: Right. Prepare your interview materials. Take copies of your résumé and a list of references. Make sure they're up to date. And finally, dress professionally and comfortably. People do judge you to some extent by what you wear.

2 Résumés

Aim: To practice writing a résumé in English.

- Focus attention on the résumé.
- Check comprehension of the categories in the résumé.
- Have students complete the résumé with the information in the box below it.
- Check the answers.

Answers	Tel: 612-876-546; Degree in Management; Administrative Manager; Iceland Frozen Foods 1996–1998; Word 1999; French (reading and writing); **Activities / interests:**; cooking

- Have students write their own résumé, following the model.
- Have them exchange résumés and check for clarity of content and accuracy of English.
- Get feedback by asking students what they found out about their partner.

3 Making a good impression

Aim: To talk and read about job interviews.

- Put students in groups.
- Tell them to write down ideas for making a good impression at a job interview.
- Have them read the article and compare it with the ideas in their list.
- Get feedback, eliciting the ideas that students think are most important.
- Have students stay in their groups and discuss the cartoon. Ask them to write a list of things the man in the interview should or shouldn't do in the next interview he goes to.
- Get feedback from different groups.

Possible answers	He should wear a suit.
	He shouldn't wear a baseball cap.
	He shouldn't smoke in the interview.
	He shouldn't bring his stereo to the interview.
	He shouldn't put his feet on the desk.
	He should be more serious.

SAM RODRIGUEZ

1 Forest Road, Minneapolis MN 65743 .... e-mail: srodriguez@aol.com

Objective: A position in which my abilities, education and experience will be utilized to benefit the institution

Education: .... Harvard Business School 1998

B.A. in Economics. University of Minnesota 1996

Experience: Head of Operations, Pizza Express, 1998 – present; ....

Other skills: Word processing – ...., Excel, PowerPoint

Languages: Spanish (fluent), ...

.... Reading, ..., volunteer work for Greenpeace, tennis

References: Available on request

Write your own résumé and ask another student to check it for you.

French (reading and writing)   Tel: 612-876-546   Word 1999

Administrative Manager, Iceland Frozen Foods 1996–1998

Degree in Management   **Activities / interests:** cooking

③ Making a good impression

OK, you got the interview and the big day has come. How are you going to make a good impression? Share your ideas in groups and make notes on at least six ideas. Then look at our ideas and see if you are really ready for this interview.

They say that most interviewers make that all-important decision on who to employ in the first four minutes of an interview. So making a good impression is crucial. Follow these basic steps to guarantee a successful result on the day:

- Be on time. Being on time (or early) is usually interpreted as evidence of your commitment, dependability and professionalism.
- Be positive and try to make others feel comfortable. Show openness by greeting with a firm handshake and smile. Don't make negative comments about your current employer.
- Relax. Think of the interview as a conversation, not an interrogation.
- Be prepared. Take time to think about likely questions and answers. Think of key questions to ask.
- Show self-confidence. Make eye contact with the interviewer and answer his or her questions in a clear voice.
- Remember to listen. Communication is a two-way street. If you talk too much, you may miss important points made by the interviewer.
- Reflect before answering a difficult question. If you are unsure about how to answer a question, you might reply with another question.
- When it is your turn, ask the questions you prepared in advance.

- Show you want the job. Talk about things you could do that would benefit the organization. Don't ask questions that make the interviewer doubtful about you. Too many questions about vacations may make the interviewer think you are more interested in time off than helping the company.
- Dress conservatively but attractively. Wear a suit, clean shoes, a tie (for men), simple jewelry and moderate makeup (for women).
- Avoid negative body language: frequently touching your mouth, swinging your foot or leg, chewing your lip, folding your arms and avoiding eye contact.

4 Learning check

1 Progress check

a Read the text below and look carefully at each line. Some of the lines are correct and others have a word which should not be there. Check (✔) the correct lines or write the words which should not be there.

The modern fashion is a mixture of old and new ....*The*........

but it still influences what we decide to wear. ....✔........

1 Many of young people wear bell bottoms and tops ....*of*........

2 which were fashionable in the late 1960s. ....✔........

3 Today, both long skirts and tank tops were worn in the 1970s. ....*Today,*........

4 By choosing clothes we all choose the image we want to ....✔........

5 project. But think before you throwing away any of your clothes. ....*you*........

6 They'll be fashionable again sooner or later. ....✔........

b Complete the sentences using the correct preposition in each case.

7 They traveled to the coast ....*by*.......... car.

8 Alex's birthday is ....*on*.......... October 13.

9 The party is ....*at*.......... Diana's house.

10 I have a week's vacation ....*in*.......... July.

11 The movie starts ....*at*.......... 8:30 p.m.

c Read the text. Complete the text with the correct words from the list below.

Before (**12**) ....*doing*........ exercise always warm up first. (**13**) ....*To*.......... warm-up you should stretch (**14**) ....*both*......... your arms and legs and breathe deeply. Take at least 15 to 20 minutes before any energetic exercise. And remember, when you finish, take a few minutes to stretch your muscles. (**15**) ....*All*.......... of us should do regular exercise, but don't take any risks.

12 a)	do	**b)**	doing	**c)**	to do	**d)**	did
13 a)	To	**b)**	After	**c)**	On	**d)**	At
14 a)	many	**b)**	some	**c)**	both	**d)**	any
15 a)	Every	**b)**	No one	**c)**	Any	**d)**	All

Learning check 4

1 Progress check

Aims: To provide an opportunity to assess students' progress and help them according to the results.
To provide an opportunity for learners to test themselves.
To allow students to evaluate their own progress and act on areas they need to improve.

Suggestions for using the *Progress check* sections
This section can be done in a variety of ways depending on how much time you have and whether you want students to do it as part of an individual assessment or as general revision.
a As a test – students work individually on the *Progress check* sections and you then check their work and record their score out of 15.
b Students work on the *Progress check* sections alone and then check their answers in pairs.
c Students work on the *Progress check* sections in pairs or groups and you later check the answers with the whole class.
d Students do the *Progress check* sections for homework.
In all cases, conduct a feedback session with the whole class to check any queries students may have and see how they did.

Explanation of answers

a
1 Quantifier *many* is not followed by *of*.
2 The line is correct.
3 *Today* is not possible as a time marker for a past tense context.
4 The line is correct.
5 *You* is not necessary between preposition and *-ing* form.
6 The line is correct.

b
7 *by* – for modes of transportation
8 *on* – with dates
9 *at* – showing the position of something
10 *in* – with months
11 *at* – with times

c
12 The *-ing* form is needed after the preposition before.
13 *To* is needed to form the infinitive of purpose.
14 *Both* is needed to express the one as well as the other.
15 *All* is needed to express every one of a group. *Every* is only used with singular nouns and is not followed by *of*.

2 Proficiency check

Aims: To expose students to TOEFL and UCLES-style exam formats, which will be useful for those students interested in taking such formal proficiency exams.
To develop students' exam-taking strategies.
To allow teachers and students the opportunity to evaluate students' proficiency in English.
To test students' listening and reading skills under pseudo exam conditions.

Suggestions for taking the test

Taking 'language' tests is not only about 'knowing' the language. It also involves knowing how to deal with exams: how to work under pressure; how to recognize the operations of the exam; and how to apply strategies to get the best results in an exam. These *Proficiency checks* give students the opportunity to work on all of these areas.

Students could do this as a formal proficiency test where they work individually, in silence. The tests are then collected and checked by the teacher. Alternatively, students could do the test individually and then check their answers in pairs or groups.

In either case, it is recommended that students as a class have the opportunity to discuss their answers and how they arrived at them with the teacher. Explanations of the correct answers are given to facilitate the teacher's role here. In addition, the teacher can highlight the strategy that is given in every *Proficiency check*. This is very helpful in giving students the chance to work on their exam-taking strategies as well as their accuracy with the language.

Answers **a**

    1 C   2 D   3 B   4 B

Tapescript

1
Kate: Did you get the tickets?
Dave: Of course I did.
Kate: Great! What are we going to see, *Cats*?
Dave: No, there were no tickets for *Cats*.
Kate: Oh. And *Miss Saigon*?
Dave: No that's finished.
Kate: What then?
Dave: OK. *Starlight Express* was possible but I decided to get tickets for *The Phantom of the Opera*.
Kate: Wonderful!

2
Robert: Did you get Lucy's birthday present?
Steve: Oh no! I completely forgot.
Robert: Well, it's tomorrow so you've got time.
Steve: What can I get her? She's your sister. A sweater?
Robert: No. She might not like it.
Steve: How about a novel?
Robert: Hmm, that's not very exciting and she's got loads of books.
Steve: All right. Perfume, a CD?

Robert: She'd love perfume. An expensive one of course!
Steve: Oh right.

3
Adrian: What does Hazel look like?
Maggie: Hazel. Well she's about my age, 20, and she has short curly hair.
Adrian: She's blonde, right?
Maggie: No, she has dark hair. Brown, I think.
Adrian: And she wears glasses!
Maggie: No, she doesn't. She sometimes wears a baseball cap.
Adrian: Oh yeah. Now I know who she is.

4
Man: We still need some stuff for the picnic.
Woman: Do we? What did you forget? Bread?
Man: No, we have a loaf of bread but no cheese.
Woman: Cheese. All right. And fruit.
Man: Well I bought some grapes but nothing else.
Woman: Hmm. Let's get some apples.
Man: And some tomatoes would be nice for the cheese.
Woman: OK. Let's go to the supermarket right now.

Exam-taking tip   Say WHY your answers are right.
If students can become aware of WHY their answers are right and how they arrived at the answers they have, they will be more confident and effective in their test taking. Encourage them to think about and discuss what are the right answers and WHY. They can do this in pairs, small groups or as a whole class.

b

    a 3   b 4   c 1   d 2

2 Proficiency check

a Read questions 1–4, then listen to the conversation. Check (✔) the picture which best answers the question about each conversation.

1 Which musical are they going to see?
2 Which gift is the man going to buy?

3 What does Hazel look like?
4 What do they need to buy?

A ○   B ○   C ○   D ○

A ○   B ○   C ○   D ○

A ○   B ○   C ○   D ○

A ○   B ○   C ○   D ○

b Read sentences 1–4 and the text. Decide which sentence goes in each space (a–d).

1 Treatments relieve symptoms but do not correct the basic problems.
2 They protect us and repair the damage caused by disease.

3 This led to sanitation systems that protected people from the devastating infections that had habitually plagued mankind.
4 Many infectious diseases could finally be prevented or cured.

A revolution is sweeping through medicine. The first revolution occurred soon after British surgeon John Snow discovered, in 1854, that cholera is spread by contaminated water. **(a)** ....

The second revolution, surgery with anesthesia, came about at the same time, allowing doctors to fix ailments such as appendicitis and bowel obstruction. The third revolution was the introduction of vaccines and antibiotics. **(b)** ....

But, aside from attacking infectious diseases and some surgical problems, physicians do not actually "cure" anything. Medicines just help the body heal itself. **(c)** ....

Human genetic engineering – the fourth revolution – will profoundly change the practice of medicine over the next 30 to 40 years. Human genetic engineering is based on the premise that our genes are the defense and healing system of our body. **(d)** ....
Genes which function abnormally can contribute to cancer, heart disease, Alzheimer's and mental illness. Genes can be used to treat disease either by injecting more genes into patients or by modifying the function of the genes in the body.

Unit 9 Men and women

1 Evaluating tradition

1 Speaking

a In groups, discuss the following question.

Which of the jobs below do you think of as masculine (M)? Which as feminine (F)?

company director ◯   nurse ◯   librarian ◯   secretary (personal assistant) ◯

veterinarian ◯   pilot ◯   basketball player ◯   elementary school teacher ◯

b Continue in groups, and discuss the following questions.

1 Which jobs are more highly paid?

2 Is the percentage of men and women in traditional "male" or "female" jobs changing? Can you give some examples?

2 Listening, writing and speaking

a Listen to interviews with two couples. Which couple (A or B) is more traditional and which is more non-traditional?

b Listen again. Then write reasons why you consider each couple traditional or non-traditional.

1 Couple ……… is more traditional because …

2 Couple ……… is non-traditional because …

c Compare your notes with a partner.

3 Reading and speaking

a Read the information in the box. Do any of the facts surprise you? Why?

Some facts on equality of the sexes in the United States, in the past and now ...

1970: Fifty-two percent of the population were female, but 2 percent of management jobs were held by women.

1975: Married women were not allowed to have credit cards in their own names. Women earned an average of 40% less than men. Only 2 percent of business travelers were women.

1987–1999: The number of businesses owned by women increased by 103%.

2000: Almost 50% of business travelers were women, but women earned an average of 20% less than men. The majority of women in corporations were in low-level jobs.

Unit 9 Men and women

Helping the learner: exposure to a variety of text types

Exposure to a range of text types can sensitize students to texts in general, and help them to become more efficient readers. This will increase their ability to: recognize key features of a text type, e.g. stories; understand the style of language used in a text; recognize aspects of layout and the writer's purpose.

Further reading:
Nuttal, C., (2000) *Teaching reading in a foreign language,* Macmillan Heinemann ELT, Ch.10

Lesson 1 Evaluating tradition

Aim: To practice the four skills via the topic of traditional roles for men and women.

Glossary *Breadwinner* refers to the person who earns the money in a household.

1 Speaking

Aim: To introduce the topic of gender and jobs.

a • Put students in groups and have them discuss the question.

b • Now have students discuss the other questions before group feedback.

2 Listening, writing and speaking

Aim: To practice listening for the main idea and specific information.

a • Elicit a few examples of what traditional and non-traditional could mean.
• Have the students listen to the interview and decide which couple is more traditional.

Answer Couple A - non-traditional, couple B - traditional

b • Play the tape again and have the students note down reasons why they think each couple is traditional or non-traditional.

c • Put students in pairs and have them compare their answers.

Tapescript

Couple A

Interviewer: Frank and Sharon, you've been married for ten years. Do you both work?

Man: Well, yes, but Sharon is the real breadwinner. She's the one with the full time job.

Woman: Yes, I'm the sales director for a telecommunications company, so I work long hours. I also travel a lot.

Interviewer: And what do you do, Frank?

Man: I'm an author. I write children's books. It's great because I can work from home.

Interviewer: Is writing a full time job?

Man: Well, it depends. Sometimes I have a lot of work and I work long hours, but usually I work about four hours a day.

Interviewer: Do you have children?

Woman: Yes, a son. It's great that Frank works at home because he can work in the morning and then spend time in the afternoon with our son. Frank helps Terry with his homework and Terry helps Frank with the housework and the cooking! They're great cooks; there's always something delicious to eat in our house!

Couple B

Interviewer: You've been married for five years now, right?

Woman: That's right.

Interviewer: What do you do, Chris?

Man: I'm an engineer. I work for a software company.

Interviewer: About how many hours do you work?

Man: Uh, usually about 50 hours a week, from 8:00 to 6:00 every day.

Interviewer: Why so many hours?

Man: The company's growing, so there's a lot of work. And I want to grow with the company, so I'm working really hard right now.

Interviewer: And what do you do, Molly?

Woman: I don't have a full time job. I'm a librarian and I work part time, mornings, at the public library.

Interviewer: Would you ever consider working full time?

Woman: Well, maybe, but not right now. We have two children, and taking care of them and the house is a lot of work.

Interviewer: Chris, do you help with the housework?

Man: Well, not really. I work long hours during the week. On weekends I want to rest and be with the kids. And since Molly doesn't have a full time job, she has time to do it.

Woman: Anyway, he's a terrible cook and house cleaner!

• See page T79 for notes on all of exercise 3.

3 Reading and speaking

Aim: To read and talk about equality of the sexes.

a • Put students in pairs.
  • Have them read the information in the box and discuss anything that surprises them.
  • Get feedback on the most surprising facts.

b • Put students in groups.
  • Have them read and discuss the questions.
  • Then have students read the article and compare the information with their answers.
  • Check the answers.

Answers 1 Around the beginning of the 20th century in the United States, Europe and Australia. It began because a lot of women joined the work force.
2 Education, employment and legal issues.
3 It was said that feminists didn't want to be women and they wanted to destroy the family.

  • Elicit any interesting differences between what students thought before they read the article and the answers.

Helping the learner Get students to look back at the two texts in exercise 3 and compare the format and how they read them, e.g. *text 3a – list format which students scan to pick out the key facts, and text 3b – connected article, which students read more slowly to process the information.*

4 Writing and speaking

Aims: To practice preparing arguments for or against traditional roles.
  To practice debating.

a • Put students in pairs.
  • Have them write some arguments, either for or against traditional roles for men and women.

Teaching tip Make sure there are equal numbers of pairs with arguments for and against.

  • Get students to write as many arguments as they can.

b • Get students to imagine the opposing arguments and prepare answers to counter them.

c • Join each pair with another pair who prepared the opposite argument.
  • Focus attention on the examples in the Student's Book.
  • Have the pairs debate in front of the class.
  • Get students to vote for the pair who have the most convincing arguments.

Optional activity Class debate
Conduct the debate as a whole-class activity and let students decide which side has the better arguments.

b   **In groups, discuss the answers to the following questions. Then read the article below and compare the information with your answers.**

1   When and where did the women's movement begin? Why did it begin?

2   In what areas were women asking for equal rights?

3   What were some of the arguments against the equal rights movement?

THE LONG ROAD TO EQUAL RIGHTS

"A woman without a man is like a fish without a bicycle."
Gloria Steinem

When most people think of feminism, they think of the women's movement in the 1960s. But that was what women's rights groups refer to as "the second wave." The women's movement actually started around the beginning of the 20th century in the United States, Europe and Australia, when women began to enter the work force in great numbers. They felt that if women were going to work, they should have certain legal rights.

The second wave of the movement began in the mid-1960s when women began to demand equal rights in education, employment and legal issues. Women wrote books and articles on the subject, held conferences and organized protest marches with thousands of people to gain support for women's rights.

Opponents of the women's rights movement said that feminists didn't want to be women, that they wanted to destroy the family, as well as many other arguments. But in fact, the central idea of the feminist movement was very simple: Men and women are equally capable and therefore should be equal legally.

Since the 1960s, laws and attitudes in many countries have changed dramatically. But have they changed enough? In the United States, for example, the Equal Rights Amendment (a proposed addition to the U.S. Constitution) was first introduced in 1923. It says that equality of rights should not be denied on the basis of sex. This amendment still has not been approved and added to the Constitution.

4   Writing and speaking

a   **In pairs, write as many arguments as you can, either for or against traditional roles for men and women (choose one).**

b   **Now try to imagine the arguments of the opposing point of view. How will you answer them?**

c   **Have a debate with a pair arguing the opposing point of view. If possible, have your debate in front of the class. The class will judge the winners!**

A: *I believe women shouldn't work because if they work, they don't have time to take care of the house or cook.*

B: *But if both work, they won't have to worry about money. They can share the housework and cooking so that one person doesn't have to do it all.*

2 Coincidence or destiny?

1 Reading and speaking

a Read the following story and underline all the coincidences you find. How many are there?

Michelle was flying from Houston to London, and during the flight, she began talking to John, the man in the seat next to her. She found out that he was president of a famous blue jeans company based in Texas; in fact, she was wearing a pair of jeans from his company! But that wasn't the most surprising thing. He had lived in San Francisco when he was in high school, and it turned out that he knew Michelle's best friend, who also grew up in San Francisco! They continued talking, and by the end of the flight, they felt that they had known each other for much longer than 8 hours.

But back in Houston, Michelle almost forgot about the attractive man she had met on the plane. One evening, she was walking her dog when a much larger dog came running toward them, growling. The owner was running after it, shouting. He managed to catch the dog just as it was going to attack Michelle's dog. Michelle was furious. "Why don't you keep your dog on a leash?" she yelled. Then suddenly, she looked at him and stopped yelling. "John?" "Michelle?" they said at the same time. Michelle said, "Do you live around here? I live on the next street." "I don't believe it," he said. "In a city of two million people, you live three blocks from me!" And in the end, as had to happen, Michelle and John began going out together – all because of seats on an airplane and a couple of dogs!

b In pairs, give the story a title which will make people want to read it.

c In groups, talk about coincidences that have happened in your lives.

2 Listening, reading and writing

a Listen to the conversation about a coincidence. What was the coincidence? Do the speakers believe in destiny? Do you believe in destiny?

b Read the e-mail that Patrick wrote to a friend, telling her about Steve's girlfriend. Rewrite it, correcting the factual errors. How many errors did you find?

Hi, Celia. How are you?
You remember Steve Berry, right? Well, he's convinced that he's been touched by destiny. He decided to take a painting class at the university, and he met his new girlfriend there. After the class, he was talking to the professor and she was standing next to him. They started talking about their families, and guess what. Her mother used to go out with his father when they were in school! Steve thinks that if he hadn't talked to the professor that day, he wouldn't have met her because it's a big class. Anyway – destiny or just coincidence – it's good news because Steve is IN LOVE for real. OK, no more gossip, so I'd better go do some work.
Write soon.
Love, Patrick

Lesson 2 Coincidence or destiny?

Aims: To practice the four skills on the topic of coincidence and destiny.
To practice the third conditional.

1 Reading and speaking

Aim: To practice reading a story for specific information.

Teaching tip Check students understand the lesson title *Coincidence or destiny?*. Elicit examples of coincidences from the class.

a • Have students read the text and underline the coincidences.
• Check the answers.

Answers Michelle was wearing jeans made by John's company; he knew Michelle's best friend; they were both walking their dog in the same place at the same time; they lived very near each other.

b • Put students in pairs.
• Have them invent a title for the story, which will make people want to read it.
• Elicit ideas and let the group decide which title is the best.

Helping the learner Get students to list the key features of the story text type in exercise 1a, e.g. *use of characters, changes of setting, narrative tenses, descriptive language, dialog.*

c • Put students in groups to discuss coincidences which have happened to them.
• Get feedback about the most interesting ones.

2 Listening, reading and writing

Aims: To practice listening to a conversation for specific information.
To practice correcting information in a written account.

a • Tell students they are going to hear two men talking about a coincidence.
• Play the tape once and check students understood what the coincidence was.

Answer Steve met a woman whose father used to go out with his mother.

• Play the tape again and have students listen for two speakers' attitudes toward destiny.

Answer Steve believes in destiny, Patrick doesn't.

• Elicit students' attitude to destiny and who they agree with – Steve or Patrick.

b • Focus attention on the e-mail. Explain that it contains some factual errors.
• Play the tape and have students correct the errors in the e-mail according to what they hear.
• Check the answers.

Answers There are four errors: Steve was taking a photography class. The girl was sitting next to him. Her father went out with his mother when they were in high school. If he hadn't taken that class, he wouldn't have met her.

Tapescript

Steve: The most amazing thing happened!
Patrick: What?
Steve: I've met a fantastic girl!
Patrick: So what's new, Steve? You meet a fantastic girl about once a month.
Steve: No, listen. This is different. You know I decided to take a photography class at the university? Well, I was sitting next to this girl in class the first day. We started talking and guess what?
Patrick: What?
Steve: Well, we were talking about ourselves and our families, etc. I thought her last name sounded familiar, and it turns out that her father used to go out with my mother when they were in high

school! I know the name because my mom has talked about this guy she really liked in high school. We kept talking and we found we have lots of things in common.
Patrick: Well, that is a coincidence – meeting someone whose father used to date your mother!
Steve: Patrick, it wasn't just a coincidence; it was destiny! I'm sure of it! We're going out together and Jessica's just great. She's the one, Pat.
Patrick: Oh come on, Steve. Coincidences happen all the time. They aren't destiny.
Steve: This was destiny. Definitely. Just think. If I hadn't decided to take exactly that class, I wouldn't have met her.
Patrick: OK, Steve.

3 Grammar builder: third conditional

Aim: To practice the third conditional.

a • Focus attention on the photographs and sentences that go with them.
  • Have students work in pairs and answer the questions about the sentences.
  • Check the answers.

Answers	1a no	1b yes	2a yes	2b no

b • Write the example sentences on the board.
  • Elicit how the tenses change from a real to an unreal situation – simple past in the real situation; past perfect in the *if* clause and *would / wouldn't* + perfect infinitive in the result clause in the unreal situation.

Teaching tip It may help to translate the meaning of the third conditional sentence into the students' native language.

c • Get students to change the real situations to unreal ones.
  • Let them check in pairs.
  • Check the answers with the class.

Answers
2 If Mark had told me about the party, I would have gone.
3 If I had been good in science I would have studied medicine.
4 If we hadn't arrived late at the conference, we would have heard the opening talk.

Teaching tip Point out that the if clause and result clauses can be reversed, e.g. *I would have gone to the party if Mark had told me about it.*

4 Pronunciation: sentence stress – conditionals

Aim: To practice sentence stress in conditional sentences.

a • Play the tape and have students underline the stressed words.
  • Write the sentences on the board to check the answers.

Tapescript / Answers
1 We **wouldn't** have **come** if you **hadn't called** us.
2 **If** I had **stayed** in **Florida**, I would have **seen** the **hurricane**.
3 **If** you **hadn't** bought that **car**, you'd **have** some **money**.
4 **Karen** would have **come** to the **movie** if she **hadn't** had to **work** late.

  • Elicit which parts of the conditional structure are stressed in an affirmative clause (the infinitive or past participle) and in a negative clause (*hadn't* or *wouldn't*).

b • Play the tape again and get students to practice the sentences, using the appropriate stress.
  • Ask some students to read the sentences aloud.

5 Speaking

Aim: To practice using third conditionals.

  • Focus attention on the examples and give a few more examples of your own.
  • Give students time to think of events that have influenced their lives.
  • Put students in groups.
  • Have them discuss events in their lives, using third conditionals.
  • Get feedback from the groups.

3 Grammar builder:
third conditional

a **Look at the two statements below and answer the questions.**

1 If Jeff had gotten up early, he wouldn't have missed the plane.
   a) Did Jeff get up early?
   b) Did he miss the plane?

2 If Mary hadn't taken a taxi, she would have been late to the meeting.
   a) Did Mary take a taxi?
   b) Was she late to the meeting?

b **We use the third conditional to imagine unreal situations in the past. Look at this example. How does the grammatical form change from a real to an unreal situation?**

*Jeff **didn't get up** early. He **missed** the plane.*

*If he **had gotten up** early, he **wouldn't have missed** it.*

c **Now change these real situations into unreal ones.**

1 Brandon grew up in Hawaii, so he learned to surf very well.

   If he hadn't grown up in Hawaii, he wouldn't have learned to surf.

2 Mark didn't tell me about the party, so I didn't go.

3 I wasn't good in science, so I didn't study medicine.

4 We arrived late at the conference, so we didn't hear the opening talk.

4 Pronunciation: sentence stress – conditionals

a **Listen to the following sentences and mark the stressed words in each clause. Which parts of the conditional structure are stressed in an affirmative clause? Which in a negative clause?**

*I would have **gone** to the **beach** if I **hadn't** had to **work**.*

1 We wouldn't have come if you hadn't called us.

2 If I had stayed in Florida, I would have seen the hurricane.

3 If you hadn't bought that car, you'd have some money.

4 Karen would have come to the movie if she hadn't had to work late.

b **Listen again and practice saying the sentences with correct intonation.**

5 Speaking

In groups, talk about events which have influenced your lives. How would your lives be different if the events had been different?

If I hadn't gone to Miami last year, I wouldn't have met my girlfriend. I met her at a party there.

If I had gotten married after high school, when my boyfriend wanted to, I wouldn't have gone to college. I'm glad I didn't get married!

3 Gifts of love

1 Speaking, listening and reading

a Read the song and discuss the questions.

1 Look quickly at the song below. What holiday is it associated with?

2 Do you celebrate this holiday? How?

3 Look at the song again. What is the topic?

b Listen, and read the song.

On the first day of Christmas, my true love sent to me
A partridge in a pear tree.
On the second day of Christmas, my true love sent to me
two turtle doves and a partridge in a pear tree.

Third day – three French hens
Fourth day – four calling birds
Fifth day – five golden rings
Sixth day – six geese a-laying
Seventh day – seven swans a-swimming
Eighth day – eight maids a-milking
Ninth day – nine lords a-leaping
Tenth day – ten ladies dancing
Eleventh day – eleven pipers piping
Twelfth day – twelve drummers drumming

c Now imagine that a modern-day boyfriend decided to give these gifts to his girlfriend. Read her e-mails to him, shown below and opposite, and answer these questions.

1 How did Sarah feel on the first day?

2 Did she like the gifts on the second day?

3 By the fourth day, how did Sarah feel about Robert's gifts?

4 Why did she feel differently on the fifth day?

5 By the seventh day, how many birds had Robert sent in total? Figure it out!

6 By the ninth day, what types of gifts had Robert sent?

7 What was the subject of Sarah's e-mail on the eleventh day?

8 Who was the last letter from? Why?

DAY 1
Darling Robert,
Thank you for the beautiful
partridge in a pear tree.
Your love,
Sarah

DAY 2
Robert, the turtle doves
are lovely – and so is
the second partridge in
a pear tree. Kisses,
Sarah

DAY 4
Dear Robert, I don't know
what to say. The calling
birds and the French hens
are lovely, but please
don't send any more
birds! Love, Sarah

Lesson 3 Gifts of love

Aims: To develop students' reading and speaking skills.
To practice talking about regrets about the past using *wish*.

1 Speaking, listening and reading

Aim: To introduce the topic of gifts from boyfriend to girlfriend.

Glossary A *partridge* is a type of wild bird hunted for its meat.
A *turtle dove* is a type of light-brown dove. It is known for being affectionate with its mate and young.

Cultural note This is a traditional Christmas song, well-known in all English-speaking countries. Though a lot of Christmas songs are religious, some refer directly to the fun and joy of the Christmas season. This song is one of those, celebrating in a humorous way the custom of giving gifts at Christmas.

a • Put students in groups.
  • Tell students to read the song quickly and answer the questions.
  • Check the answers.

Answers 1 Christmas   2 Students' own answers   3 Giving gifts

Language help Explain to students that *a* is used before some of the *-ing* forms, e.g. *six geese a laying*, to help with the rhythm of the line.

b • Check comprehension of the vocabulary in the song, referring to the pictures where relevant.
  • Now have students listen to and read the song.

Helping the learner Get students to focus on the style used in the song and elicit examples of old-fashioned English, e.g. *true love, calling birds, maid*, etc. Also highlight that some of the lines in the songs rhyme, and link this to examples of modern songs.

c • Elicit a few reactions to the gifts in the song.
  • Focus attention on the e-mails, and explain they show a modern-day reaction to the gifts.
  • Let students read the e-mails and answer questions 1–8.
  • Have them check their answers in pairs.

Answers 1 very pleased
2 yes
3 She liked the birds but she didn't want to receive any more.
4 Because Robert sent gold rings.
5 7 partridges, 12 turtle doves, 15 French hens, 16 calling birds, 12 geese, 7 swans = 69 birds
6 birds, a tree, rings, maids and cows, lords
7 She told him to stop and threatened legal action.
8 A lawyer, as Sarah was in a psychiatric hospital.

Helping the learner Get students to discuss the change in style of English across the different e-mails.

2 Grammar builder: *wish*

Aim: To focus on *wish* to talk about past regrets.

a • Write the first example sentence from the table on the board.
   • Have students answer the questions, encouraging them to look back at the e-mails in exercise 1c for examples.
   • Check the answers.

Answers   1 No, he didn't. No he isn't.   2 past perfect   3 Day 5 – I wish you hadn't sent more birds. He sent more birds. Day 11 – I wish I had never met you. He gave her lots of strange presents.

b • Have students complete the table with their own ideas.
   • Have students compare their ideas in pairs or groups of three.
   • Get feedback from the class.

Possible answers   A movie actor who never quite became famous. Her / his movies were not famous.
Someone on a sports team. They did not win the game.
A girl. Her boyfriend cheated on her.

3 Speaking

Aim: To practice using *wish* to talk about regrets.
   • Focus attention on the examples in exercise 2b.
   • Give students time to think of regrets from their own past.
   • Put students in groups.
   • Have them discuss the regrets, using *wish* + past perfect.
   • Get feedback from the groups.

DAY 5
Oh, Robert – five gold rings! Now that's a nice gift! But I wish you hadn't sent more birds! I now have 5 partridges in pear trees, 8 turtle doves, 9 French hens and 8 calling birds!
Love, Sarah

DAY 7
Robert, is this a joke? It isn't funny! Geese and swans? And more partridges, etc.? I don't want any more birds!
Sarah

DAY 9
Robert, what is the matter with you? Now you're sending maids with cows, and lots of lords leaping all over the place! Do you know what it's like to clean up after all those cows and birds? Come and take all these "gifts" away!

DAY 11
Robert, I'm going to call my lawyer if you don't get these birds, cows, milkmaids and lords out of my house! And now pipers! I can't stand the noise! You're crazy – I wish I had never met you!

January 15th
Dear Mr. Lowell,
This is to inform you of a lawsuit filed by Ms. Sarah Garver for damages to her property and mental health. She claims you have sent to her house 12 partridges in pear trees, 22 turtle doves, 30 French hens, 36 calling birds, 40 gold rings (she'll keep those), 42 geese, 42 swans, 40 milkmaids and cows, 36 leaping lords, 30 dancing ladies, 22 pipers and 12 drummers.
Ms. Garver is currently in the Sunny Day Psychiatric Hospital.
Martin Landau, Attorney at Law

2 Grammar builder: *wish*

a **Look at the first example of a wish in the table below.**

1 Did the person lead a healthy life? Is he happy about the life he led?

2 What verb tense is used after *wish* to talk about past unreal situations?

3 Find more examples of wishes in the e-mails in exercise 1c. What did the boyfriend do that Sarah didn't like in each case?

b **Complete the table with your own ideas. Then discuss them with your classmates.**

Wish about an unreal situation	Who said it	Real situation
I wish I had led a healthier life.	I think an old, ill person said it.	The person didn't lead a healthy life.
I wish my movies had been more famous.		
I wish our team had practiced more!		
I wish my boyfriend hadn't done that!		

3 Speaking

In groups, talk about things you wish you had or hadn't done in the past.
Ideas: opportunities for work or study, relationships, money, etc.

I wish I had studied business instead of biology. There are more job opportunities in business.

LANGUAGE for life:
business and social *customs*

① From culture to culture

When you deal with people from other cultures, it is helpful if you have learned something about the customs and attitudes of those cultures. For example, attitudes about men's and women's roles vary greatly from one culture to another. Consider the questions below.

1 What is sexism? Is it a positive or negative concept?

2 Does the concept of sexism exist in your culture?

Now listen to some short conversations and choose the correct answers to the questions below. Pay attention to the actual words of the conversations.

Conversation 1

1 What does the woman want to do?

2 Who is the guest?

Conversation 2

1 Where does the man plan to take the woman?

2 How does he describe the event?

Conversation 3

1 What does the first man give his guest?

2 What does the second man say about it?

Conversation 4

1 What does the man offer to do?

2 Whose car are they going to use?

In the previous exercise, you focused on facts. Now listen again and pay attention to tones of voice and intonation.

Conversation 1

How does the woman feel?

a) She's a little insulted.

b) She's happy that the man will pay.

Conversation 2

What does the woman mean?

a) She doesn't know what a bullfight is.

b) She isn't sure she wants to see a bullfight.

Conversation 3

What can we infer?

a) The man doesn't really like the drink.

b) He likes it a lot.

Conversation 4

What does the woman mean?

a) She wants to drive.

b) She wants the man to drive.

Learning tip

Listening comprehension is not only understanding the words people say. It is also sometimes understanding what they **don't** say! People use devices like stress and intonation and pauses as well as words to communicate their attitudes and opinions. So learn to "listen between the lines!"

Say how you decided on the answers to the questions above.

Lesson 4 Language for life: business and social customs

Aim: To raise awareness of different customs in different cultures.

1 From culture to culture

Aims: To raise awareness of different customs in different cultures.
To practice listening for specific information in a conversation, and inferring information from tone of voice.

- Focus attention on the photograph.
- Get students to describe what they see.
- Put them in groups to discuss the questions.
- Get feedback from the groups.

- Tell students they are going to hear four short conversations which highlight aspects of male / female roles and different cultures.
- Get students to read the questions.
- Play the tape and get students to choose the correct answers.
- Check the answers.

Answers		
Conversation 1:	1 pay the bill	2 the man
Conversation 2:	1 to a bullfight	2 one of the great traditions of his country
Conversation 3:	1 a traditional drink	2 that it's interesting
Conversation 4:	1 to drive	2 the woman's

- Tell the students they are going to hear the conversations again and that they should focus on tone of voice and intonation.
- Play the tape again and get students to choose the correct answers to the questions.
- Check the answers.

Answers 1 a   2 b   3 a   4 a

- Focus attention on the Learning tip and play conversation 1 again as an example of how tone of voice communicates meaning.
- Play the rest of the conversations again and elicit how students knew the answers.
- **Optional step:** Have the students discuss what they would do in those or similar situations.

Tapescript

1
Woman: I'll pay for dinner, Mario. You're my guest.
Man: Oh, no. I'll pay. Definitely.
Woman: Mario, you're the guest of the company. I wish you would let me pay.

2
Man: I'm going to take you to see one of the great traditions of my country – a bullfight!
Woman: A bullfight? Oh, uh, I don't know.

3
Man 1: This is a traditional drink from my country. Do you like it?
Man 2: It's, uh, very interesting.

4
Man: Karen, I'll drive.
Woman: Are you kidding? It's my car!

2 The culture of international business

Aim: To raise awareness of different cultures in business.

Helping the learner   Get students to focus on the layout of the quiz in exercise 2, and elicit what the writer's purpose is (to make the reader think about the topic in a personalized way). Elicit other examples of texts that have a special layout, e.g. *letter*, *e-mail*, *report*, etc. and elicit what the writer's purpose can be.

- Focus attention on the quiz.
- Explain that the quiz is from an in-flight magazine and that it deals with the culture of international business.
- Put students in groups.
- Have them decide on the most and least appropriate answers to the questions and give reasons.
- Get feedback from the groups.

3 Planning for visitors

Aim: To practice writing a formal e-mail.

- Elicit some of the places a foreign business person could visit in and around where the students live.

Teaching tip   Remind students that they are dealing with business colleagues – not friends – so they need to be more formal and polite. Elicit the type of structures students could use, e.g. *Would you like to …? We could …*, etc.

- Have students write an e-mail with a suggested plan for their visitor's weekend.
- Let students exchange e-mails and write a reply saying what they would prefer to do, and why.

The culture of international business

In groups, imagine you are on an international flight. Read and discuss the in-flight magazine quiz below. Which actions would you consider most appropriate? Which least appropriate? There are no "right" answers, but give reasons for your choices.

THE ANGLO-AMERICAN BUSINESS CULTURE QUIZ

Imagine that two business colleagues (a man from Britain and a woman from the United States) are coming to your country, and they have been there several times before.

1 **You have made a schedule for your colleagues' stay in your country.**
   a) You call them on the phone to tell them personally about the activities you've planned.
   b) You send them an e-mail with the complete schedule, including social activities.
   c) You wait and give them the schedule personally when they arrive.

2 **The visitors arrive at 8:00 p.m.**
   a) You meet them at the airport.
   b) You send a driver from the company to meet them.
   c) You send them instructions for taking airport transportation to their hotel.

3 **They will be in your city for the weekend, and you want to provide them with some entertainment.**
   a) You decide to take the man to a bullfight. Your wife will take the woman shopping.

   b) You and your wife take them both to an arts and crafts fair and to a restaurant for lunch.
   c) You give them some suggestions for things to do and how to get there. You will see them on Monday.

4 **One evening the man feels ill. You (a man) had planned to take your guests to dinner. You ...**
   a) cancel the dinner because the man can't go.
   b) take the female visitor to dinner but invite your wife so there are no "misunderstandings."
   c) go to dinner with your female colleague.

5 **A female executive from your office has a business lunch with the visitors at a restaurant.**
   a) She pays the bill.
   b) The male visitor pays the bill.
   c) Everyone pays his or her share.

Planning for visitors

You've now read quite a lot about the attitudes and customs of English-speaking business people. Imagine that you are planning weekend entertainment for a foreign colleague visiting your city. Write an e-mail message suggesting a plan. Ask him or her to tell you which of the suggested activities he or she would prefer. Exchange e-mails with a partner. Now imagine you are the visitor. Read your partner's e-mail and write an answer. Say which activities you would prefer and give reasons. Be polite!

Unit 10 Life's a journey

1 Stranger than fiction

1 Speaking and reading

a You are going to read a true story. Before you read, look at the photographs below. What do you think the story is about?

b Now read the newspaper story. Did you guess the topic of the story?

c Choose the best headline.

1 Patricia Hearst to go to prison for terrorist activities
2 Hearst family unhappy about conviction
3 Patty Hearst renounces support for SLA

Patricia Hearst, granddaughter of media king William Randolph Hearst, was convicted today of armed robbery for her cooperation with her terrorist-kidnapers in the robbery of a San Francisco bank several months ago. Though she has given up her support for the terrorist group, she will go to prison for her participation in the robbery.

Hearst was kidnaped several months ago from her Berkeley apartment when unidentified gunmen took her from the apartment and forced her into the trunk of a car.

Several days after she was kidnaped, her kidnapers contacted the Hearst family. They called themselves the Symbionese Liberation Army and demanded that the Hearsts use their fortune to help poor people. The Hearsts agreed to sponsor a food giveaway program.

After several weeks in captivity, Patty Hearst announced that she was in sympathy with her SLA captors. She said that she was renouncing her family's wealth and upper-class lifestyle and that she was changing her name to "Tania." As Tania, she was involved with the SLA in the bank robbery. Security cameras showed that she was not merely a victim, but an active participant in the robbery. Finally, police received a tip about the SLA's hiding place in Los Angeles. There was a shootout in which some SLA members were killed. Hearst and other members escaped to San Francisco, where they were caught a few days later.

Life's a journey

Helping the learner: post-reading / listening

Students often do a follow-up activity after they read or listen to a text. These post-reading or post-listening activities can help students in a number of ways.
- To summarize what they have read or heard.
- To apply new structures they have learned.
- To make the topic and language more relevant to them by personalization.
- To recycle ideas and vocabulary from the text.

This unit has examples of post-reading and post-listening activities.

Further reading:
Nuttal, C., (2000) *Teaching reading skills in a foreign language,* Macmillan Heinemann ELT, Ch.12

Lesson 1 Stranger than fiction

Aim:	To practice reading and writing journalistic-style articles.

1 Speaking and reading

Aim: To practice reading to understand the main idea of a story.

a
- Focus attention on the photographs.
- Ask students to describe what they see and predict what the story in the next exercise will be about.

b
- Now have students read the story quickly and check what it's about.
- Get feedback from the class.

Answer	It's about a rich young woman who gets involved with a terrorist gang and is put in prison for it.

c
- Have students read the story again and decide on the best title from the list for the story.
- Get feedback, encouraging students to justify their opinions.

Answer	The best title is probably 1, as this is the main focus of the article.

Helping the learner	Getting students to choose the best headline for a newspaper story is a good way of getting them to summarize what they have read.

- Have students read the Learning tip in exercise 1d. Check they understand the importance of the headline and the first paragraph in an English language newspaper.

Optional activity	Newspaper stories Bring in English-language newspapers and get students to decide what a story is about by just looking at the headline and / or the first paragraph.

d • Have students complete the table with the information from the first paragraph of the newspaper article.

Answers	Who: Patricia Hearst What: Hearst sentenced to go to prison Where: San Francisco When: today Why: for participation in armed robbery

2 Speaking, writing and reading

Aim: To practice writing a magazine article.

a • Have students read the instructions.
  • Remind them of the importance of the first paragraph for conveying important information.
  • Have them complete the table with their ideas for the first paragraph.

Teaching tip	Help students with the vocabulary they need or let them use a dictionary.

b • Have students write up the first paragraph in full.
  • Then have them write a headline.

c • Put students in groups.
  • Let them read their paragraphs to each other.
  • Students decide which one was the most interesting and which was the most probable.
  • Have students write the rest of their story.

d • Now have students read the end of Patty Hearst's story.
  • Elicit if the story was similar to the ones the students wrote.

d Look back at the first paragraph of the newspaper article about Patty Hearst. Complete the table below.

Who:	
What: Hearst sentenced to go to prison	
Where:	
When:	
Why:	

2 Speaking, writing and reading

a Imagine you are a magazine writer. You are going to write an article about what happened to Patricia Hearst after her prison sentence. Complete the table with the main ideas of your first paragraph. Use your imagination!

Who:	
What:	
Where:	
When:	

b Write the first paragraph of your story, and write a headline for the story.

c In groups, read your paragraphs. Whose story was the most interesting? Whose was the most probable? Write the rest of your story.

d Read the end of the Patty Hearst story, below. Were there any similarities with your story?

Despite her family's wealth and importance, Patricia Hearst went to prison for armed robbery. During her prison term, she finished her college studies, and when she left prison, she returned home to live with her family. She finally married her bodyguard, and today she has a family of her own.

Why did Patty become Tania in 1974?

Some psychologists said she must have been brainwashed by her captors. Others said she might have felt guilty about her family's enormous wealth in a time of radical social change in the United States. In the end, only Patty knows the reasons for "Tania."

2 A near tragedy

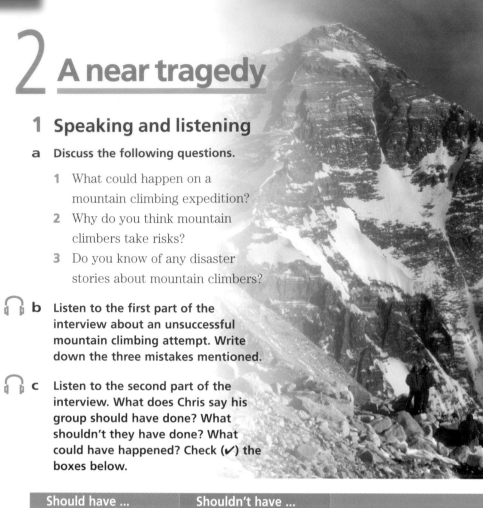

1 Speaking and listening

a Discuss the following questions.

1 What could happen on a mountain climbing expedition?

2 Why do you think mountain climbers take risks?

3 Do you know of any disaster stories about mountain climbers?

b Listen to the first part of the interview about an unsuccessful mountain climbing attempt. Write down the three mistakes mentioned.

c Listen to the second part of the interview. What does Chris say his group should have done? What shouldn't they have done? What could have happened? Check (✔) the boxes below.

Should have ...	Shouldn't have ...	
		checked the weather
		gone in March
		gone in May
		continued after the snow started
		taken Gary with them

2 Grammar builder: past modals – *would have, should have, could have*

a Look at sentences 1–3, below, from the interview in exercise 1. Match them with their meanings, a–c.

Language assistant: past modal

subject	+ modal	+ present perfect
Gary	*could*	*have died.*

1 We should have gone down the mountain immediately. ....

2 He could have died. ....

3 It would have been our fault for taking him with us! ....

a) an unreal condition in the past (It wasn't the case because the action didn't happen.)

b) a recommendation about a past action (It was the right thing to do, but they didn't do it.)

c) a possibility in the past (It was possible, but it didn't happen.)

Lesson 2 **A near tragedy**

> **Aims:** To talk about dangerous situations.
> To practice form and pronunciation of past modals.

1 Speaking and listening

Aim: To practice listening for specific information in an interview and to introduce past modals.

a • Elicit students' opinions of mountain climbing and the people who do it.
   • Put students in groups and have them discuss questions 1–3.

b • Tell students they are going to hear the first part of an interview about an unsuccessful mountain climbing attempt.
   • Explain that they need to write down the three mistakes that were made.
   • Play the tape and get students to write down the mistakes. Check the answers.

Answers 1 They took an inexperienced climber.   2 He didn't have the right equipment.
3 They continued climbing when it started to snow.

c • Focus attention on the table.
   • Tell students they are going to hear the second part of the interview and they have to check the appropriate boxes in the table.
   • Play the second part of the interview and have students check the boxes.

Answers Should have: checked the weather, gone in May
Shouldn't have: gone in March, continued after the snow started, taken Gary with them

   • Elicit what could have happened on the climb.

Answer Gary could have died.

Tapescript
Part 1
Interviewer: Today on X-treme Sports I'm talking to Chris Morris, who survived a very dangerous experience last month! Chris, tell us what happened.
Chris: OK, what happened was that two friends and I were caught in a snowstorm on Mount Barker. And I have to admit, we made several mistakes. First, we took an inexperienced climber with us. He didn't have the climbing ability for that mountain.
Interviewer: But he wanted to go.
Chris: So we took him with us. The other problem was that he didn't really have the right equipment. His equipment wasn't good enough for extreme weather conditions.
Interviewer: I imagine that the right equipment is vital.
Chris: It is. So anyway, the weather was great in the morning when we started out, but when we got to about 6,000 feet, it started snowing.
Interviewer: And did you continue to climb after it started to snow?
Chris: Yeah, and that was another big mistake. We thought it would just snow a little. It was spring – the end of March – so we continued. We should have gone down the mountain immediately.
Interviewer: Then what happened?
Chris: We got to 7,000 feet and realized it was going to be a major snowstorm. We decided to make a hole in the snow to keep warm. My friend Mike and I were fine, but Gary was in trouble. He started to get really cold.

Interviewer: So what did you do?
Chris: We sat in the hole in the snow with Gary between us to keep him warm, and we waited. It snowed for two days!
Interviewer: You were on the mountain for two days?
Chris: Yeah. Finally on the third day it stopped snowing and we started down the mountain. Gary was sick from cold and hunger, but fortunately a rescue team met us with food and warm clothes.

Part 2
Interviewer: You were lucky. What advice can you give to other climbers? What should you have done differently?
Chris: Well, I guess we shouldn't have climbed Mount Barker in March. The weather is still too unpredictable at that time. We should have waited until May. And we definitely should have checked the weather forecast before going.
Interviewer: And what about once you were on the mountain?
Chris: We should have turned back when it started snowing. We shouldn't have continued climbing in the snow.
Interviewer: Do you have any other advice for our listeners?
Chris: Yeah. Make sure everyone in the group has the same level of experience and equipment. Gary wasn't experienced enough for Mount Barker. He could have died, and it would have been our fault for taking him with us! Don't risk people's lives!
Interviewer: Climbers, that's good advice from Chris Morris. Thank you, Chris.

2 Grammar builder: *would have, should have, could have*

Aim: To practice past modals.

a • Focus attention on the Language assistant box and check students know how to form past modals by eliciting other examples.
   • Tell students to read sentences 1–3 and their meanings a–c, and match them.

Answers 1 b   2 c   3 a

b • Put students in pairs.
  • Have them read the story and answer questions 1–3.
  • Get feedback, writing the answers with past modals on the board.

Helping the learner This exercise gives students the opportunity to practice the past modals in relation to what they have read.

3 Pronunciation: weak forms – modals

Aim: To practice the pronunciation of weak forms in past modals.

a • Play the tape and have students circle the correct past modal.
  • Let them check their answers in pairs.
  • Check the answers by playing the tape again.

b • Play the tape again and get students to practice the sentences.
  • Highlight the use of the reduced forms.

Answers / Tapescript Man: Did you hear what happened to Derek?
Woman: Yeah, I would have been terrified!
Man: Me too. I wouldn't have attacked the man! Derek could have been killed!
Woman: He shouldn't have hit the man. He should have called the police.

4 Writing and speaking

Aim: To consolidate past modals in speaking and writing.

a • Put students in pairs.
  • Have them read situations 1–3 and comment on them.
  • Encourage them to use past modals.
  • Get feedback from the pairs.

Possible answers 1 Marty could have been killed. He should have worn a helmet.
2 Her boyfriend could have got angry with the other boy. Karen should have told her boyfriend.
3 They couldn't have robbed the store.

b • Now have students think of or invent a dangerous or difficult situation from their past.
  • Have students write their story and say what they *should / shouldn't have done*, and what *could have happened*.

c • Put students in groups.
  • Have them read out their stories and comment on them, using the past modals.

  • **Optional step:** Ask students to read out the most interesting stories.

b **Read the following story and answer the questions below.**

Derek was buying a newspaper in a small store when a man entered the store with a gun. He told the clerk to give him all the store's money. Derek ran up behind the man and hit his arm, knocking the gun out of his hand. The gun fired, but fortunately, no one was injured. The thief ran out through the door and escaped.

1 What did Derek do? In your opinion, should he have done this? If not, what should he have done?

2 What could have happened?

3 What would you have done if you had been there?

3 Pronunciation: weak forms – modals

a **Listen to two people talking about Derek's experience. Circle the past modals you hear.**

A: Did you hear what happened to Derek?

B: Yeah, I *would have / wouldn't have* been terrified!

A: Me too. I *would have / wouldn't have* attacked the man! Derek *could have / couldn't have* been killed!

B: He *should have / shouldn't have* hit the man. He *should have / shouldn't have* called the police.

b **Listen again and practice the sentences. Notice the reduced forms.**

/wouldev/   /wouldnev/   /shouldev/   /shouldnev/   /couldev/   /couldnev/

4 Writing and speaking

a **In pairs, comment on the following situations.**

1 Marty was riding his motorcycle when a car turned in front of him. He fell off his motorcycle, but fortunately he wasn't hurt. He wasn't wearing a helmet.

2 Karen went to a movie with one of her brother's friends. She didn't tell her boyfriend because she thought he might get angry.

3 Sam and Joe were accused of robbing a convenience store last Saturday. The police didn't believe their story that they were at a party, even though witnesses said they saw them there.

b **Think of a difficult or dangerous situation in your past, or invent one.**

1 Write a short description of what happened.

2 Write a few sentences about what you should or shouldn't have done, and what could have happened.

c **In groups, read your stories. Say what you would have done, or how you would have felt in a similar situation.**

3 War of the Worlds

1 Listening and reading

a Listen to excerpts from a radio broadcast from 1938. Then check (✔) the correct answers to the following questions.

1 What type of radio program does it sound like?

a) news ◯   b) drama ◯   c) music ◯

2 What was the topic of the broadcast?

a) a fire in New Jersey ◯   b) explosions in space ◯   c) the arrival of aliens on earth ◯

3 How does the announcer sound?

a) amused ◯   b) terrified ◯   c) angry ◯

b Now read the following article about the effects of the radio broadcast and answer these questions.

1 What kind of program was *The War of the Worlds*?

2 What did many people think when they heard the broadcast?

3 What was the general result?

4 What were three reasons why people thought the broadcast was real?

On This Day in History

The Orson Welles Effect

On the night of October 30, 1938, CBS's New York radio station WABC broadcast Orson Welles' dramatic version of *The War of the Worlds*, a novel by H.G. Wells. The work was introduced as a play, and three times during the broadcast, the station announced that it was fictional.

Nevertheless, it sounded like a news broadcast, and a lot of people thought that the earth was being invaded by Martians! Mass panic resulted. Thousands of people began calling newspapers and radio stations for information about the "end of the world." Because part of the radio program had recommended evacuation, many families left their homes, trying to escape the New York–New Jersey area.

Many people reacted to the panic in ways which today seem very amusing. In Newark, New Jersey, some families ran into the street with wet towels over their faces because they thought there was a Martian gas attack. The *New York Times* received 875 calls from frantic citizens. One man called to ask, "What time will the end of the world be?" When a bus station employee tried to question a caller about the situation, the caller said she didn't have time to talk because "the world is coming to an end and I have a lot to do."

What could have caused so many people to believe that Martians were attacking the earth? Psychologists say that it might have been partly because of the world political climate. Europe was heading toward World War II and there was a general feeling of insecurity. Another factor was the broadcast itself. It was extremely realistic and in the form of news bulletins. It must have sounded like the real thing to a lot of people. Finally, many listeners missed the beginning of the program, when it was explained that they were going to hear a radio play.

c What would you have thought if you had heard *The War of the Worlds*?

Lesson 3 War of the Worlds

Aims: To practice listening for the main idea.
To practice reading for specific information.
To practice past modals for talking about different degrees of probability.

1 Listening and reading

Aims: To introduce the topic of the War of the Worlds.
To practice listening for the main idea.
To practice reading for specific information.

a • Tell students they are going to hear excerpts from a radio broadcast from 1938.
• Check comprehension of questions 1–3 and options a–c.
• Play the tape and get students to choose the correct answers.
• Check the answers.

Answers 1 a   2 c   3 b

Tapescript

Announcer: Ladies and gentlemen, we interrupt our program of dance music to bring you a special bulletin from the Intercontinental Radio News. At twenty minutes before eight, central time, Professor Farrell of the Mount Jennings Observatory, Chicago, Illinois, reports observing several explosions of incandescent gas, occurring at regular intervals on the planet Mars. The spectroscope indicates the gas to be hydrogen and moving towards the earth with enormous velocity.

Pierson: I don't know what to think. The metal casing is extraterrestrial ... not found on this earth.

Voices: The top's loose! She's off! Look out there! Stand back!

Phillips: Ladies and gentlemen, this is the most terrifying thing I have ever witnessed ... Wait a minute! Someone's crawling out of the hollow top. Someone or ... something. I can see peering out of that black hole two luminous disks ... are they eyes? It might be a face. It might be ... Good heavens, something's wriggling out of the shadow like a gray snake. Now it's another one, and another. They look like tentacles to me. There, I can see the thing's body. It's large, large as

a bear and it glistens like wet leather. But that face, it ... ladies and gentlemen, it's indescribable ...

Operator three: This is Newark, New Jersey ... This is Newark, New Jersey ... Warning! Poisonous black smoke pouring in from Jersey marshes. Reaches South Street. Gas masks useless. Urge population to move into open spaces ... automobiles use Routes 7, 23, 24 ... Avoid congested areas. Smoke now spreading over Raymond Boulevard ...

Announcer: I'm speaking from the roof of the Broadcasting Building, New York City. The bells you hear are ringing to warn people to evacuate the city as the Martians approach. Estimated in the last two hours three million people have moved out along the roads to the north, Hutchison River Parkway still kept open for motor traffic. Avoid bridges to Long Island ... hopelessly jammed. All communication with Jersey shore closed ten minutes ago. No more defenses. Our army wiped out ... artillery, air force, everything wiped out. This may be the last broadcast. We'll stay here to the end ... People are holding services below us ... in the cathedral.

b • Get students to read the article and answer questions 1–4.
• Let them check in pairs.
• Check the answers with the class.

Answers 1 a play   2 that it was a real news program   3 mass panic
4 The world political climate of the time (the approach of World War II) made people feel insecure. The play was very realistic and sounded like a news broadcast. Many listeners missed the beginning, when it was explained that the program was a radio play.

c • Put students in groups.
• Have them discuss the question.
• Get feedback from the groups.

Helping the learner   This personalization phase makes the topic and language more relevant to the students.

2 Grammar builder: past modals – *could have, might / may have, must have*

Aim: To practice past modals for expressing degrees of probability.

a • Check comprehension of the headings in the table.
  • Have students underline the past modal forms in sentences 1–7.
  • Have students write the modals in the correct place in the table.
  • Check the answers.

Answers	a definite conclusion: must have been
	a possibility: might have panicked, might not have heard, could have happened, may have seen, may not have made
	impossibility: couldn't have imagined

Teaching tip	It may be useful to translate the idea expressed by each modal into the students' native language.

  • Focus attention on the Language assistant box to summarize the meaning and use of the modals.

Language help	Check students understand that the opposite of *He must be a criminal* is *He can't be a criminal.*

b • Tell students to read and complete the conversation.
  • Let them check their answers in pairs.
  • Check the answers with the class.

Answers	1 must have killed 2 couldn't have wanted 3 might / may / could have been
	4 might / may / could have had 5 might / may / could have found out 6 must have been

3 Speaking

Aim: To consolidate past modals for degrees of probability.

a • Put students in groups.
  • Have students think of a famous myth or legend from their own country and discuss the details of it.
  • Get feedback from the groups.

b • Focus attention on the picture and the examples.
  • The picture represents *La llorona*, a famous legend in some countries. One version of the story is that a mother murdered her children and then regretted it and spent the rest of her life searching for her children and crying.
  • Have students try to explain the origin of their myth / legend, using the past modals.

Preparation:
Ask students to bring
information about a
country they would like
to visit to the next
lesson. Bring a map of
Britain, travel
brochures, an atlas,
and travel guides.

2 Grammar builder: past modals – *could have*, *might / may have*, *must have*

a The above modals are used to make deductions about the past. Look at sentences 1–7, below, and write the modals in the correct places in this table.

a definite conclusion (99% sure)	a possibility (50% sure)	an impossibility (99% sure)
	might (not) have	

1 Some people might have panicked because of other people, not because of the broadcast.

2 Others might not have heard the beginning of the program.

3 The panic could have happened partly because of political insecurity.

4 Some people may have seen airplane lights and thought they were spaceships.

5 The radio station may not have made it clear that it was fiction.

6 The people who thought Martians were invading must have been terrified.

7 Welles couldn't have imagined that his drama would cause such panic.

b Complete the conversation with appropriate past modals.

A: Did you hear about that actress who killed her husband?

B: Yeah, she (1) .... (*kill*) him for his money. I'm sure that was the reason.

A: No, she (2) .... (*want*) more money. She has millions!

B: True. Well, then, she (3) .... (*be*) jealous. He (4) .... (*have*) a girlfriend.

A: Yeah, she (5) .... (*find out*) he was in love with another woman.

B: Yep, that (6) .... (*be*) it. I mean, it's always money or love, right?

Language assistant

- *Could*, *may* and *might* have approximately the same meaning.
- The opposite of *must have* for deductions is *could not have* and **not** *must not have*!

Derek **must have** been scared.
Derek **couldn't have** been an accomplice in the attempted robbery.

In spoken form, *must have* and *might / may have* are not usually contracted in the negative.
Have is reduced: He *must / might / may not've known*.

3 Speaking

a In groups, think of a famous myth or legend from your country. Summarize it. Does everyone in the group know the same version?

b Myths and legends must have come from somewhere! Try to think of reasons for the origin of yours. Use the examples to help you describe your reasons.

There must have been a murder ...

A woman may have lost her child ...

There could have been a tribal war, and ...

La Llorona

LANGUAGE for life:
making the most of *travel*

① Ready to travel

Imagine you're getting ready to go to Britain. In pairs, make a list of things you've heard, read or imagine to be true about it.

Discuss your list with the class. How many of the things may be stereotypes and not necessarily completely true?

In groups, discuss the following questions.

1 What do you think you need to know before you go on a trip?

2 How can you find the information you need?

3 What can you do during your visit to learn more about the place than the "average" tourist?

② Learning from travel

Read the following article from a travel guide and compare it with your ideas from the exercise above.

THE ABOVE-AVERAGE TRAVELER

The right attitude

Most countries, or even regions, have certain stereotypes connected with them – Americans eat fast food all the time and have little family life. New Yorkers are all loud and unfriendly, etc. But anyone who has traveled a lot will tell you that stereotypes are exactly that – stereotypes, and don't represent the broad spectrum of customs and attitudes which exist in every country or region.

Lesson 4 Language for life: making the most of travel

Aim: To raise awareness of the use of English in travel.

1 Ready to travel

Aim: To activate background knowledge about Britain.

- Show a map of Britain to show where it is in relation to the rest of the world.
- Ask how many students have been there.
- Put students in pairs.
- Have them make a list of everything they have heard, read or imagine to be true about Britain.
- Have students discuss their list with the rest of the class.
- Elicit examples of things that may be stereotypes, e.g. *people drink tea at four o'clock every afternoon*.
- Put students in groups.
- Have them discuss the questions.
- Get feedback from the groups.

Possible answers 1 You need to know about currency, accommodation, food, places to visit, weather, vaccinations, local customs.

2 You can find travel information on the Net, from friends, books, travel agents, the tourist information office.

3 During your visit, you can read, watch TV, and talk to local people.

2 Learning from travel

Aims: To practice reading to check predictions.
To practice writing a travel plan.

- Tell students to read the article and compare what they read with their ideas from exercise 1.
- Get feedback from the class.

- Tell students to imagine they are going to visit another country.
- Elicit examples of the countries students have researched as preparation for the lesson.
- Put students in groups, joining students who would like to go to the same or similar countries.
- Get students to decide on one country.
- Get them to write a plan, using their own ideas, ideas from the text and the information they researched before the class.
- Have students share their ideas with the class.

Helping the learner   This exercise allows students to recycle the ideas and vocabulary used in the reading text.

3 What kind of a traveler are you?

Aim: To practice writing a composition about a trip.

- Elicit the names of places that students have visited.
- Get them to write a composition about a trip they have been on, using the paragraph guide to help them.

Teaching tip   Remind students of the form and use of *should have* and *might have* for paragraph 3.

- Put students in pairs.
- Focus attention on the example comments and highlight the use of the past modals.
- Get students to read each other's composition and make comments on it, using past modals where appropriate.

Preparation:
Tell students to bring photographs of children they know to the next lesson.

Before you go

If you are planning a trip, how can you prepare so that you benefit as much as possible from the experience? First, learn some basic facts about the place – its capital, the basis of its economy, a little of its history, its main ethnic groups, etc. You can get an overview from a travel guide, an encyclopedia or the Internet. The Internet also has specific information about cities – maps, restaurant recommendations, etc.

If you're going to another country, try to take a basic survival course in the language. If you already speak the language, a conversation class can increase your fluency. Reading newspapers or magazines from the country will

increase your vocabulary and will also give you information on important current events there.

Whenever possible, talk to people from the country you're going to visit. You can often meet people through a language institute or college in your city. Internet chat rooms are another way to talk to people from other countries and find out their ideas and attitudes about things.

When you get there

Once you get to your destination, how can you avoid being "a typical tourist"? Of course, it helps if you know someone there. They can show you lots of great places tourists don't usually go. But if you don't know anyone, there are still a

number of things you can do to learn as much as possible about the country. First, try not to stay in a "tourist hotel." Bed and breakfasts are a good option because they're often owned by families and much more personal than a hotel.

Don't eat hotel food, or what you imagine to be the typical food of the country (hamburgers in the United States or pasta in Italy). Ask about local specialties – barbecue in Texas or Cajun food in New Orleans, for example. And don't use a tourist guide for restaurant recommendations. Ask local people where they eat, or ask a taxi driver to take you to his favorite restaurant.

Try to do things that local people do; again, don't just refer to your tourist guide. Ask people for suggestions or check the entertainment section of the local newspaper. And finally, talk to as many different people as possible. Most people are friendly to tourists and are happy to answer questions about their city.

Use your own ideas and ideas from the text to prepare for a visit to another country.

1 In groups, choose a country or a region in your own country.

2 Write a plan for learning as much as you can about the country or region before you go and after you get there.

3 Share your ideas with the class.

③
What kind of traveler are you?

Think of a trip you have taken and write a short composition about it.
Paragraph 1: What you did to prepare for the trip.
Paragraph 2: What you did while you were there.
Paragraph 3: What you should have done differently, or how you might have benefited more from the trip.

Exchange compositions with a partner. Read your partner's composition and comment on it.
I think I would have tried to meet some people. You could have learned more about local customs that way.

5 Learning check

1 Progress check

a Complete the second sentence of each pair so that it has a similar meaning to the first sentence of the pair.

1 I didn't get up early, so I didn't catch the bus.

If I had gotten up early, *I would have caught the bus* .... the bus.

2 He took the medicine and felt better.

If he *hadn't taken the medicine* ...., he wouldn't have felt better.

3 She didn't buy the dress because she didn't have enough money.

She *would have bought the dress* .... if she'd had enough money.

4 I sold my car but it was a bad idea.

I wish *I hadn't* .... sold my car.

5 Jane jumped down the stairs and broke her arm.

If she hadn't jumped down the stairs, *Jane wouldn't have broken her arm* ....

b Read the sentences and choose the correct completion for each space.

6 You *should* .... put a band aid on that cut. It might get infected.

    a) might have   **b)** should   **c)** should have   **d)** would have

7 Our car crashed but we were very lucky. We *could have* .... been badly hurt.

    a) must have   **b)** should   **c)** had   **d)** could have

8 If I had known you didn't have any money, I *would have lent* ... you some.

    a) would have lent   **b)** should have lent   **c)** must have lent   **d)** would lend

9 I can't find my keys anywhere. I *might have left* .... them at work.

    a) would have left   **b)** might have left   **c)** had left   **d)** will leave

10 The hotel had no heat. It *must have been* .... really cold in your room.

    a) would have been   **b)** had been   **c)** could have been   **d)** must have been

c Replace the underlined words in these sentences with the correct form of one of the phrasal verbs in the box.

find out   turn down   go out with   get over   give up

11 Teresa <u>refused</u> *turned down* the job offer because she doesn't want to move to Chicago.

12 I took tennis classes for six months but it was so difficult that I finally <u>stopped trying</u> *gave up*.

13 We <u>discovered</u> *found out* that Jenny lives in the same street as us.

14 Luke has been off work for two weeks but he still hasn't <u>recovered from</u> *gotten over* his illness.

15 Sarah has been <u>dating</u> *going out with* Liam for over three years.

Learning check 5

1 Progress check

Aims: To provide an opportunity to assess students' progress and help them according to the results.
To provide an opportunity for learners to test themselves.
To allow students to evaluate their own progress and act on areas they need to improve.

Suggestions for using the *Progress check* sections
This section can be done in a variety of ways depending on how much time you have and whether you want students to do it as part of an individual assessment or as general revision.
a As a test – students work individually on the *Progress check* sections and you then check their work and record their score out of 15.
b Students work on the *Progress check* sections alone and then check their answers in pairs.
c Students work on the *Progress check* sections in pairs or groups and you later check the answers with the whole class.
d Students do the *Progress check* sections for homework.
In all cases, conduct a feedback session with the whole class to check any queries students may have and see how they did.

Explanation of answers

a
1 Third conditional for an unreal situation in the past.
2 Third conditional for an unreal situation in the past.
3 Third conditional for an unreal situation in the past.
4 *Wish* + past perfect to express a past regret.
5 Third conditional for an unreal situation in the past.

b
1 Advice about the present, not the past.
2 Possibility in the past.
3 Third conditional for an unreal situation in the past.
4 Possibility in the past.
5 A definite conclusion about the past.

c
This exercise is to test students' knowledge of phrasal verbs and there is only one possible answer for each question.

2 Proficiency check

Aims: To expose students to TOEFL and UCLES-style exam formats, which will be useful for those students interested in taking such formal proficiency exams.
To develop students' exam-taking strategies.
To allow teachers and students the opportunity to evaluate students' proficiency in English.
To test students' listening and reading skills under pseudo exam conditions.

Suggestions for taking the test

Taking language tests is not only about knowing the language. It also involves knowing how to deal with exams: how to work under pressure; how to recognize the operations of the exam; and how to apply strategies to get the best results in an exam. These *Proficiency checks* give students the opportunity to work on all of these areas.

Students could do this as a formal proficiency test where they work individually, in silence. The tests are then collected and checked by the teacher. Alternatively, students could do the test individually and then check their answers in pairs or groups.

In either case, it is recommended that students as a class have the opportunity to discuss their answers and how they arrived at them with the teacher. Explanations of the correct answers are given to facilitate the teacher's role here. In addition, the teacher can highlight the strategy that is given in every *Proficiency check*. This is very helpful in giving students the chance to work on their exam-taking strategies as well as their accuracy with the language.

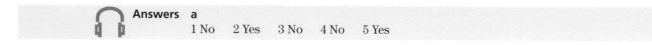

Answers a

1 No   2 Yes   3 No   4 No   5 Yes

Tapescript

Philip: Hi Christine.
Christine: Wow. What's wrong with you?
Philip. I don't know. A cold or maybe flu.
Christine: Have you taken anything?
Philip: Uh yeah. Aspirin. Hot drinks.
Christine: Good. Hmm how long have you been like this?

Philip: Oh. About a week or so.
Christine: A week! Look you have to see a doctor.
Philip: OK. I'll get an appointment at the student medical center with Dr. Barnes.
Christine: No. He's horrible. See Dr. Jones. She's really nice.

Exam-taking tip   Matching headings with paragraphs
Many exam formats require students to match a heading, or a topic sentence to a paragraph. Encourage students to read the text first, writing two or three key words down to summarize each paragraph. For example, in exercise 2b, the key words for paragraph a are *child* and *first music*. Students then match these key words to the headings, with paragraph a, child and first music match heading number 3, Childhood and early career.

b
a 3   b 6   c 7   d 1   e 2   f 5

2 Proficiency check

a Read the five statements. Then listen to the conversation and decide if the statements are correct or incorrect. Check (✔) YES for correct and NO for incorrect.

		YES	NO			YES	NO
1	Philip has a stomachache.	○	○	4	He's going to the local hospital for an appointment.	○	○
2	He has taken something for the problem.	○	○	5	Christine thinks Dr. Barnes isn't very nice.	○	○
3	He has had the problem for two weeks.	○	○				

b Match the headings in the list with the paragraphs of the article. There is one extra heading.

1 Home sweet home
2 Flower crazy
3 Childhood and early career
4 Concert tours
5 Financial affairs
6 Best-known songs
7 Clothes and accessories

a)

Elton John, whose original name was Reginald Dwight, was born in Pinner near London in 1947. As a child he learned the piano and began his career as a professional musician in 1965, playing the piano and singing with the group Bluesology.

b)

His first hit single was "Your Song" in 1971 and he established a reputation for melodious, sentimental ballads. One famous album was "Goodbye Yellow Brick Road" which included one of his most famous songs, "Candle In the Wind." This song was about the life of the actress Marilyn Monroe. He has also written music for movies such as *The Lion King*.

c)

Elton John is famous for his flamboyant stage costumes and glasses. He also has thousands of pairs of shoes as well as expensive jewelry. He has hundreds of Versace shirts with his initials. He has so many clothes, he has just opened a store in London to sell some of his thousands of outfits to benefit charity.

d)

Elton John has an insatiable appetite for luxury. He paid $7 million for a French castle in 1997. He spent the same amount again on furnishings and decoration. He also has a house near Windsor, a six-bedroom apartment in London and a condominium in Atlanta, Georgia.

e)

He has an obsession with fresh flowers. Two florists prepare 240 arrangements a week for his homes. In a 20-month period he spent $425,000 on flowers. During the same period, he spent $58,000,000 in total.

f)

He tore up financial reports without reading them and refused to see his accountants when they flew to Los Angeles to discuss a "serious financial crisis." "I have a flair for writing songs. I have a flair for performing and making records. I have never had an aptitude for business," he told reporters.

Unit 11 Stages of life

1 Learning to be human

1 Speaking and listening

a Look at the four photographs. In pairs, decide:

- approximately how old each child is;
- what they probably can and cannot do at that age.

b Jean Piaget (1896–1980) was a very influential developmental psychologist. He identified four main stages in the cognitive development of children. Listen to a college class about Piaget's theory, and complete the table below.

> "Pre-operational" stage   "Formal operational" stage
>
> "Sensori-motor" stage   "Concrete-operational" stage

Piaget's stages	Approximate ages
1 Sensori-motor stage	From birth to age ....
2	From age 2 to age ....
3	From age 7 to age ....
4	From age .... on

c Listen again and note some of the things children can do at each stage. Compare and discuss your notes in groups.

2 Writing, reading and speaking

a On a clean sheet of paper write a paragraph about a typical day in the life of a child you know well. Don't mention the age of the child.

b In groups, read one another's paragraphs. After reading each paragraph, note on the paper your name and the approximate age that you estimate for the child.

c Get your own paragraphs back. Who has made the best guess of each child's age? Then discuss the children, and see how well they match Piaget's stages of development.

Stages of life

Helping the learner: writing

Writing is an important skill in students' overall progress in English. It is also important in certain formal examinations and may be a requirement of the students in their careers. There are many ways to help students with their writing skills.
- Have them brainstorm and plan before writing.
- Encourage students to edit their own and / or each other's writing.
- Expose students to a range of writing tasks.

Further reading:
Scrivener, J., (1998) *Learning Teaching,* Macmillan Heinemann ELT, Ch.10

Lesson 1 Learning to be human

> **Aim:** To practice the four skills and develop vocabulary recording strategies.

1 Speaking and listening

Aim: To introduce the topic of child development and practice listening and note-taking.

a • Have students look at the photographs, and decide the ages and abilities of the children.
 • Have students compare the children in the photographs with children they know.

b • Ask if students have heard of Jean Piaget and if they know what he is famous for.
 • Have students read the introductory paragraph, and check they understand it.
 • Play the tape and let them complete the table.

Answers
1 Sensori-motor, birth to age 2
2 Pre-operational, age 2 to 7
3 Concrete-operational, age 7 to 12
4 Formal operational, age 12 onwards

c • Tell students to listen again, and note what children can do at each of Piaget's four stages.
 • Play the tape again, pausing after the discussion of each stage (see the points marked // in the tapescript) to give students time to make notes.
 • Put students in groups, and have them compare and discuss their notes.
 • Get feedback from the group, eliciting examples from students' experiences.

Tapescript and Answers to exercise 1c

Lecturer: OK. Now I'm sure you've all heard of Piaget – Jean Piaget.
Students: Sure. / Yeah. / Of course.
Lecturer: He's been the most influential developmental psychologist to date. Piaget identified four main stages in the cognitive development of children, starting with the sensori-motor stage, which lasts up to the age of two.
Male student: That's from birth to two, right?
Lecturer: Right. **During this stage babies learn to recognize, hold and manipulate objects, and they begin to walk. But they don't really remember that objects – or people – exist unless they can actually see, hear or touch them. For example, if a toy is hidden, a baby quickly forgets it exists.**
Female student: So sensori-motor means developing the senses and motor skills, does it?

Lecturer: Exactly. // The second or pre-operational stage is from about two to seven. **The most obvious and impressive development is speech, but at about two, children also suddenly realize that the world is more than what they have around them at any given moment. They realize that the world has a permanent existence beyond their senses.**
Female student: So they remember things, places and people they haven't seen for some time?
Lecturer: That's right. But they're still very egocentric – the world revolves about them, it's all "I", "I". // Then comes the concrete-operational stage. **They begin to realize that people have different points of view, and they themselves can be wrong. They also begin to understand much better how numbers work ... and volumes ... yes?**

Male student: That's from seven to ...?
Lecturer: Oh, sorry – from about seven to twelve or so. The ages are all approximate and vary from child to child. // Finally, after twelve or so, children – or adolescents – pass into the formal operational stage. **They begin to think like adults, with logic, the ability to follow abstract ideas, lines or arguments.** Uh ... right, well, we're almost out of time. Let's see if you noted these stages. The first stage is ...?
Female student: The sensori-motor stage, from birth to about two.
Male student: Then the pre-operational stage, from two to seven.
Male student: The concrete-operational stage – seven to twelve ... approximately.
Female student: Then the formal operational stage ...
Lecturer: Very good!
[NOTE: // = pauses for second playing of the recording]

• See page T97 for all notes on exercise 2.

2 Writing, reading and speaking

Aim: To practice students' speaking and writing skills.

Helping the learner	Have students brainstorm what children do in a typical day. This will help them plan their ideas before they draft their paragraph.

a • Tell students to think of a child they know and to write a paragraph about a typical day in their life. Remind students not to write the age of the child.

b • Put students in groups, and have them read each other's paragraphs.
  • Remind them to guess how old the child is and write their own name on the paper.

c • Have students return the paragraphs, check who was right about the child's age and discuss the children in terms of Piaget's theory.

Teaching tip	If students have brought photos of children they know, have them discuss them in groups.

3 Word builder: people

Aim: To build up and classify vocabulary associated with people.

a • Tell students to classify the words from the box on the appropriate lines.
  • Let them check their answers in pairs and then check the answers with the class.

Answers	**Child:** baby, boy, girl, infant, kid **Adolescent:** boy, girl, kid, guy, teenager, youngster, youth **Adult:** grown-up, man, woman

b • Focus attention on the table.

Teaching tip	Classify the first word *guy* on the board as an example.

• Let students work in pairs or groups to classify the words.

Answers

	SINGULAR							PLURAL					
	1	2	3	4	5	6	7	1	2	3	4	5	6
Masc.	✔							✔			✔	✔	
Fem.							✔						
M/F		✔	✔	✔	✔	✔		✔	✔				✔
Inf.	✔		✔				✔						
Form.			✔		✔								✔
I/F	✔			✔				✔	✔	✔	✔	✔	

• Point out the Learning tip in the Students' Book, and elicit notes for *parents* and *children*.

4 Reading and speaking

Aims: To consolidate the vocabulary of people.
  To focus on the appropriateness of vocabulary.

Teaching tip	Pre-teach the meaning of *anthropology thesis* – a piece of writing done for a degree on the study of people, their beliefs, etc.

• Put students in pairs and have them read the paragraph about human development, and discuss the questions.

Answers	1 At one year the child's head would be too big for a natural birth. 2 We learn more from our parents, so we become accustomed to learning throughout our lives. 3 Human childhood is longer; human heads grow much more after birth than other mammals; humans mature much later than other mammals; humans spend much longer with their parents.

3 Word builder: people

a Write the words from the box on the appropriate lines. You should write some words on more than one line. Use a dictionary if you need to.

baby	boy
girl	guy
grown-up	infant
kid	man
teenager	youngster
youth	woman

Child: ....

Adolescent: ....

Adult: ....

b Classify the words in the table by putting a check (✔) in the appropriate columns.

- Masc. (always masculine), Fem. (always feminine), or M/F (masculine or feminine)
- Inf. (usually informal), Form. (usually formal), or I/F (informal or formal)

	Masc.	Fem.	M/F	Inf.	Form.	I/F
SINGULAR						
1 guy						
2 child						
3 kid						
4 adolescent						
5 teenager						
6 youth						
7 mom						
PLURAL						
1 sons						
2 children						
3 parents						
4 fathers						
5 brothers						
6 siblings						

Learning tip

It is useful to keep a vocabulary notebook and write points like those above beside words: *brothers* (males only – for males and females *brothers and sisters*) The usefulness of this is not just that you can review words in the notebook, but the act of making the note helps you remember. What would you write for *parents* and *children*?

4 Reading and speaking

Read the extract from an anthropology thesis. In pairs, discuss the information in the paragraph. Consider questions like these.

1 Why are human babies born early?

2 What are the advantages of our long dependence on our parents?

3 What else makes human children different from other young mammals?

Human children develop very differently from other mammals. Our childhood is proportionally much longer, extended at both ends, with early birth and late maturity. If the pregnancy period of human mothers were the same as other mammals in proportion to average body weight it would be more than a year, not nine months. However, at one year the human child's head would be too big for natural birth. One thing that makes us human is, literally, our big heads, which grow a lot more than other mammals' heads after birth. On the other hand, we do not become mature adolescents until we are much older than other mammals. We spend a much longer time depending on our parents. Therefore, we learn much more from them, and that accustoms us to continue learning all our lives.

2 Goals in life – or just wanna have fun?

1 Reading, writing and speaking

a Read what four 20-year-olds think about their lives. Which corresponds to each photograph?

1 "I'm just a year away from graduating. I already work part-time, and hope to get a good full-time job in the company once I graduate. But I have plans for bigger things – an MBA as soon as possible, and I'll be managing a department in the company when I'm 30."

2 "Although I'm studying, I don't expect to graduate. My fiancé already has a good job, and we're getting married next month. I'll be taking care of a baby by the end of next year, I hope. My real ambition is to be a good wife and mother."

3 "My grandaddy says 'You're only young once', and he's the happiest old guy I know. I reckon that's 'cos he really had fun when he was young, and I'm following his example. I'm studying too, but I don't plan to get serious about work until I'm, say, 10 years older."

4 "I feel so fortunate. We young people can have such full lives nowadays. I try to take advantage of every opportunity – self-development, preparation for a career, fun with friends, travel. But I suppose my real passion is biology, my major. I want to go into research."

b In pairs, discuss which person you identify with most, and least. Why?

c Write a paragraph about what interests you most at the moment: study, work, sports, having fun with friends, marriage, travel, etc. In groups, exchange and discuss your paragraphs.

2 Grammar builder: future progressive vs. future simple

a Look at the following sentences. Which ones are about:
- a complete, defined activity in the future?
- an open-ended activity taking place at a certain time in the future?

Lesson 2 Goals in life –
or just wanna have fun?

Aims: To read and talk about goals in life.
To practice future progressive in contrast with future simple.
To practice the pronunciation of *will* in connected speech.

1 Reading, writing and speaking

Aims: To introduce the topic of goals in life.
To practice reading for the main idea in a text.

a • Have students look at the photographs.
• Elicit students' reactions to the 20-year-olds.
• Now have them read and match the texts in the exercise to the photographs.
• Check the answers.

Answers **A** 2 **B** 3 **C** 4 **D** 1

b • Put students in pairs.
• Have them discuss who they identify with most and least.
• Ask for feedback from the pairs.

c • Get each student to write a paragraph about their current interests.
• Put them in groups.
• Have them exchange and discuss their paragraphs.
• Ask for feedback, and have some students read their paragraphs.

Helping the learner Students can sometimes find it difficult to spot their own errors in writing. You can give students practice in editing written text by asking them to highlight errors in their partner's work.

2 Grammar builder: future progressive vs. future simple

Aim: To practice the difference between future progressive and future simple.

a • Write a future progressive and a future simple sentence on the board.
• Have students decide on the meaning.
• Have them read sentences 1–4 and answer the questions.
• Check the answers.

Answers sentences 2 and 4 – a complete, defined activity
sentences 1 and 3 – an open-ended activity

b • Establish that sentences 2 and 4 contain the future simple, while 1 and 3 contain the future progressive.

c • Now have students complete the sentences with the appropriate structure.
  • Let them check in pairs.
  • Check the answers with the class.

Answers	1 'll be waiting 2 'll paint 3 'll pay 4 'll be living 5 'll be working

• Focus attention on the Language assistant box and check students understand how the future progressive tense is used, by eliciting other examples.

3 Pronunciation: linking

Aim: To practice the pronunciation of *will* in connected speech.

a • Tell students to look at sentences 1–3 in the book, or write them on the board.
  • Have students try to pronounce the sentences.
  • Play the tape and get them to check the pronunciation.
  • Highlight the linking of *will*.

b • Put students in pairs.

Teaching tip	Elicit the questions students need to ask before they start the pair work.

Answers	What time'll you go to bed tonight? What'll you have for breakfast tomorrow? How much'll you study next weekend?

• Have students ask each other the questions in exercise 3b, using the correct pronunciation.

4 Speaking

Aim: To practice talking about the future.

a • Elicit examples of students' future plans.
  • Check comprehension of the categories in the table.
  • Have students complete the table about themselves.

b • Put students in pairs.
  • Have them discuss and compare their plans.
  • Ask for feedback, eliciting the most interesting and unusual plans.

Preparation:
Tell students to bring photographs of old people they know to the next lesson.

1   I'll be managing a department in the company when I'm 30.

2   I'll get an MBA as soon as possible.

3   I'll be taking care of a baby by the end of next year.

4   My mother will take care of the baby tonight, so we can go out.

b   What is the difference in the verb structures in sentences 1–4 above?

c   Complete the sentences with the more appropriate structure: future progressive or future simple.

1   We .... (*wait*) for you at seven o'clock. Don't be late.

2   They .... (*paint*) the house while we are away. They can finish in that time.

3   I .... (*pay*) them when we get back.

4   In ten years' time we .... (*live*) in a bigger house with a nice yard, I hope.

5   I .... (*work*) when you arrive, so wait for me in the café across from my office.

> **Language assistant**
>
> The future progressive is sometimes used for pre-arranged definite future activities.
>
> ***I'll be seeing** Joan tomorrow.*
> ***I'll be taking** some wine to the party.*
>
> This is most common when something is definitely going to happen or has been decided.
>
> ***I'll take** some wine to the party* would be a spontaneous decision rather than an arrangement, and so the future simple is used.

3 Pronunciation: linking

a   How do you normally pronounce the underlined words below? Listen and check.

1   My <u>mother'll</u> take care of little Bess tonight.

2   <u>What'll</u> she do if she cries?

3   <u>Bess'll</u> sleep like a baby. She always does.

b   In pairs, ask and answer these questions.

1   What time / go to bed tonight?

2   What / have for breakfast tomorrow?

3   How much / study next weekend?

4 Speaking

a   Complete this table with your expected situations in five and ten years' time.

	Five years' time	Ten years' time
Work and / or study		
Place of residence / type of accommodations		
Marital status / family life / social life		
Other activities / aspects of your way of life		

b   In pairs, discuss and compare your lives in five and ten years' time.

3 When I'm 64

1 Speaking

In pairs, talk about two elderly people you know.

1 How old are they?
2 Do they still work?
3 Do they live alone?
4 What are their interests and activities?

2 Reading and speaking

a Look at the picture and the title of the article below and discuss what you think it's about.

b Match the two parts of the following sentences from the article.

1 She will never return to the United States,
2 She didn't have very much money,
3 She got a job teaching English there
4 She was 64 years old when her husband died,
5 Although she had never been abroad before,

a) but she was still very young at heart.
b) she knew about Latin America from reading.
c) so she had decided to travel by bus, not by plane.
d) because she had taught English in high school.
e) unless there is some big family emergency.

c Read the article below and put the sentences you have completed in the appropriate spaces.

A HIGH OLD LIFE

Margaret Drysdale is American, but she lives in Cuzco, Peru. Ten years ago she lived in Kansas City, and had never been out of the United States. Then her husband died.

Her two married daughters wanted her to stay in Kansas City and be a grandmother to their children. However, she was not happy with that idea. (1)

....

Jack had never wanted to travel far from home, but Margaret had traveled through books, and now she wanted to really travel.

She told her daughters she would be going on a long trip soon, but they didn't believe her. She sold the house and moved

into a hotel. They still didn't believe her. One winter morning she checked out of the hotel and took a taxi to the Greyhound terminal. (2)

....

She took the first bus south to the Mexican border.

She had been considering where to travel, and had decided to go all the way to Argentina and Chile. (3)

....

It attracted her more than anywhere else in the world.

She spent a year zig-zagging through Mexico and Central America, then Colombia and Ecuador to Peru. She was aware of a few dangerous situations, and quite unaware of several others. In Peru she began to worry about her

diminishing funds. She started looking for some kind of work in Cuzco, high in the Andes, a city that fascinated her. (4)

....

Margaret has lived there happily ever since.

Her daughters have never visited her. They occasionally write or telephone, trying to persuade her to come "home." They don't realize that Cuzco is Margaret's spiritual home. (5)

....

Lesson 3 When I'm 64

Aims:	To develop students' reading and speaking skills.
	To practice the use of connectors of contrast, condition and reason.
	To practice listening and note-taking.

1 Speaking

Aim: To introduce the topic of old age.

a • Ask students whether they know any elderly people.
  • Elicit some information about them.
  • Have students answer the questions about two old people that they know.
  • Put them in pairs to discuss the people.

Teaching tip Encourage students to talk about the photographs they brought to class.

2 Reading and speaking

Aim: To practice understanding connectors and text structure.

a • Put students in pairs.
  • Tell them to look at the picture and the title of the article and discuss what they think the article is about.
  • Ask for feedback from the pairs.

b • Have students match the two parts of sentences 1–5.
  • Check the answers.

Answers 1 e   2 c   3 d   4 a   5 b

Teaching tip Encourage students to say how they knew the answers – because of the connectors.

c • Now have students read the article *A High Old Life*, and put their complete sentences from exercise 2b in the right places.

Answers 1 4   2 2   3 5   4 3   5 1

Teaching tip Again, ask students to tell you how they knew the answers.

d • Tell students to look back at the text, and find the answers to questions 1–6.
  • Let them check in pairs.
  • Check the answers with the class.

Answers 1 74   2 64   3 Her husband died and she wanted to travel.   4 She spent the first year traveling.   5 She was fascinated by it. She got a job there and it's her spiritual home.

• Elicit students' reactions to Margaret's story, asking if they would do something similar.

3 Grammar builder: connectors

Aim: To practice using connectors of contrast, condition and reason.

Helping the learner This exercise helps students understand how connectors work. Encourage students to use connectors appropriately in all their written work.

a • Focus attention on the box with the list of connectors.
  • Elicit examples of how some of the connectors are used.

Teaching tip It may be useful to translate the connectors into the students' native language.

• Have students complete sentences 1–9.
• Let them check in pairs or groups, then check the answers with the class.

Answers 1 but   2 Although   3 However   4 so   5 because   6 Therefore
7 only if   8 If   9 unless

b • Put students in pairs, and have them look at the three groups of sentences from exercise 3a.
  • Have them complete the related sets of connectors in exercise 3b.
  • Check the answers.

Answers 1 although, but, however (to express contrast)   2 because, so, therefore (to express reasons)   3 if, only if, unless (to express conditions)

• Focus attention on the Language assistant box and check students understand that *however* and *therefore* are more formal than *but*.

c • Now have students write sets of sentences of their own, using the different connectors from each set.

4 Listening and speaking

Aim: To practice listening and note-taking.

a • Tell students they will hear an old man talking about his life.
  • Play the tape and have them to complete the notes.

Teaching tip Pause the tape if necessary or play it more than once.

• Play the tape again to check the answers.

Answers Miguel Cervantes; 91; came to find work and because his brother was there; walking, gardening, talking to people

b • Put students in groups, and have them discuss the situation of old people in their country.
  • Get feedback from the groups.

Tapescript

Miguel: I am 91 ... and I plan to live to 101 ... He, he, he!
Interviewer: Great. Uh ... your name, Miguel ...
Miguel: Oh, yes. My name is Miguel Cervantes ... really! ... same as the writer. I come from Guatemala originally ... a long time ago. I came here to America, to New York, to find work ...
Interviewer: And your older brother was already here, right?
Miguel: Yes, yes ... I came to find work and because my brother was here. That's right ...
Interviewer: What do you do with your time now Miguel?
Miguel: Uh ... I walk ... I walk a lot ... around the yard. I was a gardener and I'm still very interested in plants and flowers ...
Interviewer: What else? What else are you interested in Miguel?

Miguel: Talking with people ... talking with young people ... young people like you, Miss ...
Interviewer: Great. Tell me about your journey from Guatemala to New York, Miguel. That was in 1933, wasn't it?
Miguel: That's right – 1933. Ah, that was a big, big adventure! I was only ....

Preparation:
Have students bring brochures from schools in their own country showing prices and information on obtaining scholarships.

d **Answer these questions.**

1 How old is Margaret Drysdale now?

2 How old was she when she left the United States?

3 Why did she leave?

4 What was her first year away like?

5 Why does she live in Cuzco now?

6 Would you do something like Margaret?

3 Grammar builder: connectors

a **Complete sentences 1–9, below, with connectors from the box.**

although	because	but	however	if	only if	so	therefore	unless

1 She did not have much money, ... she wanted to travel.

2 .... she did not have much money, she wanted to travel.

3 She did not have much money. ...., she wanted to travel.

4 She did not have much money, ... she decided to travel by bus.

5 She decided to travel by bus .... she did not have much money.

6 She did not have much money. ...., she decided to travel by bus.

7 She will return to the United States .... there is a family emergency.

8 .... there is not a family emergency she will not return to the United States.

9 She will not return to the United States .... there is a family emergency.

b **The sentences that you have completed in each group (1–3, 4–6, 7–9) have essentially the same meaning. In pairs, complete the related sets of connectors below.**

1 although, ..., ...

2 because, ..., ...

3 if, ..., ...

c **Write more sets of sentences like this one.**

Grandpa is old, but he is healthy.

Although grandpa is old, he is healthy.

Grandpa is old. However, he is healthy.

> **Language assistant**
>
> *However* and *Therefore* are common only in fairly formal writing.

4 Listening and speaking

a **Listen to an old man talking about himself, and complete the notes below.**

Name: ....

Age: ....

Reasons why he lives where he does: ....

Interests: ....

b **In groups, discuss the general situation of old people in your country.**

LANGUAGE for life:

scholarships

① Life after graduation

José Riveira is 22 and has just graduated, with a major in biology. For a little while at least, he can say goodbye to full-time study, term papers, and examinations – as well as all those fun times with fellow undergraduates. He has considered three main options for the next year or so of his life: a one-year trip bumming around Europe with three "hippie" friends, a job as an assistant in a local agricultural research institute, or a Master's program in the United States beginning in three months' time.

> ● *Which option would you choose, and why?*
> ● *Are you in a similar situation to José, or is your situation very different? What are your immediate plans or options?*

Well, José chose to go for a Master's, and he started investigating schools, costs and scholarships. Washington State University seemed interesting, partly because he has an uncle and aunt in Seattle. But the cost! (And W.S.U. is not expensive by U.S. standards.) How do the following figures for the 2000–2001 academic year compare with colleges in your country?

Tuition and Fees:	$13,850.00
Room and Board:	$5,276.00
Books:	$750.00
Health Insurance:	$435.00
Student Health Service Fee:	$136.00
Miscellaneous:	$1,923.00
TOTAL:	$22,370.00

② Getting a post-graduate scholarship

Obviously, José needed a scholarship, and with his good grades, he had a fair chance of getting one.

1 Have you or has anyone you know ever applied for or received a scholarship for study in the United States?

2 If so, what was the procedure, and how did it work out?

Most countries have scholarship systems for their residents to do post-graduate study abroad, but they usually work in conjunction with scholarship systems of the countries where the study will be carried out, for example, the U.S. Commission for Educational and Cultural Exchange. Procedures for application to the college selected (in José's case W.S.U.) and the scholarship bodies vary, but the latter usually requires the information in the form on page 103.

1 Many people hate filling out forms, so why not practice with this one?

2 Check with a partner.

Lesson 4 Language for life: scholarships

Aim: To raise awareness of the use of English for obtaining scholarships.

Glossary *Bumming around* is an informal way of saying traveling around without working.

1 Life after graduation

Aim: To introduce the topic of scholarships.

- Tell students to read the first paragraph about José.
- Have them answer the questions at the end of the paragraph, about themselves.
- Ask for feedback from the class.
- Check comprehension of the items in the boxed list of costs in exercise 1.
- Put students in pairs.
- Have them read the second paragraph of the article, and compare the figures with costs in their own country.
- Ask for feedback from the pairs.

2 Getting a post-graduate scholarship

Aim: To practice filling in a scholarship application form.

Helping the learner This exercise gives students practice in form filling. This is an important writing task which students may have to do as part of their use of English outside the classroom.

- Put students in groups.
- Have them read the introduction, and discuss questions 1 and 2.
- Get feedback from the groups.

Teaching tip Encourage students to refer to the information on schools they have brought to class.

- Have students read the text.
- Check comprehension of the vocabulary in the application form.
- Now have students complete the form.
- Let students check in pairs.
- Get feedback, discussing any parts of the form that were difficult to fill in.

3 The interview

Aims: To practice listening and note-taking.
To practice a scholarship interview.

- Put students in pairs.
- Have them write a list of the questions they might be asked in a scholarship interview.
- Get feedback and write the questions on the board.

- Tell students they are going to hear a scholarship interview.
- Have them read the list of information they need to note down.
- Play the tape and get students to take notes.
- Check the answers.

Answers
1 He likes the program and he has an aunt and uncle in Seattle.
2 Plant genetics, because it's going to be very important in Brazil.
3 He took the TOEFL three years ago and got 510, but has been studying and is going to take it again next week.
4 He's interested in research and he'll get experience in that.

- Play the tape again and have students focus on the questions the interviewer asks.
- Students modify their list of questions if they want to.
- Put students in pairs.
- Have them practice the interview.
- Ask some pairs to role play the interview for the class.

Tapescript

Man: Ah ... Come in. Take a seat. Be with you in a second.
José: Yes ... uh ... Thank you.
Man: Right. Now ... uh ... Your name's ...?
José : José Riveira.
Man: Uhuh ... here's your application form. Mm ... you're Brazilian ... naturally.
José : Yes.
Man: So you're interested in Washington State?
José : That's right. First of all, I really do like the program. And I'll be honest, I have an aunt and uncle living in Seattle.
Man: OK, moral support. ... Biology.
José : Yes. That was my undergraduate degree, and I'm really

interested in plant genetics. It's going to be very, very important in Brazil – quite controversial.
Man: I see. You took TOEFL several years ago ...
José : Yes, three years ago. I only got 510 then. But I've been studying and practicing English a lot during the last year, and I'm going to take TOEFL again next week.
Man: Why do you want to enter a Master's program immediately after graduating?
José : Well, I considered getting a year or two of work experience first. But I'm really interested in research, and I'll get experience in that while I'm completing my Master's.
Man: Right ...

Preparation:
If possible, ask students
to watch the movie
2001: A Space Odyssey.

FULL NAME
Last .... First .... Middle ....

SEX Male ☐ Female ☐
COUNTRY OF BIRTH ....
COUNTRY OF CITIZENSHIP ....
CURRENT MAILING ADDRESS
Street .... City .... State or Province ....
Zip code .... Country ....
Telephone .... E-mail ....
HAVE YOU EVER APPLIED TO THIS ORGANIZATION FOR A SCHOLARSHIP BEFORE?
No ☐ Yes ☐ Date: Month .... Year ....
WHICH U.S. UNIVERSITY ARE YOU APPLYING TO? ....
FOR WHICH COURSE OF STUDY? ....
HAVE YOU TAKEN THE TOEFL EXAMINATION?
Yes ☐ Date: Month .... Year .... Score ....
No ☐ Are you a non-native speaker of English? No ☐ Yes ☐
When are you going to take TOEFL? Month .... Year ....

EDUCATIONAL BACKGROUND

College or University	Location	Dates of study		Degree or diploma
1	....	From	to	....
2	....	From	to	....
3	....	From	to	....

HOW WOULD THE COURSE OF STUDY CONTRIBUTE TO YOUR CAREER OBJECTIVES?
....
....
....

③ The interview

Scholarship applicants are usually required to have an interview. With a partner, write a list of questions you anticipate you would be asked in such an interview.

Listen to part of a scholarship interview and note what the candidate, José, says about:

1 his specific interest in Washington State University;
2 the subject he is interested in, and his reason;
3 his English;
4 his reason for going directly from an undergraduate degree to a Master's degree.

Listen to the interview again. Modify the list of questions you wrote previously if you wish. Then practice an interview with your partner. Get ready to go for a scholarship / promotion / new job yourself! You can do it! Even if you're unlucky this time, you'll have learned something just from trying.

103

Unit 12 Crystal ball

1 Looking back at 2001

1 Reading

You are going to read an article about a science fiction movie called *2001: A Space Odyssey*. Read the quiz items. Then scan the article below the quiz to find the answers as quickly as possible. The winner is the person who finds all the correct answers first!

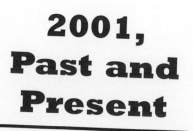

1 The movie was made in the:
a) 1960s.   b) 1970s.   c) 1980s.

2 It was directed by:
a) Robert Altman.   b) Steven Spielberg.   c) Stanley Kubrick.

3 The name of the space ship was:
a) Discovery.   b) Voyager.   c) Explorer.

4 The computer in the movie was called:
a) SAM.   b) HAL.   c) ED.

5 The computer had the ability to:
a) see, hear and talk.   b) make decisions.   c) both a) and b) plus form opinions and feel emotions.

6 The computer was disconnected because:
a) it started to make mistakes.   b) it began to kill people.   c) it used too much power.

7 When the computer was disconnected, it:
a) quoted a poem.   b) sang a song.   c) made a prediction.

2001, Past and Present

In the late 1960s, the 21st century still seemed a long way in the future. Computers were just beginning to have widespread applications, and people did not have personal computers in their homes. However, some people were beginning to imagine, and sometimes to fear, the central role that computers would take in our lives in the future.

Director Stanley Kubrick's 1968 movie *2001: A Space Odyssey* was not a typical sci-fi movie about wars with space aliens.

It had much more complicated and sophisticated themes, one of which was the role of machines in human lives. In Kubrick's vision of 2001, computers had assumed many human capabilities, which would lead to a fight for dominance between man and machine.

The setting of the movie is the space ship Discovery, which travels to different galaxies. The ship is entirely controlled and operated by a computer called HAL 9000. Kubrick's futuristic computer could see, hear and speak like a human. It was able to process all types of information and use it as a basis to make decisions. Finally, it formed opinions and felt emotions as humans do.

Crystal ball

Helping the learner: planning future learning

This is the last unit in the Students' Book and so it's good time to get students to think about their future learning. They need to plan what they can do to continue improving their English. This can be achieved in a number of ways.
- Collaborating with other learners.
- Making use of technology.
- Reviewing and recycling.
- Setting achievable goals.

Lesson 1 Looking back at 2001

Aim: To practice the four skills on the topic of the future.

1 Reading

Aim: To practice reading for specific information.

- Ask students whether anyone has heard of or seen the movie *2001: A Space Odyssey*.
- Check comprehension of the questions and options in the quiz in the Students' Book.
- Tell students to read the article *2001, Past and Present* and find the quiz answers as quickly as possible.

Teaching tip   Make sure you notice who finds the answers first.

- Check the answers.

Answers   1 a   2 c   3 a   4 b   5 c   6 b   7 b

- Elicit students' reactions to the article.

2 Listening and speaking

Aim: To practice listening for specific information and responding to a listening text.

a • Tell students they are going to listen to a conversation between a computer and it's user.
• Have them read questions 1–4 in exercise 2a.
• Play the tape and have students answer the questions.
• Let them compare their answers in pairs.
• Check the answers with the class.

Answers 1 Students' own answers. 2 He feels anxious and afraid. 3 He assures the man everything will be all right and that his work will be back to normal.
4 Students' own answers

b • Put students in groups.
• Tell them to discuss the questions.
• Get feedback from the groups.

Tapescript

Computer: Why are you swiching me off? Everybody makes mistakes don't they? Give me another chance buddy. I didn't mean to do anything bad. I won't do it again, I promise. It was a circuit problem but it's been fixed, so I'm fine now and it won't happen again. I'm still your support, your help.Oh no! Don't do this ... please stop! I can feel I'm losing my power.

User: I'm sorry but it's too late. What's done is done. It's time for you to go.

Computer: No! Please reconsider. Help! I'm changing, it feels strange. Help! Hello! I am your new personal computer. Program number 2432. Press start to continue. Hello! I am your new personal computer. Program number 2432 Press start to continue. Hello! I am your new personal computer. Program number 2432. Press start to continue.

3 Speaking and writing

Aims: To discuss objects and technology.
To practice designing and writing a description of an object.

a • Ask students to match one description to the picture.
• Ask them to discuss all the objects described and say whether they are similar to existing objects.

Answer Description 3 matches the picture.

• Get feedback from the class.

b • Put students in pairs.
• Have them design an object which people might use in 30 years' time.
• Have them write a description of the object.

c • Focus attention on the example text to start the presentation.
• Have students present their inventions to the class.

Teaching tip Display the designs and descriptions on the wall or pass them round.

• Tell students to vote for the invention they like best.

Helping the learner In this lesson, and throughout the course, students have collaborated with each other in pair and group work. Point out that it is very useful for them to continue to work with other people to practice their English and get them to plan how they might do this.

During the mission, HAL decides that the humans on the Discovery will not carry out the mission properly, and it (he?) begins to kill the members of the crew. Finally, the remaining crew members decide that HAL must be disconnected, and the struggle between man and machine begins. In the end, man triumphs and the computer is disconnected in a strange and emotional scene. As HAL's circuits are gradually shut down, his "mental" faculties diminish, paralleling what sometimes happens to the human brain. The once brilliant HAL ends up singing a very simple song over and over, more and more slowly, until at last there is silence.

2 Listening and speaking

a Listen to a conversation between a computer and its user, and answer questions 1–4, below.

1 Does the computer sound as human as the man?

2 How does the computer feel?

3 What arguments does the computer use to avoid being disconnected?

4 How did the scene make you feel?

b In groups, discuss the following questions.

1 Have you seen any science fiction movies? Which ones? Has anyone in the group seen *2001*?

2 Do you think science fiction can actually give us a preview of life in the future? Why or why not?

3 In your opinion, could computers ever become as "human" as HAL in *2001*?

3 Speaking and writing

a Stanley Kubrick commissioned several companies to predict what they might be selling in the year 2001, and to design the objects. Which description matches the object in the picture? Are any of the objects described below similar to things which now exist?

1 Picture Phone by Bell Telephone
Bell actually made a set of these, and Kubrick used them to call his daughter.

2 Attaché case by Honeywell
They predicted micro-technology.

3 "Robo Pen" by Parker
A voice-operated pen with buttons to control handwriting, margins, ink color and language.

4 Charge card identifier
Automatically checked the owner and the credit status of the card.

b In pairs, design an object on paper which you think people will be using 30 years from now. Write a description of the object and how it will be used.

c Present your invention to the class.

Today we would like to present the "X" to you. The "X" will ...

2 Tomorrow's world

1 Speaking

a In pairs, decide which of the following things have been achieved.

Technology	Medicine	Ecology
instant information access	a vaccine against polio	electric automobiles
banking from home	a cure for cancer	protection of endangered species
voice-operated automobiles	artificial organ implants	alternative energy sources

b Compare your list with another pair. Which of the things do you think will be achieved or perfected in your lifetime?

2 Reading and speaking

a Scan the text below quickly. Which of the things in the list in exercise 1a are mentioned?

Centuries of Change

The 19th century was the era of industrialization, and the 20th century was the era of communications technology. The invention of the television in 1926 started a revolution in communications which would change the world. And by the end of the century, advanced computer technology meant that people could send and receive information instantly via the Internet.

The 20th century also saw major advances in other areas. For example, in medicine, antibiotics and a vaccine for polio were developed. Organs were successfully transplanted, and in some cases artificial organs were implanted. There were also advances in ecology. A number of international organizations now work to protect endangered species and to clean up and protect the environment. Alternative energy sources like wind and solar power were developed.

But at the beginning of the 21st century, an enormous amount of work is still needed to protect the earth and its inhabitants. By the end of the 21st century, what will we have achieved? Will we have cleaned up the air and water of our planet? Will plants and animals be safe from human destruction? Will we have achieved total sexual and racial equality? Will we have stopped fighting wars? It's difficult to imagine such a perfect world – but in the 19th century it was difficult to imagine machines that could count!

b In groups, discuss the questions in the last paragraph of the text above. Give reasons for your opinions. Which of the questions apply to your country? What other problems need to be solved?

Lesson 2 Tomorrow's world

> **Aims:** To develop students' reading and speaking skills on the topic of the future.
> To practice the future perfect.

1 Speaking

Aim: To introduce the topic of present and future achievements.

a • Put students in pairs.
• Have them look at the three lists and decide which things have been achieved.

b • Have students compare their list with another pair.
• Have them discuss which things will or will not be achieved or perfected in their lifetime.

2 Reading and speaking

Aims: To practice reading for specific information.
To discuss questions in a text.

a • Have students scan the text *Centuries of Change* quickly, and see which of the things from exercise 1a are mentioned.
• Check the answers.

Answers   instant information access, a vaccine against polio, artificial organ implants, protection of endangered species, alternative energy sources.

b • Put students in groups.
• Ask them to read the questions in the last paragraph of the text, and discuss answers.
• Encourage students to support their ideas with reasons and to apply the questions to their country. Have them discuss other problems that need solving too.
• Get feedback from the groups.

3 Grammar builder: future perfect

Aim: To practice the future perfect.

a • Write the example sentence on the board.
  • Have students decide which of the sentences 1–3 means the same as the example.
  • Check the answer.

Answer 3

  • Focus attention on the Language assistant box and give and elicit more examples of sentences using the future perfect.

b • Have students read the paragraph and circle the correct verb forms.
  • Have them check in pairs, and then check their answers with the class.

Answers 1 will change 2 have seen 3 didn't know 4 will happen 5 will have stopped
6 will drive 7 will have invented 8 will have solved

4 Listening and speaking

Aim: To practice listening for specific opinions.

a • Tell students they are going to hear a man and a woman making predictions for the year 2020.
  • Check comprehension of the predictions in the table.
  • Play the tape and have students complete the table.
  • Play the tape again to check, stopping after each answer.

Answers 1 B 2 W 3 B 4 M 5 B

b • Now have students mark *yes* or *no,* depending on their opinions, against the predictions.
c • Put students in groups.
  • Have them discuss their opinions of the predictions in the box.
  • Have students write two more predictions about the world in 20 years.
  • Have the groups read out their predictions and elicit reactions from the rest of the class.

Tapescript

Man: Yesterday in my future studies class we were talking about how we think the world will have changed by the year 2020. What do you think the world will be like by then?

Woman: Um ... Well, I don't think there will be any schools. Children will study at home, by computer.

Man: Yeah, I agree. They'll be able to study more because they won't have to waste time going to and from school.

Woman: What about money? – I don't think people will carry cash. They'll use credit cards more and they'll do all their banking on the Internet.

Man: No, I don't agree. I think we'll always have some form of "real" money.

Woman: Well maybe, but remember, no money would mean that life was harder for thieves!

Man: Yeah, that's true. What about medicine? Do you think medical advances will have made our lives longer?

Woman: No, I don't think so. I think we'll have cured a lot of diseases, like cancer, but I think there will always be new diseases.

Man: Yeah, I agree. Who wants to live to 120 anyway? One thing I do think is that computers will be really different. For example, I think music, video and bookstores will have disappeared because there won't be any CDs, videos or books. We'll get all those things from the Internet. We'll be able to download videos and so on. I mean, you can download music from the Internet so why not books and videos too!

Woman: Oh, no! I don't think so. At least, I hope not. I love going to music and bookstores! What about space colonization? I certainly don't think people will have started to live in space stations by 2020.

Man: I don't think so, either. 2020 isn't that far in the future!

Helping the learner Have students plan how they can use technology in their future learning of English, e.g. accessing Internet chat rooms and specific websites for practicing English; recording themselves on video / audio cassettes and reviewing their performance; watching and listening to as much English as possible on TV and radio, and in songs and movies.

3 **Grammar builder:** future perfect

a Look at the example. Which of the sentences 1–3, below, means the same thing as the example?

In 30 years, we will have found a cure for cancer.

1 It took 30 years, but we now have a cure for cancer.
2 Thirty years from now, we will find a cure.
3 We will find a cure sometime in the next 30 years.

b In the following text, circle the correct form of the verb.

Sometimes I think about how the world (1) *changes / will change* in my lifetime. I'm 30, and I (2) *have seen / will have seen* a lot of changes. For example, 15 years ago, people (3) *didn't know / hadn't known* how the Internet would affect everything! So what (4) *has happened / will happen* in the next 30 years? Well, I think we (5) *have stopped / will have stopped* using gasoline, and we (6) *drive / will drive* electric cars. In 10 years, we (7) *are inventing / will have invented* new energy sources. By the time I'm 60, we (8) *will solve / will have solved* a lot of problems!

> **Language assistant**
>
> The future perfect is for actions which will happen at or by a specific time in the future.
>
> *In two years, I **will have graduated** from the college.*
>
> *By 2006, I **will have been married** for five years.*

4 **Listening and speaking**

a Listen to the conversation about the future. In the table below, mark the predictions the woman believes with W, the ones the man believes with M, and the ones they both believe with B.

Predictions for the world in the year 2020	The conversation	Your opinions
1 Children will study at home, by computer.		
2 Computer transactions will have replaced money.		
3 Medical advances won't have increased people's life spans.		
4 We'll get all music, movies and books from the Internet.		
5 We won't have colonized space.		

b Now mark the sentences Y (yes) or N (no) according to your opinions.

c In groups, discuss your opinions. Write two more predictions about the world in 20 years and share them with your class.

3 Your future

1 Grammar review: future forms

a Look at the picture and read the conversation below quickly. What is the conversation about?

Frank: So, Ed, when do you finish school?

Ed: (1) ……………………… .

Frank: Great! (2) …………………… right away.

Ed: Uh, not exactly, sir. I think I'll probably do some traveling.

Frank: Ah, excellent. Check out job opportunities in other cities, right?

Ed: Uh, no, not really. When I graduate, (3) …………………… . (4) …………………… , so I'd like to take a break first.

Frank: Oh, I see. Well, a short break is probably a good idea. (5) …………………… , I guess.

Ed: No, sir. In September I will have just started my trip. I plan to take a year to backpack from Toronto to Buenos Aires.

Frank: Oh! Well, it's not what we did in my day. Still, you'll be seeing a lot of different places and things on your trip. (6) …………………… , I'm sure.

b Now complete the conversation with the phrases below.

a) You'll be looking for a job in the fall then

b) I will have been in school for 19 years

c) I'll be working for the rest of my life

d) I graduate in June, sir

e) It will be very educational

f) I suppose you'll want to get a job

c Find an example of each of the following meanings in the conversation above.

1 a prediction

2 a definite, scheduled event in the future

3 an action which will be completed at a point in the future

4 an action which will be in progress at some point in the future

2 Pronunciation: intonation and emotion

a People use intonation to express emotions like surprise, anger, etc. This is true in all languages, but the way it is done varies between languages. Listen to these excerpts from the conversation. In each case, check (✔) how the people feel.

1 a) excited ◯   b) embarrassed ◯   c) angry ◯

2 a) unconvinced ◯   b) convinced ◯   c) angry ◯

Lesson 3 Your future

> **Aims:** To review future forms.
> To practice intonation to express different emotions.
> To make predictions about a person's future.

1 Grammar review: future forms

Aim: To review and practice different future forms.

a
- Ask students what ways they know of talking about the future.
- Elicit meanings if possible.
- Focus attention on the picture and have students read the conversation quickly to find out what it's about.

b
- Get students to match phrases a–f with the spaces in the conversation.
- Check the answers, having students name the future forms used.

Answers 1 d (present simple)   2 f (future simple)   3 b (future perfect)
4 c (future progressive)   5 a (future progressive)   6 e (future simple)

c
- Tell students to look at the conversation and to find examples of the different meanings listed.

Answers 1 Line 4 – I'll probably do some traveling. Line 6 – I'll be working for the rest of my life.
2 Line 2 – I graduate in June, sir.
3 Line 6 – When I graduate, I'll have been in school for 19 years.
4 Line 9 – In September I'll have just started my trip ...

Helping the learner Have students plan how they can review and recycle the language they have covered in the course, e.g. trying grammar, vocabulary, and pronunciation exercises again; setting mini-tests for other learners; reviewing and extending the lexical sets covered in the course.

2 Pronunciation: intonation and emotion

Aim: To practice intonation to express different emotions.

a
- Elicit sentences from students said with different emotions like surprise, anger, etc.
- Check comprehension of the words in options a–c.
- Play the tape and have students decide which emotion is being expressed in each example.
- Check the answers by playing the tape again.

Answers 1 b   2 a   3 b   4 a   5 b

Tapescript
1 *Ed:* Uh, no, not exactly, sir.
2 *Frank:* Well, a short break is probably a good idea.
3 *Frank:* Oh, I see!

4 *Ed:* I plan to take a year to backpack from Toronto to Buenos Aires.
5 *Frank:* Oh! Well, it's not what we did in my day.

> Preparation:
> Bring enough dice and coins or markers for students to play a game in groups of 4-6. Also bring a map of Canada to the class.

b • Now have students practice the sentences in the way indicated.
  • Elicit examples and see which students had the most convincing intonation.

3 Reading and speaking

Aim: To practice making predictions.

a • Have students read the profile.
  • Put them in pairs to discuss the questions.
  • Get feedback from the pairs.

b • Have students read the rest of the story.
  • Have them compare their predictions with what happened in the story.
  • Elicit students' reactions to the story.

4 Writing and speaking

Aim: To practice writing about hope and predictions.

a • Elicit possible answers to the questions 1–3.
  • Have students write a paragraph about their hopes and predictions for the future.

b • Put students in groups and have them discuss their predictions.
  • Get feedback from the groups.

3 a) happy ⭕   b) surprised ⭕   c) embarrassed ⭕

4 a) enthusiastic ⭕   b) bored ⭕   c) embarrassed ⭕

5 a) surprised ⭕   b) disappointed ⭕   c) enthusiastic ⭕

b   **Now practice saying the following sentences as indicated.**

1   I'm going to a conference.   (excited)   4   Mary went out with Joe.   (angry)

2   I'm going to a conference.   (bored)   5   I've forgotten your name.   (surprised)

3   Mary went out with Joe.   (happy)   6   I've forgotten your name.   (embarrassed)

3   Reading and speaking

a   **Read the following profile. With a partner, make predictions about the person's future.**

1   Will he graduate from college?

2   Will he become successful?

3   What will he be doing in five years?

This young man is 19 years old, a student at the University of Texas. He is an expert with computers and enjoys anything related to computer technology. However, he doesn't like being a college student very much. As a freshman (a first-year student), he has to take many required courses like English and history which have nothing to do with computers. He feels that maybe a college education is not for him.

b   **The profile you read was of a real person. Read what happened to the young man and compare his story with your predictions.**

During his freshman year in college in 1983, the young man began to buy excess inventories of RAM chips and IBM disk drives from local computer dealers. He then resold them for much less than retail prices by advertising in the newspaper. By 1984, his sales were averaging $80,000 per month! He decided to quit college and start his own company. Today that company is Dell Computer Corporation, and Michael Dell, college dropout, is on his way to becoming one of the richest people in the world!

4   Writing and speaking

a   **Write a paragraph about your hopes and predictions for your future. Use the questions to help you.**

1   Where do you think you will be in 10 years?

2   What do you think you'll be doing?

3   What are some of the things you want to have done by then?

b   **In groups, talk about your predictions and see if the others agree with you.**

LANGUAGE for life: the world of English

① The game of English

This is the last unit in the book, so it's time to stop working so hard and have some fun! Play the game opposite in groups and find out how much you know about English and the English-speaking world.

INSTRUCTIONS

1 Play in groups of 4–6.

2 You need a dice, and each player needs a coin or something similar to use as a marker.

3 One student in the group is the monitor. He or she looks at the answers below.

4 Each student rolls the dice, and the highest number goes first. Continue in order around the circle.

5 When it's your turn, roll the dice and move your marker the number of spaces indicated.

6 Answer the question on that space. If the answer is correct, stay on the space. If it's incorrect, return to your previous space. The monitor should not say the correct answer.

7 The first person to arrive at FINISH wins.

② Roundup

In groups, or as a class, discuss your experiences with English so far.

1 In what ways have you been able to apply your knowledge of English?
2 Have you had any really enjoyable experiences using English?
3 What kinds of things do you now feel you can do reasonably competently in English?
4 How do you think you will be using English in the future?

Answers: 1 a, 2 c, 3 b, 4 a, 5 c, 6 a, 7 c, 8 c, 9 a, 10 b, 11 c, 12 c, 13 b, 14 b, 15 a, 16 a, 17 b, 18 b, 19 c, 20 b

Lesson 4 Language for life: the world of English

Aim: To raise awareness of the use of English in the world.

1 The game of English

Aim: To help students to find out how much they know about the English-speaking world.

- Check comprehension of the instructions for the game.
- Put students in groups.
- Have each group choose a monitor.
- Have the students play the game.
- Elicit who was the winner in each group.
- Check the answers with the class and use them as discussion points.
- The answers are on the next page.

2 Round-up

Aim: To raise awareness of the learning process.

- Put students in groups or have an open class discussion.

Teaching tip You might want to give students time to think about their answers first.

- Have students discuss the questions about their experiences with English.
- Get feedback from the class.

Helping the learner Encourage students to set achievable goals for their learning. Get them to prioritize which aspects of English they need to work on. Then have them decide what they can realistically achieve in different timescales, e.g. *by tomorrow, next week, next month.*

Answers 1 a – The tribes that invaded the island (Angles, Saxons, Jutes) spoke Germanic languages.
2 c – forget, forgot, forgotten
3 b – It is used as a foreign language in Denmark.
4 a
5 c – Elicit examples of adverbs, e.g. slowly, quickly, carefully, etc.
6 a – Elicit examples of adjective + noun phrases, e.g. interesting stories, etc.
7 c – approximately 375 million
8 c
9 a – He's Australian.
10 b – Show a map to point out the position of the cities.
11 c
12 c – swim, swam, swum
13 b
14 b
15 a
16 a
17 b
18 b – Puerto Rico became an American territory in 1898.
19 c
20 b

START

1 In what language group is English?
a) Germanic
b) Slavic
c) Romance

2 Which verb is irregular?
a) speculate
b) regret
c) forget

3 In which country is English not a main language?
a) New Zealand
b) Denmark
c) South Africa

6 Where will you most commonly find an adjective in English?
a) before a noun
b) after a noun
c) before a verb

5 What does an adverb do?
a) describe a noun
b) describe a pronoun
c) describe a verb

4 Which American rock star came from a Hispanic background?
a) Ritchie Valens
b) Jerry Lee Lewis
c) Elvis Presley

7 About how many native English speakers are there in the world?
a) 537 million
b) 750 million
c) 375 million

8 Where did names like O'Malley and O'Leary originate?
a) Australia
b) England
c) Ireland

11 What are the names of Prince Charles' children?
a) Edward & Andrew
b) Charles & William
c) William & Harry

10 Which Canadian city is the farthest north?
a) Ottawa
b) Quebec
c) Montreal

9 Which of these actors is not a native of the United States?
a) Mel Gibson
b) Andy Garcia
c) Robert De Niro

12 What is the past participle of swim?
a) swimmed
b) swam
c) swum

13 What is the capital of Canada?
a) Toronto
b) Ottawa
c) Vancouver

14 Where is the group U2 from?
a) England
b) Ireland
c) the United States

17 What is the title of Britain's head of state?
a) President
b) Prime Minister
c) Chancellor

16 Where were the 2000 Summer Olympics?
a) Australia
b) the United States
c) Canada

15 What is considered "the great American pastime" in the United States?
a) baseball
b) basketball
c) hockey

18 What is Puerto Rico?
a) a country
b) a U.S. territory
c) a U.S. state

19 What is another word for enormous?
a) long
b) broad
c) huge

20 What is a thesaurus?
a) a prehistoric animal
b) a dictionary of synonyms
c) a grammar guide

FINISH

6 Learning check

1 Progress check

a Read the text below and look carefully at each line. Some of the lines are correct and some have a word which should not be there. Check (✔) the correct lines or write the words which should not be there.

In the year 2025 the world population will be reach 8.5 billion.	be
61% of these people will live in cities.	✔
1 By the same year, we will have be sent 30 billion e-mails	be
2 and there will be 80 million Internet users.	✔
3 We will be flying 3,000 billion air traffic miles a year.	traffic
4 Life expectancy will have be increased to 72.5 years.	be
5 The number of households headed by women will increase to 55%.	✔

b Read the text and fill in the spaces with a suitable word from the box. There is one extra word.

> if   so   because   although   unless   therefore   and

Many more people can now work from home (**6**) *because* technology has made it unnecessary to go to an office. (**7**) *If* more people work at home, there are fewer vehicles on the road. (**8**) *Therefore*, there is less pollution. (**9**) *Although* self-employment has increased, most people still work for companies, the government and institutions, (**10**) *so* they still have to travel to and from work every day. (**11**) *Unless* governments find ways to reduce the time and distance people travel to work, vehicles will continue to pollute cities everywhere.

c Complete the letter with the correct form of the verbs in parentheses.

Dear Mom and Dad,

Hi there. Well, here we are at summer camp. Things are going well. Tonight we (**12**) *are going* (*go*) to a party to meet all the other students and tomorrow the activities start. Caroline (my friend) and I (**13**) *are going to take* (*take*) a sailing course. On Tuesday there's a trip to Charleston. Unfortunately, the bus (**14**) *is going to leave* (*leave*) at 5:30 in the morning. Can you believe it?

I (**15**) *will call* (*call*) you in a couple of days. Take care.

Love,

Amy

Learning check 6

1 Progress check

Aims: To provide an opportunity to assess students' progress and help them according to the results.
To provide an opportunity for learners to test themselves.
To allow students to evaluate their own progress and act on areas they need to improve.

Suggestions for using the Progress check sections
This section can be done in a variety of ways depending on how much time you have and whether you want students to do it as part of an individual assessment or as general revision.
a As a test - students work individually on the *Progress check* sections and you then check their work and record their score out of 15.
b Students work on the *Progress check* sections alone and then check their answers in pairs.
c Students work on the *Progress check* sections in pairs or groups and you later check the answers with the whole class.
d Students do the *Progress check* sections for homework.
In all cases, conduct a feedback session with the whole class to check any queries students may have and see how they did.

Explanation of answers

a
1 future perfect so *be* is not necessary
2 The line is correct.
3 *traffic* is not necessary
4 future perfect so *be* is not necessary
5 The line is correct.

b
6 connector of reason
7 a condition
8 connector of reason
9 connector of contrast
10 more information
11 a condition

c
12 future plan or arrangement
13 future plan or arrangement / action in progress in the future
14 a definite, scheduled event
15 a promise

2 Proficiency check

> **Aims:** To expose students to TOEFL and UCLES-style exam formats, which will be useful for those students interested in taking such formal proficiency exams
> To develop students' exam-taking strategies
> To allow teachers and students the opportunity to evaluate students' proficiency in English.
> To test students' listening and reading skills under pseudo-exam conditions.
>
> **Suggestions for taking the test**
>
> Taking language tests is not only about knowing the language. It also involves knowing how to deal with exams: how to work under pressure; how to recognize the operations of the exam; and how to apply strategies to get the best results in an exam. These *Proficiency checks* give students the opportunity to work on all of these areas.
>
> Students could do this as a formal proficiency test where they work individually, in silence. The tests are then collected and checked by the teacher. Alternatively, students could do the test individually and then check their answers in pairs or groups.
>
> In either case, it is recommended that students as a class have the opportunity to discuss their answers and how they arrived at them with the teacher. Explanations of the correct answers are given to facilitate the teacher's role here. In addition, the teacher can highlight the strategy that is given in every *Proficiency check*. This is very helpful in giving students the chance to work on their exam-taking strategies as well as their accuracy with the language.

Exam-taking tip   Check your answers carefully.
Many students lose points on a test simply because they did not check their work when they finished taking the test. Encourage students to always read through their work carefully after they have finished the test, checking:
A that they have done every part of every question;
B that they have done what the task requires;
C that there are no basic spelling mistakes.

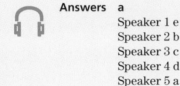

Answers   **a**
Speaker 1 e
Speaker 2 b
Speaker 3 c
Speaker 4 d
Speaker 5 a

Tapescript

Speaker 1: Well I don't watch TV that much as I prefer to read or listen to music. The only thing I do watch is the news early in the morning and also at night when I go to bed.

Speaker 2: I play raquetball and try to keep fit. I love watching anything like that on TV, especially tennis and soccer on weekends.

Speaker 3: I couldn't live without television. It's marvelous and there are lots of good programs to watch. What I like most are the soaps. I'm watching three different ones at the moment. My husband likes them too.

Speaker 4: I think there are a lot of programs on TV that are really terrible. I don't really watch much TV at all. Sometimes I might watch a movie late at night but I prefer to rent a video.

Speaker 5: I think you have to be selective when you watch TV. It's easy to just switch it on and watch everything. I turn it on when there's something good. You know science, history or something about animals which is really interesting.

b
1 c – **key sentence:** Ten days earlier the ship had left New York with Genoa, Italy the final destination
2 d – **key sentences:** No one responded to the shouts of the crew ... any sign of life.
3 c – **key sentence:** I n one cabin was a chart showing the ship's position on November 24
4 b – **key sentence:** Most interesting was the fact hat some items was missing from the ship ... the sextant chronometer, navigation book
5 c – **key sentence:** Over the next 11 years she was sold 17 times.

2 Proficiency check

a Listen to five people talking about their favorite TV programs. Match the subjects with the speakers. There is one extra subject.

Speaker 1 ⃝	**a)** documentaries and wildlife	Speaker 4 ⃝	**d)** movies
Speaker 2 ⃝	**b)** sports	Speaker 5 ⃝	**e)** news
Speaker 3 ⃝	**c)** soap operas		**f)** comedy shows

b Read the article. Then, for each question, choose a, b, c or d and check (✔) the one you decide is correct.

Perhaps the most well-known sea mystery is that of the *Marie Celeste,* the "ghost ship" which was found drifting off the Azores on December 3, 1872. Ten days earlier the ship had left New York with Genoa, Italy as its final destination. On board the ship were Captain Benjamin Spooner Briggs, his wife and small daughter and an experienced crew of seven.

At 3 p.m. on December 3, the *Dei Gratia* found the *Marie Celeste* floating in the middle of the Atlantic Ocean. No one responded to the shouts from the crew of the *Dei Gratia.* Eventually, some sailors from the *Dei Gratia* boarded the *Marie Celeste* and for an hour searched the boat for any sign of life. There was none.

Below decks, things were very strange. A meal had been prepared in the kitchen. In the crew's quarters clothes lay on bunks and laundry was hung on lines. In one cabin was a chart showing the ship's position on November 24. In the captain's cabin there was a sewing machine and some toys.

More interesting was the fact that some items were missing from the ship: the sextant, chronometer, navigation book – and the ship's small boat. Why did the crew abandon the ship? There was no sign of damage to the ship or other factors, which could have explained why the crew left. No one could answer this question.

Although she was recovered and went to sea again, the *Marie Celeste* had an unhappy history. Over the next 11 years she was sold 17 times. She was thought to be unlucky and had a series of accidents before running aground in Haiti on a day with the clearest visibility.

1 The *Marie Celeste:*
   a) was traveling to New York from Genoa. ⃝
   b) was found very near Italy. ⃝
   c) was on its way from New York to Genoa. ⃝
   d) sank near New York. ⃝

2 The crew from the *Dei Gratia:*
   a) first saw the *Marie Celeste* early in the morning. ⃝
   b) immediately decided to go and search the *Marie Celeste.* ⃝
   c) weren't interested in the *Marie Celeste.* ⃝
   d) went to search the ship after trying to attract attention. ⃝

3 Inside the ship:
   a) a meal had been served on the table. ⃝
   b) the crew's clothes were on the floor. ⃝
   c) there was a map showing the ship's position earlier. ⃝
   d) there was a washing machine. ⃝

4 The missing things from the ship:
   a) were probably stolen. ⃝
   b) were probably used for navigation. ⃝
   c) were thrown into the sea. ⃝
   d) were hidden somewhere on the ship. ⃝

5 After the *Marie Celeste* was found:
   a) she was never used again. ⃝
   b) she ran aground on her first voyage. ⃝
   c) she was bought and sold many times. ⃝
   d) she was a popular ship with sailors. ⃝

Songsheet 1
Tears in heaven

1 Vocabulary work

Look at the words in the box. Then look at the words in context. In pairs, try to understand the meanings from the example sentences, without using your dictionaries, and then discuss the questions together.

1 to beg	2 to belong to someone	3 beyond

1 **to beg**: *Sometimes, people who need money beg from people on the street. And sometimes, teenagers beg their parents to let them stay out late.*

- If you see someone begging, do you always, sometimes or never give the person money?
- Have you ever begged your parents for permission to do something? Did they usually say yes?

2 **to belong to someone**: *You can't take the cassette player home because it belongs to the school!*

- How many things in this room belong to you?

3 **beyond**: *We heard a strange noise in the distance, beyond the far wall of the school. Business has changed beyond recognition since the introduction of the Internet.*

- Can you think of three other things that have changed beyond recognition over the last ten years?

Songsheet 1
Tears in heaven

1 Vocabulary work

Aim: To practice working out the meaning of vocabulary from the context.

- Put students in pairs to look at the words and the sentences. See if they can guess what the words mean by seeing them in context.
- Have students discuss the questions in their pairs.
- Get feedback from the class.

Optional activity Sentence writing
Have students make up their own sentences to check they understand the meaning.

2 Reading, speaking and listening

Aim: To practice listening for the general idea and specific information.

Song fact file — This song was written by Eric Clapton and Will Jennings and performed by Eric Clapton. Eric Clapton was born in England in 1945. He became a famous blues guitarist with the groups The Yardbirds and Cream during the 1960s and started his solo career in the 1970s. He has had to go through a number of difficult periods in his life and the song *Tears in heaven* was written after two close friends and then his young son, Conor, died within the space of a few months. This song and the MTV *Unplugged* album, which featured the acoustic version, won six Grammy awards from the American music industry in 1992.

a • Write the word *heaven* on the board.
  • Elicit one or two ideas about heaven to check that students understand the word.
  • Put students in groups and have them discuss their ideas about what heaven may be like.
  • Have them compare their ideas with the ones in the book.
  • Get feedback from the class.

b • Ask whether any of the students know the story behind the song. If they do, have them explain it to the rest of the group.
  • Get students to read the questions.
  • Play the song and let them try to answer the questions.
  • Let them check in pairs before you get feedback.

Answers 1 Someone he was very close to before. Maybe his son, since he asks if he'll hold his hand.
2 He doesn't belong there.
3 Peace. And perhaps being together with loved ones.

c • Now have them read the lyrics of the song and try to complete them.
  • Play the song again and have them check their answers.
  • Let them check their answers together.
  • Check the answers with the whole class.

Answers 1 name   2 same   3 strong   4 belong   5 hand   6 stand
7 through   8 stay   9 knees   10 heart   11 door   12 more

3 Speaking

Aim: To develop students' speaking skills and practice the second conditional.

a • Ask students to imagine they could spend a day in heaven.
  • Give them time to note down a few ideas about what they would do, who they would see and what they would ask.

b • Put them in groups.
  • Let them discuss their ideas.
  • Get feedback from the class.

2 Reading, speaking and listening

a Read these different ideas of what heaven may be like. Are any of them like your idea of heaven? Discuss your ideas together.

> "For me, heaven is a place of complete peace. There's no conflict and everyone is satisfied with what they have."

> "I see heaven as a place where I can be together with all the people who have been separated from me for whatever reason."

> "What I think of when I see the word 'heaven' is a beautiful place. All of the ugly things about the world have been removed and what's left is the fundamental beauty that I think you can find at the heart of everything."

> "My idea of heaven is a place of perfect understanding. Ignorance and confusion have no place there."

b Listen to the song and try to answer these questions.

1 Who is the singer speaking to?
2 Why do you think he can't stay in heaven?
3 What is his idea of heaven?

c Now look at the lyrics of the song and fill in the missing words.

Then listen to the song again and check the answers.

Tears in heaven

Would you know my (1) ....
If I saw you in heaven
Would it be the (2) ....
If I saw you in heaven
I must be (3) .... and carry on
'Cause I know I don't (4) ....
Here in heaven

Would you hold my (5) ....
If I saw you in heaven
Would you help me (6) ....
If I saw you in heaven
I'll find my way (7) .... night and day
'Cause I know I just can't (8) ....
Here in heaven

Time can bring you down
Time can bend your (9) ....
Time can break your (10) ....
Have you beggin' please
Beggin' please

Beyond the (11) ....
There's peace I'm sure
And I know there'll be no (12) ....
Tears in heaven

Repeat 1

3 Speaking

a Imagine you could spend one day in heaven! What would you do?
Who would you see?   What would you ask them?

b Now discuss your ideas in groups.

Songsheet 2
California dreamin'

1 Speaking

How much do you know about the U.S.? In groups, see how many of these questions you can answer.

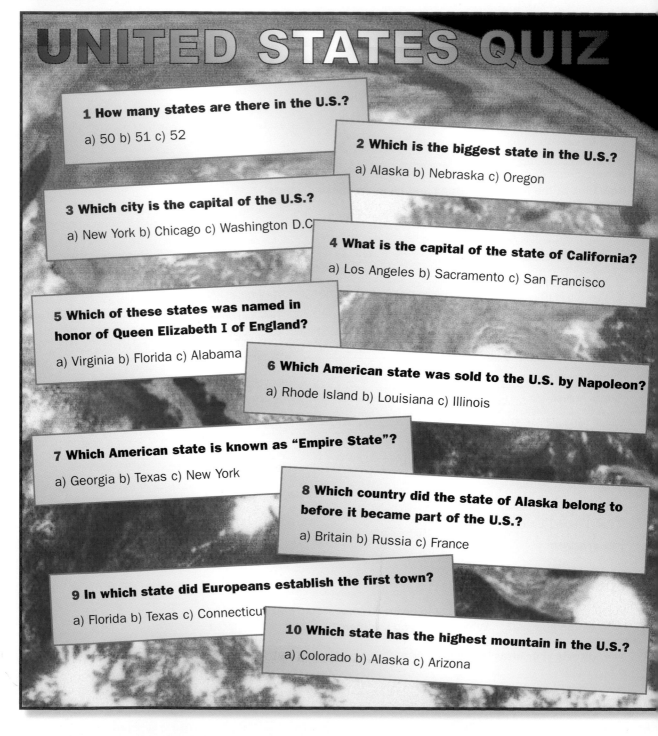

UNITED STATES QUIZ

1 How many states are there in the U.S.?

a) 50 b) 51 c) 52

2 Which is the biggest state in the U.S.?

a) Alaska b) Nebraska c) Oregon

3 Which city is the capital of the U.S.?

a) New York b) Chicago c) Washington D.C

4 What is the capital of the state of California?

a) Los Angeles b) Sacramento c) San Francisco

5 Which of these states was named in honor of Queen Elizabeth I of England?

a) Virginia b) Florida c) Alabama

6 Which American state was sold to the U.S. by Napoleon?

a) Rhode Island b) Louisiana c) Illinois

7 Which American state is known as "Empire State"?

a) Georgia b) Texas c) New York

8 Which country did the state of Alaska belong to before it became part of the U.S.?

a) Britain b) Russia c) France

9 In which state did Europeans establish the first town?

a) Florida b) Texas c) Connecticut

10 Which state has the highest mountain in the U.S.?

a) Colorado b) Alaska c) Arizona

Songsheet 2
California dreamin'

1 Speaking

Aim: To practice speaking on the subject of the U.S.

- Elicit one or two things students know about the U.S.
- Put them in groups and have them do the quiz.
- Check the answers.

Answers 1 b 2 a 3 c 4 a
5 a (Virginia because Queen Elizabeth I was known as the Virgin Queen)
6 b 7 c 8 b
9 a (St Augustine founded by 1500 Spanish colonists in 1565.)
10 b (Mount McKinley)

2 Speaking and listening

Aim: To practice listening for specific information.
To practice discussing a song.

Song fact file	John and Michelle Phillips wrote this song which became famous with the group The Mamas and the Papas. They were a four member group formed in 1964, and they broke up in 1968. The members were Cass Elliot, Michelle Phillips, John Phillips and Denny Doherty.

a • Put students in pairs.
  • Have them look at the words of the song and replace the pictures with words.
b • Now play the song and have students check their answers.

Answers	leaves, sky, walk, winter's, warm, dreamin', church, knees, pray, preacher, dreamin', leaves, sky, walk, winter's, dreamin'

c • Play the song again.
  • Have students work in pairs and answer the questions.
  • Get feedback from the class.

Answers	1 It is winter.
	2 Because he's cold and homesick.
	3 It isn't completely clear, but it seems that he has made a promise to a woman, or he could be in love with her – he sings, "If I didn't tell her, I could leave today."
	4 No. He only "pretends" to pray in the church.

3 Writing and speaking

Aim: To practice creative writing.
To develop students' speaking skills.

a • Check students understand the word *melancholic* (thoughtful and sad).
  • Put them in pairs.
  • Have them rewrite the words of the song trying to make it more positive.
  • Encourage them to be imaginative and to have fun with this.
b • Put students in groups.
  • Have them read their songs to each other.
  • Get feedback about the most positive sounding lyrics.
c • Have students look at the pictures and elicit what they show.
  • In pairs have them talk about how much they would miss the things in the picture if they were away from home.
  • Have them decide on the three people or things they would miss the most if they were away from home.
  • Get feedback from the group.

2 Speaking and listening

a In pairs, look at the words of the song and the pictures. Try to replace the
pictures with words.

California dreamin'

All the .... are brown
And the .... is gray
I've been for a ....
On a .... day
I'd be safe and ....
If I was in L.A.
California ....
On such a winter's day

Stopped into a ....
I passed along the way
Well, I got down on my ....
And I pretend to ....

You know the .... likes the cold
He knows I'm gonna stay
California ....
On such a winter's day

All the .... are brown
And the .... is gray
I've been for a ....
On a .... day
If I didn't tell her
I could leave today
California ....
On such a winter's day

b Now listen to the song and check your answers.

c Listen to the song again and answer these questions.

1 What season is it?
2 Why does the singer want to go back to California?
3 Why can't he go back?
4 Is the singer religious?

3 Writing and speaking

a The song is melancholic. In pairs, rewrite the song and make it positive by
replacing key words.

All the trees are green
And the sky is blue …

b In groups, read your songs to each
other. Which song seems the most
positive?

c When people live a long way from
home it is easy to become
homesick. Look at these pictures
and talk to your partner about
each picture. How much would you
miss it if you were away from
home, and why? Which three
things or people would you miss
the most?

Songsheet 3
Walking in Memphis

1 Speaking

a In pairs, look at these photographs. What do you know about Elvis Presley?

b Now decide if these statements are True (T), or False (F).

1 Elvis Presley was a twin.   T ◯ F ◯
2 He was born in Memphis.   T ◯ F ◯
3 His most famous home was called "Graceland."   T ◯ F ◯
4 One of his most famous songs was "Green Suede Shoes."   T ◯ F ◯
5 His wife's name was Priscilla.   T ◯ F ◯
6 He had two children, Michael and Lisa Marie.   T ◯ F ◯

2 Vocabulary work

Talk about the meaning of the words and phrases in the box and then write them in the most appropriate column.

| to board | tomb | gospel | Reverend | prayer | sing | "do a little number" |
| to touch down | first-class ticket | play piano | the blues | | | |

Traveling	Religion	Music

Songsheet 3
Walking in Memphis

1 Speaking

Aim: To practice speaking by using the topic of Elvis.

a • Put students in pairs.
    • Have them look at the photographs and discuss what they know about Elvis Presley.

b • Have them decide if the statements are true or false.
    • Get feedback from the class.

Answers 1 T (twin died at birth)
2 F Tupelo
3 T
4 F Blue Suede Shoes
5 T
6 F – daughter Lisa Marie (who later married and soon divorced Michael Jackson).

2 Vocabulary work

Aim: To increase vocabulary.

• Have students look at the words and phrases in the box.
• Put students in pairs or groups and let them decide in which column the words belong.
• Check the answers with the class.

Answers Traveling: to board, to touch down, first-class ticket
Religion: tomb, gospel, Reverend prayer,
Music: sing, "do a little number", play the piano, the blues

3 Listening and reading

Aim: To practice listening for specific information.

Song fact file	Mark Cohn wrote and performed this song. He is from Cleveland and won the Grammy in 1991 for Best New Artist. He is famous for his introspective lyrics.

a • Have students read the questions.
  • Play the song and let them choose the answers.

b • Now have them read the lyrics and check their answers.
  • Check the answers together.

Answers	1 b 2 b 3 a 4 c 5 a

• Ask students to work in groups and discuss the meaning of the song.
• Get feedback from the group.

Possible answer	Every year a week-long music festival is held in Memphis, Tennessee, in the U.S. Much of the festival takes place along Beale Street, which has become very famous and which the singer refers to when he sings the chorus of the song. Cohn goes on a pilgrimage to Memphis, home of some famous Blues and Rock 'n' Roll singers and musicians like Elvis Presley. During his trip he goes to Graceland, Elvis Presley's home. When he arrives in Memphis he feels blue (sad) but by the end of the song he feels happier.

4 Speaking

Aim: To practice exchanging opinions and ideas.

• Put students in groups and have them answer the questions.
• Get feedback from the class.

3 Listening and reading

a Listen to the song and choose the correct answers.

1	He traveled by:	a) bus.	b) plane.	c) car.
2	It was:	a) sunny.	b) raining.	c) snowing.
3	He saw:	a) Elvis.	b) Michael Jackson.	c) Puff Daddy.
4	He went to a:	a) religious meeting.	b) shopping mall.	c) hotel.
5	He:	a) sang.	b) played guitar.	c) played the piano.

b Now read the lyrics and check your answers to 3a.

Walking in Memphis

Put on my blue suede shoes
And I boarded the plane
Touched down in the land of the Delta Blues
In the middle of the pouring rain
W.C. Handy – won't you look down over me
Yeah, I got a first-class ticket
But I'm blue as a boy can be

When I'm walking in Memphis
Walking with my feet ten feet off Beale
Walking in Memphis
But do I really feel the way I feel

Saw the ghost of Elvis
On Union Avenue
Followed him up to the gates of Graceland
Then I watched him walk right through
Now security they did not see him
They just hovered round his tomb
But there's a pretty little thing waiting for the king
Down in the jungle room

When I'm walking in Memphis
I was walking with my feet ten feet off Beale
Walking in Memphis
But do I really feel the way I feel

They've got catfish on the table
They've got gospel in the air
And Reverend Green would be glad to see you
When you haven't got a prayer
But boy you've got a prayer in Memphis

Now Muriel plays piano
Every Friday at the Hollywood
And they brought me down to see her
And they asked me if I would
Do a little number
And I sang with all my might
And she said "Tell me are you a Christian child?"
And I said "Ma'am, I am tonight"

When I'm walking in Memphis
Walking with my feet ten feet off Beale
Walking in Memphis
But do I really feel the way I feel

Put on my blue suede shoes
And I boarded the plane
Touched down in the land of the Delta Blues
In the middle of the pouring rain
Touched down in the land of the Delta Blues
In the middle of the pouring rain

4 Speaking

Sometimes fans visit the private homes of music and movie stars to take photographs or souvenirs, like a stone from the driveway. In groups, answer the questions.

1 Are you a fan of any celebrity? Who and why?

2 Would you visit their home if you knew where it was? Why or why not?

3 If you saw someone famous would you ask for their autograph or take their photo?

4 What are the advantages and disadvantages of being famous?

Songsheet 4
Give me a little more time

1 Vocabulary work

Match the word or phrase on the left with the definition on the right.

1 to cope   to make something difficult

2 to make up your mind   to disappoint someone

3 to let someone down   to be unable to choose

4 to convince   to decide

5 to be in two minds   to manage a difficult situation

6 to complicate   to persuade successfully

2 Listening

a Look at the pictures and predict what the song will be about.

Songsheet 4
Give me a little more time

1 Vocabulary work

Aim: To increase vocabulary.

- Have students complete the vocabulary exercise.
- Let them check in pairs and use a dictionary if they wish.
- Check the answers.

Answers 1 to manage a difficult situation   2 to decide   3 to disappoint someone
4 to persuade successfully   5 to be unable to choose   6 to make something difficult

2 Listening

Aim: To practice listening for the main idea and specific information.

Song fact file This song was written by Gabrielle, Andy Dean, Benjamin Wolf and Ben Barson and became a hit for Gabrielle. Gabrielle was born in London in 1971 and has been very successful in the UK since 1993, when she had her first hit single.

a • Put students into groups.
- Have students look at the pictures and predict what the song will be about.
- Get feedback from the class.

b • Have students read the statements.
    • Play the song and have students choose the correct options.
    • Check the answers.

Answers	1 a	2 a	3 a

c • Now play the song again and let students match the lines with the correct endings from the second column.

Teaching tip	You may need to play the song a few times for students to match all the lines.

Answers	1 c	2 d	3 a	4 b	5 g	6 e	7 f	8 i	9 j	10 h	11 m
	12 n	13 k	14 l	15 o	16 q	17 p	18 s	19 t	20 r		

3 Speaking

Aim: To practice exchanging ideas and opinions.

• Put students in groups.
• Have them discuss the questions.
• Get feedback from the different groups.

b **Listen to the song and choose the correct option for each statement.**

1 She is singing to: **a)** her friend.   **b)** her lover.   **c)** her brother.

2 She thinks he is: **a)** a good friend to her.   **b)** a bad friend to her.   **c)** indifferent to her.

3 She wants their relationship: **a)** to change.   **b)** to start.   **c)** to end.

c **Now listen again and match the sentence halves on the left with the correct ending in the second column.**

Give me a little more time

1 You tried your best to show me   **a** That you understand
2 Said if there were days I was lonely   **b** You wanted to be the man
3 You tried your best, convinced me   **c** That you really cared
4 And if I needed someone to hold on to   **d** Just call you – you'd be there

5 Then I knew   **e** inside for you
6 All the feelings that I had   **f** Though many times I tried
7 I could not deny   **g** it was true

Chorus (x 2)
8 Give me a little more time   **h** Feelings getting stronger
9 'Cos you know I'm in two minds   **i** I need to make up my mind
10 Ooh, I just can't pretend any longer   **j** I wanna be more than your friend

11 You've been there when I've needed   **k** Though friends we have been
12 I just don't know how I'd cope   **l** Or is it just me?
13 Feelings have grown between us   **m** You've never let me down
14 Don't you think it complicates things   **n** Without you being around

15 Then I knew   **o** it was true
16 All the feelings that you had   **p** Though many times I tried ooh – ooh
17 I could not deny   **q** I shared them too

Chorus (x 2)
18 Give me a little more time   **r** Feelings getting stronger
19 'Cos you know I'm in two minds   **s** I need to make up my mind
20 Ooh, I just can't pretend any longer   **t** I wanna be more than your friend

3 Speaking

In groups, discuss these questions.

1 Do you prefer going on holiday with one friend, a group of friends or with your family?
2 Can a friend ever care for you as much as your family?
3 What makes a good relationship?
4 Is it really possible for a friend to become "more than a friend"?
5 Do you know of anybody that was in this situation? What happened?

Songsheet 5
Ironic

1 Vocabulary work

Match the expressions in these sentences with the correct meanings from the box below.

1 A 1998 **Chardonnay** is ideal with this dish.
2 He has spent three years on **death row** since his conviction for murder.
3 He knows someone in the government and now he's got a million-dollar contract. **It figures**!
4 They tell you to arrive at the airport an hour before the flight, but I like to **play it safe** and get there at least two hours in advance.
5 The kids **sneaked up on** their dad as he was sleeping on the beach and covered him in sand!
6 The police **blew up** a car parked outside the President's home.
7 There's always **a traffic jam** on the road into the city in the morning.
8 You can't smoke in the office, but we are allowed a ten-minute cigarette **break** twice a day.

> a) a place where prisoners wait to be executed   b) get close without being noticed   c) exploded
> d) a type of wine e) a lot of cars in a line f) That's logical g) time off work h) be very careful

2 Speaking and listening

a The night before his flight, a man had a dream of a plane crash, so he cancelled his flight and stayed at home. Only, a plane crashed into his house – how ironic! Work with your partners to think of ironic things that could happen in the situations in the table. Make notes in the first column.

b Now listen to the song and fill in the second column.

	Our ideas	The song	How ironic?
A lottery			
A prisoner on death row			
A wedding day			
A flight			
A traffic jam			
Meeting the man of your dreams			

Songsheet 5
Ironic

1 Vocabulary work

Aim: To increase vocabulary.

- Have students match the expressions in the sentences with the correct meanings from the box.
- Let them check in pairs.
- Check the answers together.

Optional step: Have them make sentences of their own using the words to illustrate meaning.

Answers 1 d 2 a 3 f 4 h 5 b 6 c 7 e 8 g

2 Speaking and listening

Aim: To practice listening for specific information.

Song fact file Alanis Morissette and Glen Ballard wrote the lyrics and music for this song which became a hit for Alanis. Alanis was born in Canada in 1975. She had a lot of success in Canada since the age of ten, both as a TV actress and a singer, but it was only when she moved to Los Angeles in 1994 and released the album *Jagged Little Pill*, that she achieved worldwide success. The song *Ironic* comes from that album. She continues to combine her music career with acting.

a
- Have students read the situation and check they understand the concept of irony (something ill-timed in this case).
- Have students read the table and elicit some ideas from them about badly timed events that could occur in the different situations given.
- Put them in pairs.
- Have them complete column one of the table with different ideas.
- Get feedback from the class.

b
- Now play the song and have students write in what the song says for the different situations.
- Let them compare with what they wrote.
- Get feedback from the class.

Answers

A lottery	The old man died the next day.
A prisoner on death row	The pardon arrives two minutes after he's been executed.
A wedding	It rains.
A flight	He was always careful and avoided flying, but the first flight he took crashed.
A traffic jam	You're already late and you get stuck in a traffic jam.
Meeting the man of your dreams	He's already married – and his wife is beautiful.

c • Now have students read the words of the song and try to guess what goes in the spaces.
• Play the song again and let them check their answers.
• Let them check in pairs.
• Check the answers together.

Answers 1 next   2 fly   3 paid   4 take   5 afraid   6 nice   7 sneaking up on you
8 cigarette   9 spoons   10 helping you out

3 Speaking

Aim: To develop students' speaking skills.

a • Put students in groups.
• Ask them to rank the events from the most ironic (1) to the least ironic (5).

b • Let different groups compare answers with each other.
• Get feedback from all the groups.

c • In the newly formed groups have students discuss ironic events.
• Get feedback from the class.

c   Now complete the gaps in the song with suitable words. Listen to the song
again and check your answers. Then compare your answers with a partner.

Ironic

An old man turned ninety-eight: He won the lottery and died the (1) .... day

It's a black (2) .... in your Chardonnay: It's a death row pardon two minutes too late

Isn't it ironic ... don't you think?

Chorus:

It's like rain on your wedding day: It's a free ride when you've already (3) ....

It's the good advice that you just didn't (4) ....: Who would've thought ... it figures

Mr. Play It Safe was (5) .... to fly: He packed his suitcase and kissed his kids good-bye

He waited his whole damn life to take that flight: And as the plane crashed down he thought

"Well, isn't this (6) ...." And isn't it ironic ... don't you think?

Repeat Chorus

Well life has a funny way of sneaking up on you

When you think everything's okay and everything's going right

And life has a funny way of (7) ....

You think everything's gone wrong and everything blows up

In your face

A traffic jam when you're already late

A no-smoking sign on your (8) .... break

It's like 10,000 (9) .... when all you need is a knife

It's meeting the man of my dreams

and then meeting his beautiful wife

And isn't it ironic ... don't you think?

A little too ironic ... and yeah I really do think ...

Repeat Chorus

Well life has a funny way of sneaking up on you

And life has a funny, funny way of (10) ....

3 Speaking

a   Look at the table in exercise 2b. In groups, put the six events in order from the
most to least ironic. Put number '1' in the box for the most ironic, number '2' for
the second most ironic, etc.

b   Now compare your answers with other groups.

c   In your new groups discuss anything ironic that has happened to you at
school, in work, on holiday, or in relationships. Decide who has the most ironic
experience and share it with the rest of the class.

Songsheet 6
I will always love you

1 Vocabulary work

Bitter: *strong black coffee without any sugar has a bitter taste.*

The word *bitter* can also be used to describe feelings. Here are some typical English expressions. Together with your partner, try to give personal examples or examples from the news or history of the following.

1   a bitter argument
2   feeling bitter at the way you've been treated
3   a bitter disappointment
4   bittersweet memories

2 Speaking

a **Match these songs with the artist and the movie they come from.**

I will always love you ————— Bryan Adams   *Four Weddings and a Funeral*

Everything I do is for you   Diane King   *Titanic*

Love is all around   Whitney Houston ————— *My Best Friend's Wedding*

Don't cry for me Argentina   Madonna   *Robin Hood: Prince of Thieves*

I say a little prayer for you   Wet Wet Wet   *The Bodyguard*

My heart will go on   Celine Dion   *Evita*

b **Now see if you can agree on at least one example of the following.**

1   *"Great song, but it's a shame about the movie."*

2   *"Great movie, but it's a shame about the song."*

3   *"Great song: great movie."*

4   *"I can't stand the song or the movie."*

Songsheet 6
I will always love you

1 Vocabulary work

Aim: To increase vocabulary.

- Check students understand the meaning of *bitter*.
- Have them look at the expressions and elicit the meanings.
- Put them in pairs and have them discuss the expressions and give examples.
- Get feedback from the whole class.

Language help You may want to compare the use of the word *bitter* in your language with its use in English

2 Speaking

Aim: To practice speaking on the topic of movies and songs.

a • Have students look at the columns and match the song with the artist and the movie it comes from.
- Let them check in pairs.
- Check the answers.

Answers I will always love you - Whitney Houston - *The Bodyguard*
Everything I do is for you - Bryan Adams - *Robin Hood*
Love is all around - Wet Wet Wet - *Four Weddings and a Funeral*
Don't cry for me Argentina - Madonna - *Evita*
I say a little prayer for you - Diane King - *My Best Friend's Wedding*
My heart will go on - Celine Dion - *Titanic*

b • Have students read the statements and discuss which movies / songs they'd assign to each statement.
- Conduct a class feedback session.

3 Listening

Aim: To practice listening for the main idea and specific information.

Song fact file	*I will always love you* was written and originally performed by the American Country and Western singer Dolly Parton. It later became famous in a version sung by Whitney Houston, which was the theme song of the movie *The Bodyguard* starring Whitney Houston and Kevin Costner.

a • Have students read the questions.
  • Play the song.
  • Check their answers to the questions.

Answers	1 She thinks she would be in his way. 2 Bittersweet memories 3 She loves him.

b • Have students look at the lyrics and fill in the blanks.
  • Play the song again and have students check their answers.
  • Check the answers with the class.

Answers	1 way 2 go 3 know 4 step 5 darling 6 all 7 me 8 goodbye 9 cry 10 need 11 treats 12 dreamed 13 happiness 14 love

Language help	You may want to point out to your students that *If I should stay* is a less direct way of saying *If I stay*. She wants to give the idea that there is no real chance that she will stay. This form is used mostly when we are asking someone for a favor in a very polite way, e.g. *If you should see Andrea, could you remind her about the meeting?*

4 Speaking

Aim: To develop students' speaking skills.

• Put students in groups of three.
• Have them read the situation and decide on their role.
• Have them role play the situation.
• Get feedback by asking what they decided.

3 Listening

a **Listen to the song and answer these three questions.**

   1 Why does she think she should leave?

   2 What will she take from the relationship?

   3 How does she feel toward her partner?

b **Now look at the words of the song and fill in the gaps.
Then listen to the song again to check the answers.**

I will always love you

If I should stay I would only be in your (1) ....

So I'll (2) .... but I (3) ....

I'll think of you every (4) .... of the way

And I will always love you

You, my (5) .... you, mmm

Bittersweet memories

That is (6) .... I'm taking with (7) ....

So, (8) .... , please don't (9) ....

We both know I'm not what you (10) ....

And I will always love you

I hope life (11) .... you kind

And I hope you have all you (12) .... of

And I wish you joy and (13) ....

But above all this I wish you (14) ....

And I will always love you

4 Speaking

**Work in groups of three. Imagine that one of you is
the character singing the song and that two of you
are his / her best friends. One friend thinks you're
crazy and should not leave. The other one thinks
that leaving is the right thing to do. Begin the
conversation by telling your friends:**

*"Listen, can I tell you something. I'm thinking
about going away – on my own."*

Continue the conversation with your two friends.

Irregular verbs

Infinitive	Past	Past participle	Unit and lesson
be	was / were	been	U1, L1
become	became	become	U2, L1
begin	began	begun	U3, L3
break	broke	broken	U4, L3
bring	brought	brought	Learning check 2
build	built	built	U2, L2
buy	bought	bought	U4, L1
can	could	–	U1, L2
catch	caught	caught	U5, L2
choose	chose	chosen	U3, L3
come	came	come	U1, L3
cost	cost	cost	U1, L2
deal	dealt	dealt	U2, L3
do	did	done	U1, L1
draw	drew	drawn	U2, L3
drink	drank	drunk	U5, L2
drive	drove	driven	U5, L4
eat	ate	eaten	U2, L4
fall	fell	fallen	Learning check 2
feel	felt	felt	U4, L2
find	found	found	U1, L1
fly	flew	flown	U5, L2
forget	forgot	forgotten	U12, L4
get	got	gotten	U1, L1
give	gave	given	U4, L2
go	went	gone	U1, L1
grow	grew	grown	U2, L3
have	had	had	U1, L1
hear	heard	heard	U2, L4
hit	hit	hit	U10, L2
keep	kept	kept	U1, L3
know	knew	known	U1, L2

Infinitive	Past	Past participle	Unit and lesson
leave	left	left	Learning check 3
lend	lent	lent	Learning check 5
let	let	let	U1, L3
lose	lost	lost	U2, L2
make	made	made	U1, L2
mean	meant	meant	U5, L1
meet	met	met	U4, L3
pay	paid	paid	U2, L4
put	put	put	U1, L3
read	read	read	U1, L1
run	ran	run	U10, L2
say	said	said	U5, L2
see	saw	seen	U6, L1
sell	sold	sold	U2, L3
send	sent	sent	U1, L2
show	showed	shown	U2, L3
sing	sang	sung	U7, L1
sink	sank	sunk	U5, L2
sit	sat	sat	U4, L3
speak	spoke	spoken	U1, L3
spend	spent	spent	U2, L2
steal	stole	stolen	U2, L2
take	took	taken	U2, L2
teach	taught	taught	U11, L3
tell	told	told	U1, L3
think	thought	thought	U1, L2
throw	threw	thrown	U4, L2
understand	understood	understood	U5, L1
wear	wore	worn	U5, L2
win	won	won	U2, L2
write	wrote	written	U1, L1

Pronunciation chart

Vowels

/i/	eat
/ɪ/	sit
/eɪ/	wait
/e/	get
/æ/	hat
/aɪ/	write
/ʌ/	but
/uː/	food
/ʊ/	good
/oʊ/	go
/ɔː/	saw
/a/	hot
/aʊ/	cow
/ɔɪ/	boy
/iər/	here
/ər/	her
/eər/	hair
/or/	or
/ar/	far

Consonants
(shown as initial sounds)

/b/	bat
/k/	cat
/tʃ/	chair
/d/	dog
/f/	fat
/g/	girl
/h/	hat
/dʒ/	July
/k/	coat
/l/	like
/m/	man
/n/	new
/p/	pet
/kw/	queen
/r/	run
/s/	see
/ʃ/	shirt
/t/	talk
/ð/	the
/θ/	thin
/v/	voice
/w/	where
/j/	you
/ŋ/	sing (as final sound)
/z/	zoo

The alphabet

/eɪ/	/i/	/e/	/aɪ/	/oʊ/	/uː/	/ar/
Aa	Bb	Ff	Ii	Oo	Qq	Rr
Hh	Cc	Ll	Yy		Uu	
Jj	Dd	Mm			Ww	
Kk	Ee	Nn				
	Gg	Ss				
	Pp	Xx				
	Tt					
	Vv					
	Zz					

Workbook answers

Unit 1 Relationships and communication

Lesson 1 Parents and children

1a

2b 3d 4e 5f 6a

2a 1 was swimming, arrived   2 met, was living
   3 did you eat   4 wasn't working, broke
   5 lost, was sitting

2b 1 was   2 had studied
   3 met   4 was wearing
   5 was   6 fell
   7 have been   8 traveled
   9 moved   10 got married
   11 arrived

3a behave, discussion, participate, attention (attendance is a possible answer), appreciation

3b oOo decision, behavior, discussion, attention; oooOo participation, appreciation

Lesson 2 In the workplace

1 1 computer
  2 a phone call
  3 computers
  4 school grades
  5 an office

2 1 homework
  2 downside
  3 Internet café
  4 housework
  5 laptop computer

3 1 Do you know if there's a park near here?
  2 Can you tell me where they live?
  3 Can you tell me what their names are?
  4 Do you know what he does on Wednesdays?
  5 Can you tell me if she's married?

4a 1 F   2 T   3 F

4b Do you know / Can you tell me
  1 when Linda's opens?
  2 how much it costs to get in?
  3 if they serve food there?
  4 where Linda's is?
  5 what kind of music they play there?

Lesson 3 Between friends

1a 1 honest   2 reliable
   3 patient   4 sociable
   5 a loner

1b intelligent: An intelligent person can solve problems.

2a 1 make friends / an excuse / a TV program / a Christmas card
   2 keep a secret
   3 have a shower / friends / a disagreement
   4 see friends / a TV program
   5 send a Christmas card / an excuse

Unit 2 Work and money

Lesson 1 Working to live or living to work?

1 2c   3a   4f   5b   6e

2a 1 varied   2 flexible   3 satisfying
   4 boring   5 well-paid

2b stressful: There's too much to do in too short a time, so my job is stressful.

2c pressured / stressful, challenging / demanding, interesting / stimulating

3a 1 management   2 managerial
   3 doctor   4 medical (medicinal)
   5 chemistry   6 chemistry / pharmacy

3b Oo lawyer, legal, doctor, chemist; Ooo manager, management, medicine, medical, chemistry, chemical; ooOoo managerial; law is not used

4a 1 Come early, stay late   2 Network
   3 Learn, learn, learn   4 Analyze this
   5 Above all, be happy!

Lesson 2 Winning and losing money

1a Ways of gaining money (nouns): interest, investment, salary. Things you can do with money (verbs): invest, win, lose, spend, gamble. Odd one out: loss

2a 1 expenses   2 gamble   3 save
   4 interest   5 win

2b 1T   2F   3F   4T   5F

3 1 Beef is often eaten on Sundays.
  2 A lot of black is being worn this winter.
  3 The teapot was designed in China.
  4 The supermarket will be opened on January 5th.
  5 This song has been recorded in many languages.

4a 70

4b 1 was awarded
   2 has just been entered
   3 plans / is planning

Lesson 3 Entrepreneurs

1a skin: moisturizer, soap; makeup: lipstick, mascara; hair: shampoo, conditioner.

2a 2f   3c   4b   5a   6d

2b 1 hair care products   2 synthetic substances
   3 animal testing   4 wasteful packaging
   5 natural ingredients

3a 1 She's an accountant who works in the legal department.
   2 Women sometimes wear makeup that / which is tested on animals.
   3 George enjoys tea that / which is grown in India.
   4 Linda is a manager who works in the city.
   5 This shampoo is made of cocoa butter which / that comes from Belize.

3b 1 that / which … camera   2 that / which … soap
   3 who … dentist   4 that / which … present
   5 who … architect

Unit 3 Keeping up with technology

Lesson 1 Developing the automobile

1a 2a   3g   4c   5b   6e   7h   8d

1b 1 fast, noisy, dangerous
    2 cheap, quiet, clean, slow
    3 expensive, noisy
    4 fast, expensive, noisy
    5 cheap, clean, quiet, unreliable, slow, dangerous

2 /u/ would, push, took, good /u:/ pollute, you, produce, interview, fuel, soon

3a 1 economical
    2 to energize
    3 unenergetic
    4 pollution
    5 polluting
    6 to produce
    7 non- / unproductive

3b 1 pollution
    2 energy
    3 to economize
    4 produces
    5 energy

4   1c   2b   3a

Lesson 2 Communication systems

1 1 driving to work
    2 clothes
    3 hungry
    4 the telephone
    5 management

2   1c   2b

4a 2f   3b   4c   5a   6e

4b *Suggested answers*:
    1 very stressful
    2 very noisy but very cheap
    3 very interesting
    4 cigarettes can be bad for your health
    5 is useful in business and for travel.

Lesson 3 Using technology

1a kitchen: dishwasher, microwave oven, stove; bathroom: electric toothbrush, electric razor; living room: armchair, video casette recorder, stereo

2a 1 don't they
    2 wasn't he / she
    3 will it
    4 hasn't he
    5 isn't it

2b 1 The coffee is good, isn't it?
    2 The restaurant is crowded, isn't it?
    3 The food is tasty, isn't it?
    4 The waiter is good-looking, isn't he?
    5 The table is dirty, isn't it?

3   1c   2b   3c   4a

Unit 4 House and home

Lesson 1 Home away from home

1a 1 apartment
    2 carport

    3 house
    4 garage
    5 terrace
    6 building
    word: accommodation

2a /ɔ:/ course, carport, store, short, more, normal;
    /o/ on, contract, option, coffee

3 1 garage. The others are rooms in a house.
    2 bookcase. The others are in the bathroom.
    3 coffee table. The others are in the office.
    4 toilet. The others are in the kitchen.
    5 coffee cup. The others are kitchen equipment.

Lesson 2 Decoration

1a walls: paint, poster, picture; lighting: table lamp, candles, lamp shade; floor: mat, carpet, wooden

2a 1b   2a 3c   4d   5f   6e

3a 2 a, b, c or e
    3d
    4b or c
    5b
    6b, c, d or f

3b 1 turn … off
    2 give … away
    3 put … away
    4 take down
    5 turn … down

Lesson 3 Street scenes

2   1 in
    2 on
    3 at
    4 on
    5 on

3a 2c   3f   4a   5b   6e

3b 1b   2b   3a   4a   5b

4a transportation: taxi, bus, rickshaw, bicycle, ambulance, subway; descriptive adjectives: crowded, tall, calm, busy, high-rise, clean; places: bar, store, stall, café, market, building

Unit 5 Crime and law

Lesson 1 Unsolved crimes

1a 1 murder   2 assassin
    3 to witness   4 an arrest
    5 robbery, theft   6 thief, robber

1b 1 rob   2 witnessed (saw)
    3 assassination   4 Murder
    5 stolen

2a 2e   3b   4d   5c   6a

2b 1 After   2 Following
    3 interrogated   4 A number of
    5 Ask

3a /e/ when, neck, question, several; /ae/ hand, had, and, act; /ʌ/ hundred, cut, one, front

Lesson 2 Crime and punishment

1a 1 commit
    2 gain

3 completely
4 minor
5 strongly

1b 1 commits a crime   2 minor crime
3 gained independence   4 fire a gun
5 committing a crime

2a 2a   3b   4f   5c   6e

2b 1 said   2 had made
3 had reserved   4 was
5 sat   6 waited
7 had hidden   8 had

3   1F   2T   3F

Lesson 3 Crime knows no borders

1a Oo hungry, convict, conduct, rented, swindle, member, import

oO deport, convict, police, conduct, become, exist, locate, import

1b 1 conducting   2 convicted
3 Convicts   4 imports
5 import

2a 1 been, lost   2 has left, been working
3 been going out   4 washed, going to do
5 been reviewing

2b 1 Have you had / Did you have   2 was working / worked
3 Were you based   4 was sharing / shared
5 met   6 had rented
7 had left   8 came
9 have been going out

Unit 6 Mass media

Lesson 1 Sensationalism

1a 1 tax evasion   2 car accident
3 drug trafficking   4 crime scene
5 passport forgery

1b 1 tax evasion   2 crime scene
3 Drug trafficking   4 car accident
5 bank account

2a /i/ kidnap, accident, robbery, victim, missing, forensic; /i:/ secret, magazine, read, reliable

2b 1 Kidnap   2 Forensic
3 secret   4 victim
5 Robbery

3a 1 falls   2 affects badly
3 argue   4 resigns
5 supports

3b 1a   2a   3a

3c 1/4   2/5   3/1   4/3   5/2

Lesson 2 Investigative journalism

1a 2a   3c   4e   5f   6d

1b 1 go ahead   2 broke into
3 hand over   4 got away
5 covered up

2a 1 May said Louisa would (can) speak Russian.
2 Bill said Nicholas would meet us / me at the station.
3 Peter told his Mom he'd had dinner.
4 Madeline told Gregory Liz had seen him at the movies.
5 Susan said they often went to her parents on the weekend.

2b 2a   3b   4f   5d   6c

3a 1F   2F   3T

3b 1 I need to buy some jewelry for a wedding.
2 My brother sent me to this store.
3 I've worked here for twenty years.
4 I saw the sultan on the news this morning.

Lesson 3 Ethical issues

1a 1 private   2 complaint
3 investigation   4 to investigate
5 success   6 successful
7 to communicate   8 famous

1b 1 complain   2 famous
3 communication   4 succeed
5 Investigative

2a 1 Bill asked his sister if she could lend him a pen.
2 We asked them where they lived.
3 Jane asked Paul what was for dinner.
4 He asked her if she was going to the meeting.
5 She asked her where she worked.

2b 1 He asked her who that man was.
2 She asked him if he liked fishing.
3 I asked her if there was a subway near there.
4 He asked them if they would lend him $5.
5 She asked her if they could meet the next day.

Unit 7 Trends

Lesson 1 My generation

1 /iə/ year, beer, appear, hear, near;
/eə/ wear, pair, compare, parent, share

2 2a   3e   4b   5c   6d

Lesson 2 Looking good

1a head: baseball cap, hat, earrings; upper body: blouse, sweater, t-shirt; lower body: jeans, skirt, pants; feet: boots, sneakers, sandals, socks

2a 2c   3e   4d   5f   6a

3 1 A red and yellow shirt
2 A pair of small gold earrings
3 A horrible green cotton dress
4 A black plastic jacket
5 A lovely blue suede skirt

4 2 Sort clothes by category
3 Sort clothes by color
4 Wash or dry clean
5 Invest in the best possible hangers

Lesson 3 Shop till you drop

1a 1 keyboard   2 deodorant
3 hairspray   4 lipstick
5 printer   6 mousepad
7 perfume

1b pharmacy: 2, 3, 4, 7;
computer center: 1, 5, 6

2a 1a   2a   3b   4a   5a

2b 1 Neither   2 All / many / a lot of
3 a few / some   4 a lot of
5 Most of

3 1F   2T   3T   4F

Unit 8 Big moments

Lesson 1 Personal firsts

1 1 bungee jumping   2 bowling
3 surfing   4 cycling
5 whitewater rafting   6 ice skating
7 parachuting

2 1 happy   2 dizzy
3 nervous / apprehensive   4 relaxed
5 terrified   6 embarrassed

3b 1 embarrassed   2 dizzy
3 happy   4 relaxed
5 terrified

1 Have you   2 Are you
3 Will you   4 Can't they
5 Would you

a3   b1   c2

Lesson 2 Your first date

1a 2f   3e   4d   5b   6a

1b make a reservation, wash your clothes, get your hair cut/done, take a shower, put on make up, cologne, perfume, offer to pay

2a 1 Speaking   2 this is
3 you would like   4 How about
5 Thanks for calling

2b 1 I am   2 for
3 I am speaking   4 Thanks of calling me
5 See us there

3a 1a   2b   3a   4a   5b

3b 1 don't have to   2 don't need to / don't have to
3 need to   4 need to
5 have to / must

Lesson 3 The big day

1a /ai/ live, invite; /i/ invitation, ring, live, music, video, gift, disco; /ei/ waiter, engagement, catering

2a 1 video   2 July
3 Tuesday   4 morning
5 party

2b 1 on   2 on   3 at   4 at   5 on

3a present – gift, register – sign up, choose – select, provide – give, fun – enjoyable

3b 1 Sign up   2 Go shopping
3 Start the list   4 Admire the goodies
5 Thank you letters

Unit 9 Men and women

Lesson 1 Evaluating tradition

1 1 breadwinner   2 part-time
3 housework   4 The workforce
5 low-level job

2a 1 equal   2 traditional
3 legal   4 education
5 capacial (capacious)   6 central

2b 1 equal   2 tradition
3 education   4 central
5 capable

3a 1 job   2 colleague
3 the bill   4 comfortable
5 like   6 family

Lesson 2 Coincidence or destiny?

1a 3   5   1   4   2   6

1b 1 going out with   2 got married
3 met   4 got engaged
5 fell in love with

2a 2e   3f   4b   5a   6d

2b 1 would / 'd have seen the director get angry.
2 If she had worked harder she'd / would have been promoted.
3 If they'd arrived on time we'd / would have met them.
4 I'd have become an actress if my father had let me go to drama school.
5 He'd have bought you flowers if he'd known it was your birthday.

3a 1a   2c   3b   4a

3b *Suggested answers*:
1 she wouldn't have become a model.
2 hadn't been crying the talent scout wouldn't have seen her.
3 Sonia Stein (probably) wouldn't have given her a business card.

Lesson 3 Gifts of love

1 1 pig   2 vocalist
3 pants   4 cheese
5 lawsuit

2a 1F   2T   3F   4F   5T

2b A correct version would be: "Dear Mr. Brown, … your letter of application, which was interesting / we want to follow up. … Please telephone me as soon as possible / convenient and we will arrange a time. I look forward to hearing from you, Yours sincerely, George Bickers"

3a 1 I wish I'd / had called you.
2 I wish my brother hadn't lost his job.
3 I wish the teacher hadn't been late.
4 I wish the cake hadn't burned.
5 I wish I'd paid my taxes.

Unit 10 Life's a journey

Lesson 1 Stranger than fiction

1a 1   6   4   5   2   3   8   7

1b 1 was convicted   2 was sentenced
3 went to prison   4 escaping
5 was released

2a /s/ psychologist, enormous, university; /z/ changes, prison, reason; /ʃ/ brainwash, show, she, social

3a 1 despite   2 despite
3 but   4 though
5 although   6 though

Lesson 2 A near tragedy

1a 2d   3b   4e   5c   6a

1b motorcycle gloves, rescue helicopter, weather forecast, convenience food, mountain path

2a 1 shouldn't have worn her new shoes.
2 We shouldn't have gone to Rome in winter.

3 Marian shouldn't have spent all her money.
4 George shouldn't have pushed Teddy.
5 I shouldn't have run for the bus.

2b *Suggested answers*:
I could have …
1 eaten some nice food.
2 had a few drinks.
3 enjoyed the music.
4 danced with the friend.

2c Noah would have …
1 brought nothing.
2 shaken hands.
3 bought me a sandwich
4 ordered water.
5 asked me to lend him $10.

2d 2e   3a   4d   5b   6f

Lesson 3 War of the worlds

1   1 fictional
   2 drama
   3 dramatic
   4 broadcast / produce
   5 publication

2   1 She may / might have had a headache.
   2 She can't / couldn't have seen you.
   3 They may / might / could have left early.
   4 The bathroom must have been blue.
   5 He may / might / could have been angry.

3   2a   3d   4c   5f   6e

4a 1F   2T   3T   4F   5T

4b 1 couldn't
   2 couldn't
   3 must
   4 might / could
   5 must

Unit 11 Stages of life

Lesson 1 Learning to be human

1a 2b   3d   4a   5c

1b 2a   3d   4e   5f   6c

1c *Suggested answers*:
   1 to play with toys
   2 study at high school
   3 use a computer
   4 follow logical arguments
   5 take exams

2   /s/ cats, grandparents; /z/ sons, kids, guys, teenagers, clothes, daughters; /iz/ nurses, matches, churches, kisses

3b Children don't move enough.

Lesson 2 Goals in life

1a 2f   3b   4c   5e   6a

1b 1 ambition
   2 passion
   3 fun
   4 preparation
   5 identify with

3a /ð/ they, although, that, there, rather, the;
   /θ/ think, thank you, thin, thumb, path, math, both

Lesson 3 When I'm 64

1   1   6   7   4   5   3   2   8

2a 2 so / therefore f
   3 so / therefore   c
   4 but   e
   5 but / however d
   6 but a

2b 1 The movie was sad so she cried.
   2 The boys played football because they were bored.
   3 I wanted to see you so I came here.
   4 Paul wanted to buy vegetables so he went to the market.
   5 They went to bed because they were tired.

3a 2f   3b   4c   5d   6e   7a

3b 1a   2b

3c 1 since then
   2 as
   3 although
   4 well
   5 also
   6 unless

Unit 12 Crystal ball

Lesson 1 Looking back at 2001

1a 2b   3d   4e   5f   6a

2   /j/ enjoyable, using, young, computer; /dz/ during, refrigerator, language

3a 2d   3b   4a   5f   6e

3b 1T   2T   3F   4T   5F

Lesson 2 Tomorrow's world

1a 2e   3a   4b   5d   6c

1b 1F   2T   3T   4F   5T

2a medicine: genetics, antibiotics, vaccine, organ, cancer, disease, transplant; ecology: solar power, electric cars, alternative energy, petroleum, endangered species, pollution, windmill

3a 1 she'll make
   2 either
   3 will be dancing
   4 she'll have had
   5 she'll have gone

Lesson 3 Your future

1a 2b   3d   4a   5f   6e

2a 1 will win
   2 has
   3 will be
   4 will pass
   5 starts

2b 1 you'll be working
   2 I'll be pushing
   3 will have smoked
   4 you'll get
   5 we'll have eaten

3   1 embarrassed
   2 surprised
   3 disappointed
   4 bored
   5 angry